A JOURNEY INTO
THOMAS HARDY'S POETRY

A JOURNEY INTO THOMAS HARDY'S POETRY

Joanna Cullen Brown

Allison & Busby
Published by W.H. Allen & Co. Plc

An Allison & Busby book
Published in 1989 by
W.H. Allen & Co. Plc
Sekforde House
175/9 St John St
London EC1V 4LL

Copyright © 1989 Joanna Cullen Brown

Printed and bound in Great Britain by
Mackays of Chatham Plc, Chatham, Kent

ISBN 0 85031 883 1

For
JNC and APC
best of parents

'One can read him for years and years and still be surprised, and I think that's a marvellous thing to find in any poet.'

Philip Larkin.

Why Hardy's Poetry?

Thomas Hardy is a twentieth-century best-seller. People who like very different kinds of reading seem to get fascinated by his novels. Many, in recent years, have begun to turn their eyes to his poems.

But Hardy was a very private and complex person, and a man who, though his feelings were deep and intense, prized understatement and reticence. The riches of his poetry, and his ideal of human life, often become apparent only as one reads below the surface of his poems. There one finds not only his honesty, as he constantly explored and faced up to truth and reality, but his compassion for the disadvantaged, his joy in living, his wit and irony and sense of the absurd – and a surprisingly modern approach to life that confronts many of the dilemmas of twentieth-century men and women. Those who look for beauty will also be satisfied.

This is a guidebook for any reader who wants to make the journey of understanding into Hardy's poems. They will not disappoint.

CONTENTS

NOTES AND ACKNOWLEDGEMENTS

Poem titles are given in italics. The text is taken from *The Complete Poetical Works of Thomas Hardy*, ed Samuel Hynes (3 vols, Oxford 1982–5.) Hardy's letters can be found in several books, but have been collected so far (up to 1925) in 6 volumes, ed Purdy and Millgate (Oxford 1978–87). Abbreviations for titles of books frequently mentioned are as follows:

Life	F.E. Hardy *The Life of Thomas Hardy 1840–1928* (in one volume, London 1962)
Notebooks	*The Personal Notebooks of Thomas Hardy*, ed R.H. Taylor (London 1978); original documents in the Dorset County Museum.
Lit. Notes	*The Literary Notebooks of Thomas Hardy*, ed Björk (London 1985); original documents in the Dorset County Museum.
Orel	*Thomas Hardy's Personal Writings*, ed H. Orel (Kansas 1966, London 1977)
Millgate	Michael Millgate, *Thomas Hardy: A Biography* (Oxford 1982)
Dennis Taylor	Dennis Taylor: *Hardy's Poetry, 1860–1928* (London 1981)
PTH	*The Poetry of Thomas Hardy*, ed Clements and Grindle (London 1980).
Casebook	*Thomas Hardy: Poems*, ed Gibson and Johnson. (Casebook Series, London 1979)
Agenda	Thomas Hardy Special Issue, Vol 10, Nos 2–3, 1972 ed Davie.

Many other books or essays on Hardy's poetry which I find helpful or illuminating are referred to, but I have deliberately excluded a long (and perhaps daunting) separate bibliography, which may easily be found elsewhere.

Thanks are due to the following for permission to quote:

Oxford University Press for passages from *The Collected Letters of Thomas Hardy*, ed Purdy and Millgate (1978–87); E.L. Hardy, *Some Recollections*, ed Hardy and Gittings, (1961); Michael Millgate, *Thomas Hardy: A Biography* (1982);

Edinburgh University Press for Graham Dunstan Martin, *Language, Truth and Poetry* (1975);

Macmillan Publishers Ltd, for *The Literary Notebooks of Thomas Hardy*, ed Lennart Björk; *Thomas Hardy: Poems*, ed Gibson and Johnson; F.E. Hardy, *The Life of Thomas Hardy*; Tom Paulin, *The Poetry of Perception; Personal Notebooks of Thomas Hardy*, ed R.H. Taylor; Dennis Taylor, *Hardy's Poetry*, 1860–1928; *Thomas Hardy's Personal Writings*, ed Harold Orel;

Penguin Books Ltd for A. Alvarez, *The New Poetry* (1962);

Chatto and Windus/Hogarth Press, and the Estate of Marcel Proust, for Proust, *Remembrance of Things Past*, tr C.K. Scott-Moncrieff and Terence Kilmartin (1981);

Routledge and Kegan Paul Ltd for Donald Davie, *Thomas Hardy and British Poetry*;

Vision Press, London; Totowa, N.J.: Barnes and Noble Books, 1980 for *The Poetry of Thomas Hardy*, ed Patricia Clements and Juliet Grindle;

Grafton Books, a division of the Collins Publishing Group, for quotation from Jean Brooks, *Thomas Hardy: The Poetic Structure*;

Agenda for articles by Donald Davie, Thom Gunn, David Wright and William Pritchard; *Victorian Poetry* for articles by FR Giordano, Jr, and William Buckler;

Faber and Faber Ltd for Douglas Dunn, *Elegies*;

SPCK for Lesslie Newbigin, *Foolishness to the Greeks*.

I should like to thank my fellow students of St Hilda's College, Oxford for their studentship, granted me for 1982–3, which first gave me space to work on Thomas Hardy's poetry.

I am grateful to my husband Bernard for his help with the index – and for so much besides.

1

HARDY'S WORLD:

Inexplicable Relations

I recently met a Modern Languages student who through his leisure reading had become hooked on Hardy's poetry. It spilled out in most of his conversations because he could not help it. The poem that at that stage was never far from his mind, and which he thought was one of the finest poems ever written, was "I Look into my Glass". I was moved by this, because although I think this too, I was almost surprised that a man in his early twenties could share the feelings of a man nearer sixty. (Philip Larkin also thought Hardy was not a young person's poet; yet he too discovered Hardy's poems when he was a young man.)

This is the poem.

I LOOK INTO MY GLASS

I look into my glass,
And view my wasting skin,
And say, "Would God it came to pass
My heart had shrunk as thin!"

For then, I, undistrest
By hearts grown cold to me,
Could lonely wait my endless rest
With equanimity.

But Time, to make me grieve,
Part steals, lets part abide,
And shakes this fragile frame at eve
With throbbings of noontide.

We must, I think, be stirred by this poem, even at a first reading. Yet in many ways it could seem unpromising. The first stanza is almost nothing but bare, ordinary monosyllables, which only gradually give way later to a handful of words of a more lyrical quality. It appears so simple, the metre so regular, in a way so bald, that no great craft may seem (unless we try to rewrite it ourselves) to have been necessary to put it together. There is no melodrama, and no rhetoric trying to persuade us how we should feel. Perhaps these are virtues. In those simple opening monosyllables there is truthfulness unadorned, experience unedited, an emotion laid bare, offered with dignity and restraint but no self-pity. Read again, the very simplicity of the opening lines takes on a power from that dignity, and from the long vowels, and the lift given by "into" and "wasting" among the single syllables. The deep emotion carries us straight over to the second stanza, where everything begins to open out: though still without self-pity, there is more explanation. There are longer words, like "lonely" and "endless", with liquid "l's" and feminine (unstressed) endings which soften the earlier harshness – until the lines broaden out into the full space and poise of "equanimity". The reader is surprised by this unexpected, unique word of five syllables: but it transforms the poem and seems to bring in the music of the spheres. It is this glimpse of equanimity, of a fate accepted with what Donald Davie in another context calls "the reposefulness of the irremediable",[1] that makes the last stanza so unbearable. The grief and the longing are drawn out in the lines' patient pauses:

> But Time, to make me grieve,
> Part steals, lets part abide.

They sing in the long meditative vowels of "grieve" and "steals" and "eve", which then mingle with the slow "i" of "Time", "abide", "noontide", and "fragile" so that these vowels, and the liquid consonants, seem to surround us wherever we turn; and the trill of the "fragile frame" catches sadly with the trill of "throbbings" in a controlled intensity.

The strength of the emotion, undoctored, and its evident sincerity, is something in Hardy which appeals to all ages. The theme of the poem – "this curse of his heart not ageing while his frame moved naturally onward", as he put it in The Well-Beloved, – might only appeal to those who have begun to experience the phenomenon. One day Hardy recorded in his diary an occasion when he felt it himself: it may have been the germ of the poem.

> *Oct 18* Hurt my tooth at breakfast-time. I look in the glass. Am conscious of the humiliating sorriness of my earthly tabernacle, and of the sad fact that the best of parents could do no better for me... Why should a man's mind have been thrown into such close, sad, sensational, inexplicable relations with such a precarious object as his own body![2]

In 1892, when he wrote this, Hardy was 52. (His birth date, in June 1840, makes quick reckoning easy.) Six years were to pass before he astonished English-speaking readers by publishing his first volume of poems: most had pigeon-holed him for ever as a rustic, and increasingly tragic, novelist. Although he had begun to write poems as early as the 1860s, and continued to include some of these, often revised, with newer ones in every succeeding volume until his death in 1928, most of his greatest poetry was written after about 1912, when he was already in his seventies – an unusual achievement in itself. Yet even from the first, in the 1860s, questions like this about the "inexplicable relations" between mind and body and their setting within time had begun to exercise him. He was to spend the rest of his long life pondering them, constantly exploring the nature of reality and the paradoxes of the human condition.

An understanding of this dawns gradually as one reads and re-reads among Hardy's hundreds of poems. But first the reader is caught up into his world: a world distinct enough, rich enough in depths and contrasts and patterns and landscapes, for one to be able to draw it, walk in it, feel its freshness, sun, wind and rain, light and darkness, green and gray, hear its sounds – and begin to see some of its implications. No less distinct are his domestic interiors: rooms where clocks and old furniture gleam in mirrors and candlelight, where stairways mount and descend almost hypnotically, where closed doors mask the sounds of music and laughter or "shaken words bitter to madness." The floors, witness to long past scenes, are "footworn and hollowed and thin", and in the hearth embers glow like memories.

From this room we look out through the casement (our vision framed by our attitudes and preconceptions), and the world has two faces. One is the green and golden world of summer and lavish autumn, sweet piercing birdsong, love and happiness and high-piled clouds. There are towers and spires in the landscape, fairgrounds and railways, and humble cottages where the stone threshold dips from the steady passage of feet over the centuries. Tracks cross the heathland, peopled with moving figures of all ages and conditions; in the distance a river glints on its way to the sea.

The other face of this world through which humans journey is sombre, a dun and dreary landscape. Storm clouds belly down, wind and rain scourge the traveller, the leafless trees thresh as if in bodily pain. Where the moon washes the scene with its greenish-yellow light, patterns of all kinds, patterns of life and understanding, emerge and grow and seem to crowd the mind – dappled moonshades, the intricate lacing of branches across the sky, the woven textures of leaves, cobwebs picked out by frost. The highroads and the telegraph wires criss-cross on the slopes, the railway cutting marks a gash across the valley. This is a real world, a world of contrasts and dissonance, where the technology that has built the *Titanic* for the favoured few meets the deceptive quiet of the hidden vales, where a horse may still plough at the speed of a man's walk.

Like the patterns, these pictures grow in the mind as one poem is added to another: one begins to be magnetised into Hardy's world. Here is a hint of its flavour.

THE SHIVER

Five lone clangs from the house-clock nigh,
    And I woke with a sigh;
Stars wore west like a slow tide flowing,
And my lover had told yesternight of his going, –
That at this gray hour he'd be hasting by,

Starting betimes on a journey afar: –
    So, casement ajar,
I eyed in the upland pasture his figure,
A dim dumb speck, growing darker and bigger,
Then smalling to nought where the nut-trees are.

He could not bend his track to my window, he'd said,
    Being hurried ahead:
But I wish he had tried to! – and then felt a shiver,
Corpse-cold, as he sank toward the town by the river;
And back I went sadly and slowly to bed.

What meant my shiver while seeing him pass
        As a dot on the grass
I surmised not then. But later I knew it
When came again he; and my word outdrew it,
As said he: "It's hard for your bearing, alas!

"But I've seen, I have clasped, where the smart ships plough,
        One of far brighter brow.
A sea-goddess. Shiver not. One far rarer
In gifts than I find thee: yea, warmer and fairer: –
I seek her again; and I love you not now.."

Without lingering too long, one can observe some of the
familiar features of Hardy's world: the window framing a figure
in the landscape, the prophetic clock, the stars and tide, the gray
hour that speaks of inner fears matching the outer setting, as the
"corpse-cold" shiver images the rippling river's chill and the
coming death of love. Here is the tragic belatedness of
understanding – "I surmised not then. But later I knew it." Here
is Hardy's characteristic noting of precise details, often in terms
of parts of the body: "I *eyed* ... his figure", and "One of far
brighter *brow*." Here is the deliberately ordinary diction and
tone seen in "I Look into my Glass" – "And back I went sadly
and slowly to bed" – yet given piquancy by unusual words like
"smalling", and favourite words which we come to add up, like
"gray", "dim", "track", "sank", and the critical "smart".
    Another glimpse of the Hardy scene comes in "The
Prospect", a poem he wrote soon after the death of his first wife.

THE PROSPECT

The twigs of the birch imprint the December sky
        Like branching veins upon a thin old hand;
I think of summer-time, yes, of last July,
        When she was beneath them, greeting a gathered band
        Of the urban and bland.

Iced airs wheeze through the skeletoned hedge from the north,
        With steady snores, and a numbing that threatens snow,
And skaters pass; and merry boys go forth
        To look for slides. But well, well do I know
        Whither I would go!

December 1912

We must take note of the pattern, which so often is an image for how an experience takes root and grows in human minds and lives. Here the experience is first seen with Emma under the summer-clad trees: it ends with the totally different world he inhabits after her death, a December of heart and season with the bare twigs branching like the veins of his old hand. The veins and twigs share the same pattern, seem to be linked as the inner world of his feeling with the outer world he lives in; he sees the change of pattern, from leafy dapple to cold winter outline – and as he looks down at his hands, he realises how he has aged as the world has changed.

Frost and ice always filled Hardy with dread. Here they provide another link between the human and his natural setting, in the body-images of the wind snoring and wheezing like a person. The hedge pattern is "skeletoned" and stark like the birches, tracing the death that has happened, the other death he wishes would now take place.

Yet still the rest of the world goes round; merriment and cheerful activity bubble on as usual for those whose experience has not yet brought them to winter. In Hardy's world the gray and the green co-exist, the green world so beautiful that if he had his way, if he could be "head-god", he would change everything:

> Even half-god power
> In spinning dooms
> Had I, this frozen scene should flower,
> And sand-swept plains and Arctic glooms
> Should green them gay with waving leaves,
> Mid which old friends and I would walk
> With weightless feet and magic talk
> Uncounted eves.[3]

* * * * * *

In a world of discrepancies and dissonance, this clash of contrasts – between the fevered hopes and the chilling of the years; between the human mind and body against time and its natural setting; the clash of an individual made in one frame while the universe and society are locked in another – this brings a cry of human anguish across the scene, a cry that cannot be easily answered.

> But Time, to make me grieve,
> Part steals, lets part abide,
> And shakes this fragile frame at eve
> With throbbings of noontide.

Hardy did not turn away from the depths of human suffering, since it was a part of living experience and as such must be accepted and examined – and where possible relieved. As he put it tersely in the second of his three "In Tenebris" poems, "if way to the Better there be, it exacts a full look at the Worst." So when the black night of pain came upon him he did not silver it, but suffered it until it passed. There are bitter moments and bleak places in the landscape. But it is precisely because he valued life and acutely felt its joys that their transience and despoiling made him grieve. The other side of the landscape still "glows with a gleam;" it is still "emblazoned with blessings", green with the pulse of life, gnarled with a wry humour at the endearing follies of humanity – and, despite the bitter moments, still threaded with an instinct hope.

> This after-sunset is a sight for seeing,
> Cliff-heads of craggy cloud surrounding it.
> – And dwell you in that glory-show?
> You may; for there are strange strange things in being,
> Stranger than I know.[4]

* * * * * *

This is the world a reader may first come to know when she or he spends time with Hardy's poetry – a world where, using his gifts of mind and spirit, and every resource of poetry, he searches all human experience and the mysteries beyond; where each poem adds pervasively to the others, and the beauty or integrity or insight of one flows into the current of them all. It is a world where one probably begins by recognising signals: the gloss of rich green leaves, the gleam of water and sunlight, the binding mesh of patterns and weaves and pilgrim tracks, the glow of love and song, fellowship and the living past; or the deadly black and white of frost and hostility, the fall of leaves and skeleton trees where no birds sing, the ashes of love betrayed and the wan gray of fading hope; the ironies of mirrored and inverted meanings, the ominous revelations of moon over water – and the awakening, too late, to the unnoticed changes that have transformed the world and ourselves. (If all this seems deadly serious, we shall also enjoy Hardy spoofing himself and his tragedies.)

But these signals are only flags flying at the top of a mast – a mast which leads straight down into real life, probing the shadowy hold of human consciousness. The green and the gray, the patterns, the mirrors and the stairs are symbols carrying deeper significance. The landscape is more than it appears: it is somewhere which is shown to influence our thinking and life; somewhere which may reflect our inner state; somewhere in which the poet is always prospecting to find meaning and analogies with human experience.

Hardy's poetry offers a world of complex and varied mood and texture, of flashes of beauty, true experience, reality and salty humour, quirkiness and tenderness. There can be few human beings to whom it does not speak with sympathy and authority.

To see if this is true, try reading (if you can without indigestion) the five poems which follow. They have nothing in common but their author, and are chosen simply as varied poems which might appeal to different people.

THE RUINED MAID

"O 'Melia, my dear, this does everything crown!
Who could have supposed I should meet you in Town?
And whence such fair garments, such prosperi-ty?" –
"O didn't you know I'd been ruined?" said she.

– "You left us in tatters, without shoes or socks,
Tired of digging potatoes, and spudding up docks;
And now you've gay bracelets and bright feathers three!" –
"Yes: that's how we dress when we're ruined," said she.

– "At home in the barton you said 'thee' and 'thou',
And 'thik oon', and 'theäs oon', and 't'other'; but now
Your talking quite fits 'ee for high compa-ny!" –
"A polish is gained with one's ruin," said she.

– "Your hands were like paws then, your face blue and bleak,
But now I'm bewitched by your delicate cheek,
And your little gloves fit as on any la-dy!" –
"We never do work when we're ruined," said she.

- "You used to call home-life a hag-ridden dream,
And you'd sigh, and you'd sock; but at present you seem
To know not of megrims or melancho-ly!" -
"True. One's pretty lively when ruined," said she.

- "I wish I had feathers, a fine sweeping gown,
And a delicate face, and could strut about Town!" -
"My dear - a raw country girl, such as you be,
Cannot quite expect that. You ain't ruined," said she.

Westbourne Park Villas: 1866

GREAT THINGS

Sweet cyder is a great thing,
  A great thing to me,
Spinning down to Weymouth town
  By Ridgeway thirstily,
And maid and mistress summoning
  Who tend the hostelry:
O cyder is a great thing,
  A great thing to me!

The dance it is a great thing,
  A great thing to me,
With candles lit and partners fit
  For night-long revelry;
And going home when day-dawning
  Peeps pale upon the lea:
O dancing is a great thing,
  A great thing to me!

Love is, yea, a great thing,
  A great thing to me,
When, having drawn across the lawn
  In darkness silently,
A figure flits like one a-wing
  Out from the nearest tree:
O love is, yes, a great thing,
  A great thing to me!

Will these be always great things,
  Great things to me?...
Let it befall that One will call,
  "Soul, I have need of thee":

What then? Joy-jaunts, impassioned flings,
    Love, and its ecstasy,
Will always have been great things,
    Great things to me!

ON A DISCOVERED CURL OF HAIR

When your soft welcomings were said,
This curl was waving on your head,
And when we walked where breakers dinned
It sported in the sun and wind,
And when I had won your words of grace
It brushed and clung about my face.
Then, to abate the misery
Of absentness, you gave it me.

Where are its fellows now? Ah, they
For brightest brown have donned a gray,
And gone into a caverned ark,
Ever unopened, always dark!

Yet this one curl, untouched of time,
Beams with live brown as in its prime,
So that it seems I even could now
Restore it to the living brow
By bearing down the western road
Till I had reached your old abode.

February 1913

SNOW IN THE SUBURBS

    Every branch big with it,
    Bent every twig with it;
  Every fork like a white web-foot;
  Every street and pavement mute:
Some flakes have lost their way, and grope back upward,
    when
Meeting those meandering down they turn and descend
    again.
  The palings are glued together like a wall,
  And there is no waft of wind with the fleecy fall.

A sparrow enters the tree,
  Whereon immediately
A snow-lump thrice his own slight size
Descends on him and showers his head and eyes,
  And overturns him,
  And near inurns him,
  And lights on a nether twig, when its brush
Starts off a volley of other lodging lumps with a rush.

The steps are a blanched slope,
  Up which, with feeble hope,
A black cat comes, wide-eyed and thin;
  And we take him in.

THE WHITEWASHED WALL

Why does she turn in that shy soft way
  Whenever she stirs the fire,
And kiss to the chimney-corner wall,
  As if entranced to admire
Its whitewashed bareness more than the sight
  Of a rose in richest green?
I have known her long, but this raptured rite
  I never before have seen.

– Well, once when her son cast his shadow there,
  A friend took a pencil and drew him
Upon that flame-lit wall. And the lines
  Had a lifelike semblance to him.
And there long stayed his familiar look;
  But one day, ere she knew,
The whitener came to cleanse the nook,
  And covered the face from view.

"Yes," he said: "My brush goes on with a rush,
  And the draught is buried under;
When you have to whiten old cots and brighten,
  What else can you do, I wonder?"
But she knows he's there. And when she yearns
  For him, deep in the labouring night,
She sees him as close at hand, and turns
  To him under his sheet of white.

I suppose that most readers would find something here, even at a first reading, that moves them to laughter, sadness, compassion, or thought. But as always with poetry there is much more to be had than a single reading will yield. For one thing, it is not until we have read a number of Hardy's poems that we realise that "Snow in the Suburbs" is one of the places where he is actually poking fun at his usual tragic preoccupations and images (of which more later). For another, it becomes more apparent that, as has been said, he is above all concerned, by every available means, to investigate reality. He is constantly re-shaping meaning, constantly pushing back the limits of our understanding, constantly enquiring into the "inexplicable relations" of human life in the world. The complexity of his thought leads him to find ways of underlining his meaning which may not show up – of which we may indeed have no ghost of a notion – until we have known the poem some time: as the unnoticed cobweb caught in the corner of the pane may be startlingly revealed by raindrops or frost; or the dusk-softened lines of the landscape, the lines on a face, be laid bare by the fiery light of sunrise. So the fun of "The Ruined Maid" can be enjoyed at one reading; but if we look only at what Hardy called the poetic veneer and not at the poetic texture, ignoring the hidden ways he uses to convey the implications of the story, we miss some of the best jokes and our understanding is shallow.

One of these ways, for example, is a subtle use of rhythm. In "The Ruined Maid" much of this is evident: we enjoy the build up of the first three lines in every stanza, as the voluble country girl expresses her amazement, followed by the sudden drop of temperature in the brief sardonic replies of the "Maid". Much of the delicious contrast between the two girls and their situation is conveyed by this antiphon of dialect and refinement, eager questioning and laconic replies, and by, for example, different positioning of the caesurae, or places where a natural pause comes in the line. By the penultimate stanza the caesurae's shifts are crucial; and then:

> "My dear – a raw country girl, such as you be,
> Cannot quite expect that. You ain't ruined," said she.

How different the "my dear" of this patronising reproof from the identical words (but then so innocently admiring) of the first line; how uncompromising is the final statement. (Yet it is typical of Hardy that he throws us the hint of a qualm in the Maid's lapse into the dialectal "be" of her past – for nothing in life is clear-cut or quite what we think.)

Then one also realises that this kind of rhythm, with a refrain in each stanza, recalls other poems:

> O where hae ye been, Lord Randal, my son?
> O where hae ye been, my handsome young man? –
> "I hae been to the wild wood; mother, make my bed soon,
> For I'm weary wi' hunting, and fain wald lie down."

Or

> When captains courageous, whom death could not daunte,
> Did march to the siege of the city of Gaunte,
> They mustered their soldiers by two and by three,
> And the foremost in battle was Mary Ambree.

Hardy is using something very near one of the old ballad metres. The ballad and refrain were poems for entertainment, as this is; they also suggest old time country simplicity and folklore, where commonly-held opinions and values might not have changed for generations. The country girl's traditionalist background, her unconscious concern to do the right thing and live by the rules of her upbringing, is reflected by her unmusical, rule-of-thumb stresses at the end of lines, made just because she thinks they ought to be there: Hardy spells them out as "prosperi-ty", "compa-ny" and subsequent similar words. But he has not finished yet. He has set up in the reader's mind, by association with balladry and its rhythms, a range of meanings which he left unsaid in so many words; but there is still something else he wants to raise. It is clear that the Ruined Maid herself is far from collecting the wages of sin, as Victorian morality would have had her do – rather, her infamous flouting of the moral law appears to have brought her only the shine of worldly success. There is no pious comment from the poet; yet, discussing all this in her fascinating essay on Hardy's meanings through rhythms, S.C. Neuman points out that the moral has come in through the back door of the metrics: for, instead of any open moralising, Hardy has enjoyed a little technical joke. He has chosen a modification of the ballad metre which is the Long Measure well known in hymns.[5]

You may think that this is far fetched, a mere invention of academic rummaging and dissection; or that if it is so, it happened purely by accident, without Hardy knowing what he was doing. Not so; "ye'll no fickle Thomas Yownie." Hardy didn't publish his first volume of poems until he was 58; he had written novels (and poems) for nearly thirty years and reflected profoundly on words and their ordering for nearer forty. In an important passage of his autobiography, he rather wearily tackled some of the imperceptive and uninformed criticism that had greeted *Wessex Poems*:

> In the reception of this and later volumes of Hardy's poems there was, he said, as regards form, the inevitable ascription to ignorance of what was really choice after full knowledge. That the author loved the art of concealing art was undiscerned.[6]

He continues specifically about rhythm, and about the close relationship he had discovered between architecture, his first professionally practised art, and poetry: "both arts, unlike some others, having to carry a rational content inside their artistic form." So the form of the poem (which includes its rhythm) must carry meaning; and as surely as Hardy was always exploring reality, he was also constantly exploring manifold ways of expressing it.

*   *   *   *   *   *

It is the kind of writing, the kind of wit, that exists in the creation of "The Ruined Maid", that reveals something of the many levels of Thomas Hardy's thinking, and makes his poetry not only an experience of life, but also a journey of discovery. A map is never a substitute for the glories of travel, but sometimes a few pointers on it can suggest features that might have been missed, or clarify the significance of the sweep of earth and sky.

I intend to pick flowers along the way. We are not going on an exhaustive route march across Hardy's world – that could take a lifetime. We are exploring for the fun of it, to extend the boundaries of experience, and to be exhilarated by what we see. We shall dally with people and places and time, ghosts and memory, and by the end of the journey I think we shall find that Thomas Hardy has brought us wisdom, disturbance, and repose.

Notes

1 Donald Davie, *Thomas Hardy and British Poetry* (London 1973), 58

2 *Life*, 251. Hardy himself wrote all but the last two chapters. Further passages omitted before publication (either by Hardy or by his second wife Florence after his death) can be found in *Notebooks*.

3 *Could I But Will*

4 *He Prefers Her Earthly*

5 S.C. Neuman, "Emotion put into Measure", in *PTH*, 44

6 *Life*, 301

2

PLACES AND PEOPLE

One of the features most evident in Hardy's world is that places matter. His sharp awareness of his surroundings makes the reader highly conscious of the setting for each poem, whether domestic or natural – of its associations with people and the past, of the way it may change or remain static, out of step with those people, and of its importance as an influential part of every experience: the "real" arena, known by our senses, where a particular moment of individual vision may take place. Hardy wrote three poems about Keats, for example, which were all inspired by places, including Keats' house at Hampstead. Many of his poems are memorably set in houses or rooms – with titles like "In a Waiting-Room", "The Ageing House", "Honeymoon Time at an Inn" – and there are constant references to doors and floors, stairways and windows. But his feeling for houses was much deeper than a merely architectural one.

TO A WELL-NAMED DWELLING

Glad old house of lichened stonework,
What I owed you in my lone work,
   Noon and night!
Whensoever faint or ailing,
Letting go my grasp and failing,
   You lent light.

How by that fair title came you?
Did some forward eye so name you
   Knowing that one,
Stumbling down his century blindly,
Would remark your sound, so kindly,
   And be won?

Smile in sunlight, sleep in moonlight,
Bask in April, May, and June-light,
   Zephyr-fanned;

Let your chambers show no sorrow,
Blanching day, or stuporing morrow,
While they stand.

That this house, described in the mellow, contented rhythms of
the poem, has a sound (even if only in its name, which is never
actually told) as well as an atmosphere and a look, need not
surprise us: Hardy's discernment of sounds and their meanings
was unusually developed.[1] This is particularly apparent in a
poem inspired by his birthplace at Higher Bockhampton, a place
which, understandably, had increasing reverberations for him
throughout his life.

SILENCES

There is the silence of a copse or croft
   When the wind sinks dumb,
   And of a belfry-loft
When the tenor after tolling stops its hum.

And there's the silence of a lonely pond
   Where a man was drowned,
   Nor nigh nor yond
A newt, frog, toad, to make the merest sound.

But the rapt silence of an empty house
   Where oneself was born,
   Dwelt, held carouse
With friends, is of all silences most forlorn!

Past are remembered songs and music-strains
   Once audible there:
   Roof, rafters, panes
Look absent-thoughted, tranced, or locked in prayer.

It seems no power on earth can waken it
   Or rouse its rooms,
   Or its past permit
The present to stir a torpor like a tomb's.

As often, Hardy zooms in like a photographer's lens from a wide
arc of view to one concentrated point; and the parts of a room or
a house have become like people, with a life of their own. Roof,
rafters, panes . . . They have watched over the centuries and the

life within those walls; have shaken to the throb of music and merriment; but now – as we stand, looking up at them in a kind of wonder, they are locked in silence, locked in a world of their own, a world of the past. They mirror our feelings, mirror the old man with his vast chamber of hoarded memories, alone there in the empty room, the silence now carrying all the weight of his years and the generations before him. The atmosphere in this poem is so powerful that one may tend to ignore its structure. The rhymes seem so effortless, as inevitable as the silence; the choice of words, made so economical by the short lines, seems so exactly right, whether in the rather stately language of, for example, "Dwelt, held carouse", or the more everyday phrases like "Once audible there." Then come perhaps the most evocative lines of the poem, where the words grow on us at each reading: the repeated consonants of "roof" and "rafters", the open lingering vowel of "panes", those three words taking the eye upward to where the magical "absent-thoughted" – (a twist away from the more usual phrase which was Hardy's first printing) – and the "tranced, or locked in prayer", seem to evaporate into the air. Varying stresses too are used with the impeding force of those alliterative consonants to enhance the effect he wants: the last three lines paint in rhythm and sound the heaviness of this hush of death.

Another poem about this childhood home shows how easily he passed from the house to the garden, the domestic to the natural, and as always from the present to the past. It is as happy a scene as the last was brooding.

A BIRD-SCENE AT A RURAL DWELLING

When the inmate stirs, the birds retire discreetly
From the window-ledge, whereon they whistled sweetly
  And on the step of the door,
  In the misty morning hoar;
 But now the dweller is up they flee
 To the crooked neighbouring codlin-tree;
And when he comes fully forth they seek the garden,
And call from the lofty costard, as pleading pardon
  For shouting so near before
  In their joy at being alive:
Meanwhile the hammering clock within goes five.

I know a domicile of brown and green,
Where for a hundred summers there have been
Just such enactments, just such daybreaks seen.

Here is Hardy's delightful sense of detail, his ability to write a beautiful poem from a small incident, and his sense of the friendly, equal relationship between all living creatures. Here too is the clock which appears so often in the poems – from a preoccupation with time passing as well as the memory of an indispensably familiar companion of his childhood. One also sees the effect of his perfectionism: he never ceased to work on his poems, usually changing words and making improvements for the next edition even as the first came from the printer. In this poem line eleven was first printed:

Meanwhile the halting clock within strikes five.

The urgency and heightened vividness of "hammering" seems to match better the joyous intensity of the birds which he has built up as the poem grows. They begin by retiring discreetly and whistling sweetly, and then they flee and call and plead pardon and one finds their whistle has been a shout for joy – and the hammering clock joins, with something more homely as it "goes" rather than "strikes". The homeliness and the deceptive simplicity and ordinariness of much of his diction (or choice of words) are part of Hardy's style and philosophy, and part of his mastery of his medium, which we can look at more fully later. Some of the mastery lies too in the variations of metre and line lengths and the placing of pause and stress, as here, to achieve the right tone or atmosphere. Having given the lively hubbub of this dawn chorus, Hardy suddenly brings us quiet, and a deep, concentrated, restrained emotion:

I know a domicile of brown and green
Where for a hundred summers there have been
Just such enactments, just such daybreaks seen.

It almost seems as if time means nothing and he himself has been watching this for a hundred years.

The earliest poem Hardy appears to have written, when he was between seventeen and twenty, was also about his birthplace ("Domicilium", p 285); but he was much more concerned then with its natural setting. It is quite clear from all his writing that these vital early years of life under the stars with the rustling of hollies and the moan of the wind in the pines gave him a particular awareness of the natural world that he never lost. At the age of 65 he was noting in which order the different trees were losing their leaves that year.[2] So his sense of place is always a sense of the land or seascape and the seasons, as well as the houses and towns, the market-place or the railway cutting. It is also firmly tethered to the map, as "Geographical Knowledge" shows – a charming poem where the village postmistress at Bockhampton talks of the whereabouts of her sailor son.

GEOGRAPHICAL KNOWLEDGE
(A Memory of Christiana C-)

Where Blackmoor was, the road that led
    To Bath, she could not show,
Nor point the sky that overspread
    Towns ten miles off or so.

But that Calcutta stood this way,
    Cape Horn there figured fell,
That here was Boston, here Bombay,
    She could declare full well.

Less known to her the track athwart
    Froom Mead or Yell'ham Wood
Than how to make some Austral port
    In seas of surly mood.

She saw the glint of Guinea's shore
    Behind the plum-tree nigh,
Heard old unruly Biscay's roar
    In the weir's purl hard by....

"My son's a sailor, and he knows
    All seas and many lands,
And when he's home he points and shows
    Each country where it stands.

"He's now just there – by Gib's high rock –
    And when he gets, you see,
To Portsmouth here, behind the clock,
    Then he'll come back to me!"

A son who didn't come back, however, is the hero of one of Hardy's finest poems, and one where he is meticulous in his development of the setting, the landscape of Southern Africa. "Drummer Hodge" was inspired by the Boer War. In October 1899 Hardy was at Southampton Docks to watch the embarcation of the troops. The resulting poems were typical of the man, his sense of place, of history, of the futility of war and a merely narrow patriotism – (though paradoxically he could also hardly ever resist the glamour of war's trappings in pre-mechanised, pre-nuclear days) – and of the sufferings of individuals.

DRUMMER HODGE

I

They throw in Drummer Hodge, to rest
  Uncoffined – just as found:
His landmark is a kopje-crest
  That breaks the veldt around;
And foreign constellations west
  Each night above his mound.

II

Young Hodge the Drummer never knew –
  Fresh from his Wessex home –
The meaning of the broad Karoo,
  The Bush, the dusty loam,
And why uprose to nightly view
  Strange stars amid the gloam.

III

Yet portion of that unknown plain
  Will Hodge for ever be;
His homely Northern breast and brain
  Grow to some Southern tree,
And strange-eyed constellations reign
  His stars eternally.

This poem seems to me to be almost perfect. A finely sprung tension holds it in balance with a deep compelling emotion which never wobbles over into sentimentality. Changing the image, it is clear that the restraint shown throughout concentrates its essence and makes it the more potent. There is that sense of peace or repose which, Coventry Patmore wrote, is necessary in great art.[3] It is precise in the details which set the scene – the foreign words *kopje, veldt, Karoo*, which reinforce our acceptance of the unfamiliar stars – (to a countryman born, like Hardy, a disorientation indeed. The stars are one of his most constant images.) There is a satisfying unity as the poem begins and ends with rest under those strange-eyed constellations: they begin by being "foreign", but they end by being "his" stars and watching over the boy left in their charge. Again the apparent effortlessness of the rhymes conceals the art; so does the choice of words – like "reign", which gives what Hardy elsewhere called a "kingly effulgence" to those sovereign stars. In only a word here and there, the innocence and simplicity of the Wessex lad is conveyed: his helplessness as he is thrown in, as it were with a tag, "Just as found"; his youth and freshness, his "homely Northern breast and brain"; and his final quiet triumph. The theme of the new life springing from the grave into tree or plant, (as in the poem "Voices from Things Growing in a Churchyard") was a Hardy favourite: it is connected with his Darwinian belief that all creation, human and bird and beast, hill and wind, are one; and it is often both cause and effect of his anchorage to particular places.

In "Drummer Hodge" Hardy characteristically works outwards from the dead man in his physical setting, the individual seen in the landscape, to his universal significance as a representative of the human race in the whole cosmos. In this its range and sweep, and so its emotional and intellectual impact, are far greater than that of Rupert Brooke's later poem, "The Soldier", with which it inevitably invites comparison. Hardy's patriotism was to total humanity, not just to that part of it which was English (– was he ahead of his time?); the restraint and apparent impersonality of his poem emphasises its universality. "There is sorrow, but it is the sorrow of the spheres."[4]

The South African setting of "Drummer Hodge" is exotic compared with most of Hardy's evocations of the natural world. He could call up in a few lines the swirling sea mist that creeps round the sheep boy on the heath, or the damps of autumn as the old woman, raking up leaves in my lord's park, "sighs at life's russet hue";[5] or the wild storms (and superstitions) that drenched his native Dorset.

NIGHT-TIME IN MID-FALL

It is a storm-strid night, winds footing swift
    Through the blind profound;
    I know the happenings from their sound;
Leaves totter down still green, and spin, and drift;
The tree-trunks rock to their roots, which wrench and lift
The loam where they run onward underground.

The streams are muddy and swollen; eels migrate
    To a new abode;
    Even cross, 'tis said, the turnpike-road;
(Men's feet have felt their crawl, homecoming late):
The westward fronts of towers are saturate,
Church-timbers crack, and witches ride abroad.

This poem strains and snaps with the tug of the gale at the trees.
The winds – described with human body imagery – are powerful
and purposeful messengers, gusting everywhere at once, testing
strengths, threatening existence. Human footfalls too are
precarious with the slime of mud and the slithering eels on the
road. (This extraordinary detail is of just the kind that Hardy's
watchful eye and ear, and his historian's impulse would record.)
By the end of the word "saturate" the crack in the timbers has
already been heard; the eels and the shrieks, the uncanny hiss of
wind and rain at this Hallowe'en-tide have prepared the reader
for anything as the covens stream forth into the night.

Hardy is good at describing water, whether the "witless
babble" of pouring gutters or the cluck of the Stour scrabbling at
the piers of the footbridge; and his pictures of the sea are superb.
So is his suggestion of atmosphere.

ONCE AT SWANAGE

The spray sprang up across the cusps of the moon,
    And all its light loomed green
    As a witch-flame's weirdsome sheen
At the minute of an incantation scene;
And it greened our gaze – that night at demilune.

Roaring high and roaring low was the sea
    Behind the headland shores:

It symboled the slamming of doors,
Or a regiment hurrying over hollow floors...
And there we stood, hands clasped: I and she!

Though one can pick out some of his methods – uncommon words, coined words, contrasting lines of Latinate words and robust Anglo-Saxon monosyllables, yet another different rhyme scheme, suitably crashing stresses – they all add up to more than the sound of the racing sea, and an atmosphere that is electric. But the sea scene is, like so many of his evocations of place, only the starting point for a moment of vision, (as it was for Matthew Arnold in the experience that led to "Dover Beach"): a moment – once, long past, – when moon over water, water over moon, are conjoined, binding us under an eerie spell that falsifies all our view of the world. In "Dover Beach" Arnold sees the world in far more explicitly pessimistic terms than Hardy could be accused of. As so often, Hardy will not dogmatise, but leaves his readers in this vaporous haze of ambiguity, to see for themselves what the world and their apprehension of it really is. Both poets feel the roar and the "confused alarms" of the sea/world surging beside them: Hardy's slamming doors and drumming on hollow floors occur in more than one poem – (and in, say, the telling image in *Tess of the d'Urbervilles* when "herons came, with a great bold noise as of opening doors and shutters") – a recurrent symbolism which is also an instance of his power of raising a scene before a reader's ears and eyes.

Hardy's care (and skill) in choosing words was no accident or untrained gift. His notebooks show that from a young man, who had left school at sixteen, he had worked incessantly on words, trying out unusual combinations, experimentally rewriting parts of the Book of Common Prayer, the Bible, or lyric themes from other poets, studying and listing words. In the 1860s, when in his twenties, he was looking, amongst other things, for ways of conveying different sounds:

clanging thunder, humble bee: *pealing* waves *whooping* storm: *clicking* twigs: *flapping* of leaves: *creaking* of trunks, and *wrenching* of branches....[6]

More than forty years later, in 1910, he made a pilgrimage to the grave of Swinburne, (a poet he had much admired in his youth,) at Bonchurch on the Hampshire coast, and wrote the poem "A Singer Asleep." This visionary poem can be unravelled to reveal how he developed the structure and patterns of his poems over the years;[7] but for now let us look simply at his description of the sea, the atmosphere he creates, – and the use he made of his studies many years before.

"A Singer Asleep" begins:

> In this fair niche above the unslumbering sea,
> That sentrys up and down all night, all day,
> From cove to promontory, from ness to bay,
> The Fates have fitly bidden that he should be
> Pillowed eternally.

Eight stanzas later it ends like this:

> So here, beneath the waking constellations,
> Where the waves peal their everlasting strains,
> And their dull subterrene reverberations
> Shake him when storms make mountains of their plains –
> Him once their peer in sad improvisations,
> And deft as wind to cleave their frothy manes –
> I leave him, while the daylight gleam declines
> Upon the capes and chines.

The word explored in the 1860s has come home. I have come to find those two opening lines of the last stanza a magical accompaniment to any walk by the wild sea.

> So here, beneath the waking constellations,
> Where the waves peal their everlasting strains...

In this poem Hardy has created an organic unity between the subject and the setting, which hard scrutiny shows to be astonishingly close-knit. It is one of the finer points of his mature poetry which will be apparent when the traveller reaches the heart of Hardy country. For the moment he or she must press on in this general survey of the journey, past the places to the people – for it is easy to see that almost every one of the poems quoted above as examples of Hardy's feeling for place is also equally or primarily about people. "Scenery is fine –" wrote Keats, "but human nature is finer."[8]

It is also often pointed out that Hardy's landscape is always one with figures. So much is made of him as a countryman and nature-lover (which in some ways he was not), that one forgets that he probably cared more about people than anything else, their pasts, their relationships, and, despite their allotted ant-like role in the evolving universe, their vital individuality. *The Life of Thomas Hardy* is full of notes and comments on this theme.

> *Aug 23* (1865). The poetry of a scene varies with the minds of the perceivers. Indeed, it does not lie in the scene at all.

> *September 28* (1877). An object or mark raised or made by man on a scene is worth ten times any such formed by unconscious Nature. Hence clouds, mists and mountains are unimportant beside the wear on a threshold, or the print of a hand.[9]

So although in Hardy's world places are vital and significant, they are almost invariably places marked by people, and people who are the dominant interest. Reading through his poems one finds that words like "highway", "track", or "thoroughfare" are frequently important. The figure crossing the landscape is often on a journey or pilgrimage through life.

> And so, the rough highway forgetting,
> I pace hill and dale
> Regarding the sky,
> Regarding the vision on high,
> And thus re-illumed have no humour for letting
> My pilgrimage fail.[10]

There are landmarks on this journey, landmarks in time as in space – like the Bronze Age barrows set up on the heath near his home not only as burial places but as routemarkers for travellers. To most local people they would be merely a feature on the skyline; he values them for their human associations.

BY THE BARROWS

> Not far from Mellstock – so tradition saith –
> Where barrows, bulging as they bosoms were
> Of Multimammia stretched supinely there,

Catch night and noon the tempest's wanton breath,

A battle, desperate doubtless unto death,
Was one time fought. The outlook, lone and bare,
The towering hawk and passing raven share,
And all the upland round is called "The He'th".

Here once a woman, in our modern age,
Fought single-handedly to shield a child –
One not her own – from a man's senseless rage.
And to my mind no patriot's bones there piled
So consecrate the silence as her deed
Of stoic and devoted self-unheed.

On the same heath ran a track which the young Thomas and his
mother often walked to visit their relations in Puddletown.
Despite his keen pleasure in its historic association, it is another
that colours the place for him.

THE ROMAN ROAD

The Roman Road runs straight and bare
As the pale parting-line in hair
Across the heath. And thoughtful men
Contrast its days of Now and Then,
And delve, and measure, and compare;

Visioning on the vacant air
Helmed legioñaries, who proudly rear
The Eagle, as they pace again
                    The Roman Road.

But no tall brass-helmed legionnaire
Haunts it for me. Uprises there
A mother's form upon my ken,
Guiding my infant steps, as when
We walked that ancient thoroughfare,
                    The Roman Road.

It is the same with another woman, his beloved sister Mary, who
fills his mind as he watches the logs burning on the hearth –
branches from the very same apple tree, now felled, on which as
children they had climbed together.[11] And in the poem "Sacred
to the Memory", as he ponders the words he has put on her

gravestone, he knows that her presence is invested everywhere she has lived, and

> stands deep lined
> Upon the landscape, high and low
> Wherein she made such worthy show.

Similarly when, poking about in the rocks by the shore, he finds a rusty old relic, his mind moves at once to the person who might have owned it.

THE SUNSHADE

Ah – it's the skeleton of a lady's sunshade,
　　Here at my feet in the hard rock's chink,
　　Merely a naked sheaf of wires! –
　　Twenty years have gone with their livers and diers
　　Since it was silked in its white or pink.

Noonshine riddles the ribs of the sunshade,
　　No more a screen from the weakest ray;
　　Nothing to tell us the hue of its dyes,
　　Nothing but rusty bones as it lies
　　In its coffin of stone, unseen till to-day.

Where is the woman who carried that sunshade
　　Up and down this seaside place? –
　　Little thumb standing against its stem,
　　Thoughts perhaps bent on a love-stratagem,
　　Softening yet more the already soft face!

Is the fair woman who carried that sunshade
　　A skeleton just as her property is,
　　Laid in the chink that none may scan?
　　And does she regret – if regret dust can –
　　The vain things thought when she flourished this?

Swanage Cliffs

I have known women to take exception to the "love-stratagem" and the "little thumb", while men say that a small, neat hand tends as a fact to belong more to women than men, and is to be appreciated; the "love-stratagem" may reflect no more than Hardy's realism about the chief option open to many Victorian women. Whatever the reader's reaction, in his poems and stories he seems to enter unusually sensitively into the minds and lives of his women characters. One could argue that he was in some ways an early feminist – but this is to stray too far off the track in this rapid stride through his peopled world, where Hardy's compassionate and ironic observation gathers a cluster of memorable individuals.

JULIE-JANE

Sing; how 'a would sing!
How 'a would raise the tune
When we rode in the waggon from harvesting
By the light of the moon!

Dance; how 'a would dance!
If a fiddlestring did but sound
She would hold out her coats, give a slanting glance,
And go round and round.

Laugh; how 'a would laugh!
Her peony lips would part
As if none such a place for a lover to quaff
At the deeps of a heart.

Julie, O girl of joy,
Soon, soon that lover he came.
Ah, yes; and gave thee a baby-boy,
But never his name ....

– Tolling for her, as you guess;
And the baby too .... 'Tis well.
You knew her in maidhood likewise? – Yes,
That's her burial bell.

"I suppose," with a laugh, she said,
"I should blush that I'm not a wife;
But how can it matter, so soon to be dead,
What one does in life!"

When we sat making the mourning
By her death-bed side, said she,
"Dears, how can you keep from your lovers, adorning
In honour of me!"

Bubbling and brightsome-eyed!
But now – O never again.
She chose her bearers before she died
From her fancy-men.

NOTE – It is, or was, a common custom in Wessex, and probably other country places, to prepare the mourning beside the death-bed, the dying person sometimes assisting, who also selects his or her bearers on such occasions.

"Bubbling and brightsome-eyed!" She is totally without self-pity, this girl of joy, and so vividly and poignantly realised that the reader is magnetised into her charmed circle. Shortly before this in *Time's Laughingstocks* is "The Orphaned Old Maid", a stringent critique of the selfish father who ensures that, again, "the woman pays." A few poems later he makes one feel with the young man led up the garden path: ("Why didn't you say you was promised, Rose-Ann?") – in fact, taking this book alone, of its 94 poems only ten or eleven are not about people. The lyrical sensitivity of "The Inquiry" describes a situation common enough in the agricultural depression of the last century: but it's with the girl that we identify.

THE INQUIRY

And are ye one of Hermitage –
Of Hermitage, by Ivel Road,
And do ye know, in Hermitage,
A thatch-roofed house where sengreens grow?
And does John Waywood live there still –
He of the name that there abode
When father hurdled on the hill
    Some fifteen years ago?

Does he now speak o' Patty Beech,
The Patty Beech he used to – see,
Or ask at all if Patty Beech
Is known or heard of out this way?
– Ask ever if she's living yet,
And where her present home may be,
And how she bears life's fag and fret
    After so long a day?

In years agone at Hermitage

This faded face was counted fair,
None fairer; and at Hermitage
We swore to wed when he should thrive.
But never a chance had he or I,
And waiting made his wish outwear,
And Time, that dooms man's love to die,
Preserves a maid's alive.

There may be a hint of criticism in the wayward suitor's name: Hardy's complex thinking often results in this kind of double meaning. There are those who see Patty's surname as a "symbol of inexhaustible life," and the rather unusual reference to the "sengreens" or prolific house-leek growing on her lover's dwelling as to a form of "vegetation that mocks his infertility."[12] It may be so, for it never does to underestimate Hardy's wiles or his art. But on a different wavelength the reader is moved by this poem, by the old eternal tale of love unfulfilled, and the lasting hurt suffered by ordinary people – "not many wise ... not many mighty, not many noble" – borne with dignity and resignation. Patty's rather breathless opening, when she discovers the chance to ask after her former lover – and we share her suspense – gives way (perhaps at the pity on the traveller's face) to a restrained and simple telling of her story. There is something about the sing-song repeated vowels and consonants of "This faded face was counted fair," that suggests it is all over, all old-fashioned now – even with the rightful emphasis that brings one up short in "None fairer." The same pattern of repeated "w's" links the lovers' intention, – "We swore to wed when he should thrive" – to its failure, as "waiting made his wish outwear." It might be the stylised narration of a Greek chorus. In each stanza the rhyme bonds it all together: the sixth line always rhymes back to the second, and the ending vowels are used to suggest harmony or disarray. In the first stanza the vowel in "grow/ago" is the same as in "road/abode", as Patty remembers her John, his house, and the security of her own home. In the second, the break before "– see" delicately jars, and shows she was really thinking of another word; so the vowel sounds of "way/day" and "see/be" are out of harmony. In the third stanza we have already reached a rather dreamlike stage as we are reminded that it happened "in years agone;" and the alliteration of the "w's" and the faded face have made it into a kind of chant or word pattern only. The vowel in "thrive" again does not chime with "fair", since that is all over. It leads forward inexorably, picking up "I" and "die" and "Time", until it clangs into "Preserves a maid's *alive*" – a stressed, bright vowel of most cruel irony that always jolts this reader, at least, into final sharp awareness of the bitterness of the woman's situation. So comes one of the gifts of poetry, that even without stopping to analyse it one can be affected, and taught, by rhyme.

"The Inquiry" shows Hardy's empathy with other people's lives. In another short poem the poignancy of the incident is laced with laughter by his ever-present sense of the absurd.

AT THE RAILWAY STATION, UPWAY

"There is not much that I can do,
For I've no money that's quite my own!"
    Spoke up the pitying child –
A little boy with a violin
At the station before the train came in, –
"But I can play my fiddle to you,
And a nice one 'tis, and good in tone!"

    The man in the handcuffs smiled;
The constable looked, and he smiled, too,
    As the fiddle began to twang;
And the man in the handcuffs suddenly sang
            With grimful glee:
            "This life so free
            Is the life for me!"
And the constable smiled, and said no word,
As if unconscious of what he heard;
And so they went on till the train came in –
The convict, and boy with the violin.

If this actually happened, one wonders how many bystanders would have noticed what the tune was, let alone its irony in the situation; but Hardy was an observer of the eagle class as well as one who thrived on music and song. He also seems to have had an affinity with children. (John Middleton Murry once described how the octogenarian Hardy delighted the Murry baby by making a rabbit out of a handkerchief). Many of his poems are about children, their plight, their grace, their contribution, or

(as in "By the Barrows") their priceless worth. In Fiesole it was
a child showing him an imperial coin identical to those he had
unearthed in Dorchester, who by

> her act flashed home
> In that mute moment to my opened mind
> The power, the pride, the reach of perished Rome.[13]

In "A Last Journey", the child ministering to her dying father
hears from him of his night's (mental) activities, breezing around
Dorset to fair and friends, back to his father's old orchard, even
to London to hear the night-watchman cry the hours:

> "And then you pulled the curtain; and, ah me,
> I found me back where I wished not to be!"
>
> 'Twas told the child next day: "Your father's dead."
> And, struck, she questioned, "O,
> That journey, then, did father really go? –
> Buy nuts, and cakes, and travel at night till dawn was red,
> And tire himself with journeying, as he said,
> To see those old friends that he cared for so?"

For the child and for the dying man, the dreamed journey has
been equally real.

Another innocent questioner seems to hold all the bright
idiosyncrasy and charm of childhood in a magic bubble, pricked
only by a world-weary adult:

BOYS THEN AND NOW

> "More than one cuckoo?"
> And the little boy
> Seemed to lose something
> Of his spring joy.
>
> When he'd grown up
> He told his son
> He'd used to think
> There was only one
>
> Who came each year
> With the trees' new trim

On purpose to please
England and him:

And his son – old already
In life and its ways –
Said yawning, "How foolish
Boys were in those days!"

It's possible that this was Hardy's own belief as a child. (It is also referred to in *The Return of the Native*.) His love of birds is carried into many poems, not only those about children like "The Bird-Catcher's Boy" (one of his finest), and "The Boy's Dream." Both these poems can recall Wordsworth, whose view of Nature was so different from Hardy's. There is an almost Wordsworthian simplicity and flatness in some of these lines, and an awkwardness which reproduces the drab, restricted and "waning" life; but there is no mistaking Hardy's sympathy for the boy.

THE BOY'S DREAM

Provincial town-boy he, – frail, lame,
His face a waning lily-white,
A court the home of his wry, wrenched frame,
Where noontide shed no warmth or light.

Over his temples – flat, and wan,
Where bluest veins were patterned keen,
The skin appeared so thinly drawn
The skull beneath was almost seen.

Always a wishful, absent look
Expressed it in his face and eye;
At the strong shape this longing took
One guessed what wish must underlie.

But no. That wish was not for strength,
For other boys' agility,
To race with ease the field's far length,
Now hopped across so painfully.

He minded not his lameness much,
To shine at feats he did not long,
Nor to be best at goal and touch,
Nor at assaults to stand up strong.

But sometimes he would let be known
What the wish was: – to have, next spring,
A real green linnet – his very own –
Like that one he had late heard sing.

And as he breathed the cherished dream
To those whose secrecy was sworn,
His face was beautified by the theme,
And wore the radiance of the morn.

Hardy seems to have had an equal, though different, sympathy with the "wretched children" driven from Athelhall Park by Sir Nameless. This pompous laird congratulated himself on being without troublesome issue, and for posterity, instead, had a giant statue of himself made from alabaster:

With shield, and crest, and casque, and sword complete:
When done a statelier work was never known.

Three hundred years hied; Church-restorers came,
And, no one of his lineage being traced,
They thought an effigy so large in frame
Best fitted for the floor. There it was placed,
Under the seats for schoolchildren. And they
Kicked out his name, and hobnailed off his nose;
And, as they yawn through sermon-time, they say,
"Who was this old stone man beneath our toes?"[14]

Hardy, like Sir Nameless, had no offspring (but dragged the knight into immortality with him, after all, on the skirts of poesy.) He was, however, certainly aware of the people in his past. Poem after poem ponders on the "sires of mine now perished and forgot," and on those he had loved and outlived. Characteristically in the following poem he personifies them in the crucial physical feature, feet and voice, eyes and cheek:

SONG TO AN OLD BURDEN

The feet have left the wormholed flooring,
    That danced to the ancient air,
    The fiddler, all-ignoring,
Sleeps by the gray-grassed 'cello player;
Shall I then foot around around around,
    As once I footed there!

The voice is heard in the room no longer
That trilled, none sweetlier,
To gentle stops or stronger,
Where now the dust-draped cobwebs stir:
Shall I then sing again again again,
As once I sang with her!

The eyes that beamed out rapid brightness
Have longtime found their close,
The cheeks have wanned to whiteness
That used to sort with summer rose:
Shall I then joy anew anew anew,
As once I joyed in those!

O what's to me this tedious Maying
What's to me this June?
O why should viols be playing
To catch and reel and rigadoon?
Shall I sing, dance around around around,
When phantoms call the tune!

One must – and can – never forget that Hardy published his first volume of poems at 58, an age when family history and the past, so often ignored when we are young, begin to fascinate. It is this maturity, this sense of looking back to understand human experience, and in that act to create experience anew, that gives him his particular vantage point. It is this, as will be clear when all the strands come together, which enables him to make out of poetry and life not just, in his own words, "a sweet pattern", but actually a revelation.

Notes

1   See, for example, the opening of *Under the Greenwood Tree.*

2   *Life,* 327

3   Coventry Patmore, *Principle in Art,* chapters V and VI

4   John Middleton Murry, "The Poetry of Mr Hardy", in *The Athenaeum,* Nov 1919, quoted in *Casebook,* 85

5   *Autumn in King's Hintock Park*

6   *Studies, Specimens, etc* – a notebook in the possession of R.L. Purdy, quoted in *Millgate*, 88

7   See *Dennis Taylor*, 17–19. Hardy's letter of 13 March 1910 to Frederic Harrison shows that he had actually written much of the poem before visiting the grave.

8   John Keats, letter to Benjamin Bailey, 13 March 1818

9   *Life*, 50, 116. Since the book is written chronologically, it is easy to find the page reference by the date of a note.

10 *For Life I Had Never Cared Greatly*

11 *Logs on the Hearth*, page 80

12 Frank R. Giordano Jr, "A Reading of 'A Set of Country Songs'", *Victorian Poetry*, vol 17, Spring–Summer 1979, Thomas Hardy Commemorative Issue, 89

13 *In the Old Theatre, Fiesole*

14 *The Children and Sir Nameless*

3

TIME, GHOSTS, AND THE GROTESQUE

In old age Thomas Hardy copied into his literary notebook a phrase from Francis Bacon: "The inseparable propriety of Time, which is ever more and more to disclose Truth."[1] To read his poetry is to become almost obsessively aware of time. Time, and particularly time past, is the character who dominates it – time, that infinitely flexible, unfathomable, element, so endless to the young, almost non-existent to the old. Hardy recognises time as basic to life: when an enquirer asks what the New Dawn's business will be that day, the Dawn catalogues his coming responsibilities – for a death, a birth, some burials,

> And for several other such odd jobs round here
> That time to-day must do.[2]

When Hardy's old friend Judge Benjamin Lock died in Bridlington, the (fittingly?) prosaic poem he wrote contains not only an unexpected, marvellous, lyrical evocation of Lock's gale-swept burial place, but a typical reflection on the universal functions of Time.

"NOTHING MATTERS MUCH"

(B.F.L.)

> "Nothing matters much," he said
> Of something just befallen unduly:
> He, then active, but now dead,
> Truly, truly!
>
> He knew each letter of the law
> As voiced by those of wig and gown,
> Whose slightest syllogistic flaw
> He hammered down.

And often would he shape in word
That nothing needed much lamenting;
And she who sat there smiled and heard,
    Sadly assenting.

Facing the North Sea now he lies,
Toward the red altar of the East,
The Flamborough roar his psalmodies,
    The wind his priest.

And while I think of his bleak bed,
Of Time that builds, of Time that shatters,
Lost to all thought is he, who said
    "Nothing much matters."

It was a phrase Hardy would feel was validated by the time-scale
of history. During the preparations for building his Dorchester
home, two closely embraced skeletons were found in an ancient
barrow by the site. They prompted a characteristic poem. Their
date was estimated at 1800 B C; and he thinks of Old Testament
figures, historic lovers like Antony and Cleopatra, Paris and
Helen, Abélard and Héloise, all of whom, though seeming
distant now, were living long *after* the buried couple. And yet,
viewed in the span of history, with rocks dating back thousands
of millions of years, what are these few thousands of human
existence? "The Clasped Skeletons" (addressed directly to
them) ends like this:

So long, beyond chronology,
    Lovers in death as 'twere,
So long in placid dignity
    Have you lain here!

Yet what is length of time? But dream!
    Once breathed this atmosphere
These fossils near you, met the gleam
    Of day as you did here;

But so far earlier theirs beside
    Your life-span and career,
That they might style of yestertide
    Your coming here!

Hardy often says that measured time is a dream – "Time seemed fiction, Past and Present one." His world is not limited to the material or temporal or spatial: in one poem,[3] even the sound of a particular kiss is gone into the ether and lives on – with all the birdsong and music that ever was, as in:

IN A MUSEUM

I

Here's the mould of a musical bird long passed from light,
Which over the earth before man came was winging;
There's a contralto voice I heard last night,
That lodges in me still with its sweet singing.

II

Such a dream is Time that the coo of this ancient bird
Has perished not, but is blent, or will be blending
Mid visionless wilds of space with the voice that I heard,
In the full-fugued song of the universe unending.

Exeter

It is natural in a museum to think of time past; but Hardy also thought of it when he looked in an exhibition at paintings of (last year's) fluffy young leaves, and when he heard the birds sing in his garden.

PROUD SONGSTERS

The thrushes sing as the sun is going,
And the finches whistle in ones and pairs,
And as it gets dark loud nightingales
          In bushes
Pipe, as they can when April wears,
          As if all Time were theirs.

These are brand-new birds of twelve-months' growing,
Which a year ago, or less than twain,
No finches were, nor nightingales,
          Nor thrushes,
But only particles of grain,
          And earth, and air, and rain.

This poem – "simple only to the heedless" – (and beautifully set by both Britten and Finzi), deserves a careful look later at what the rhyme and versification tell.[4] It was almost certainly written after re-reading a similar passage in chapter XX of *Tess of the d'Urbervilles*, when Hardy was preparing a new edition of his novels. (This is one of the fascinating aspects of his developing art: how the re-reading often triggered an old memory or image and created a new poem or altered an existing one.[5]) "Proud Songsters" raises thoughts not only about birds, but about everything ephemeral: about unthinking youth who "pipe ... as if all Time were theirs"; about love and death and the muse, which poets have associated with Philomela the nightingale as far back as the old Greek legends; about the fleeting cycle of Nature and life.

But Time in Hardy's mind and poetry is much more complex. "The Clasped Skeletons" is an example of the kind of archaeological/geological time which he knew with his mind, and describes so vividly in *A Pair of Blue Eyes* when Henry Knight is literally cliff-hanging eye to eye with the fossils; but it is rare in his poetry. Nearest to it perhaps is his great sense of history. When Field-Marshal Allenby captured Jezreel in 1918, Hardy wrote a poem full of the historic past of that vital plain of Esdraelon where so many battles for supremacy had taken place. When he watched the Boer War troops embarking at Southampton, he thought of the place as

> Here, where Vespasian's legions struck the sands,
> And Cerdic with the Saxons entered in,
> And Henry's army leapt afloat. . . .[6]

So he constantly recalls the human story behind "the melancholy marching of the years." But as that line shows, he presents a rather conventionally personified Time, a being who is often of malevolent intent, as in

> But Time, to make me grieve,
> Part steals, lets part abide;

and

> Time, that dooms man's love to die,
> Preserves a maid's alive.

Similarly in two poems written when he was only 26, his feeling that the universe and humans within it are ruled by blind chance describes how "dicing Time for gladness casts a moan," and how "Sportsman Time but rears his brood to kill."[7] We hear that "Time laughed awry," and more than once comes this image:

> Yet I note the little chisel
>   Of never-napping Time
> Defacing wan and grizzel
>   The blazon of my prime.
> When at night he thinks me sleeping
>   I feel him boring sly
> Within my bones, and heaping
>   Quaintest pains for by-and-by.[8]

Time is always changing things – one could select from scores of instances in different poems:

Time unveils sorrows and secrets
Time has tired me
Time cures hearts of tenderness
Time has buried the past
Time-wraiths turn our songsingings to fear
Ah, she's a beldame now,/Time-trenched on cheek and brow.

Time separates lovers by its "dividing months" and "The grey gaunt days dividing us in twain."

All these personifications are rather dull and predictable. They seem to be what Hardy thought about Time, rather than what he felt. Often in his poetry there is such an apparent dichotomy. He explained it more than once, in phrases like "I hold that the mission of poetry is to record impressions, not convictions";[9] and particularly in the Apology to *Late Lyrics and Earlier*, where he denies that his poetry represents his "view" of life, but calls it "really a series of fugitive impressions which I have never tried to co-ordinate." So it is with Time: underneath the conventional references lie some powerful "impressions" which colour many of his poems.

One of these is the curiously claustrophobic quality that characterises his "personal" time. By "personal" I mean the time within which he feels he and all human beings live – it can almost be equated with "life". (Bergson's "duration" – the psychological arena in which we live our deepest experiences, as opposed to clock time – may be similar.) Indeed the word "within" is crucial, for one of Hardy's preoccupations is with being trapped or imprisoned. (Reading his poems with an eye to the key words is a fascinating exercise: if one just looks for the actual words, let alone implied meanings – *prison, chains, bondage, slave, thrall, cell, mew, gin, cage* – one finds how the idea accumulates.) Something of this is in the poem about his birthplace where we were locked in the silence of the years, caught in "a torpor like a tomb's." It is explicit in the poem he wrote after his mother's death.

AFTER THE LAST BREATH

(J.H. 1813–1904)

There's no more to be done, or feared, or hoped;
None now need watch, speak low, and list, and tire;
No irksome crease outsmoothed, no pillow sloped
    Does she require.

Blankly we gaze. We are free to go or stay;
Our morrow's anxious plans have missed their aim;
Whether we leave to-night or wait till day
    Counts as the same.

The lettered vessels of medicaments
Seem asking wherefore we have set them here;
Each palliative its silly face presents
    As useless gear.

And yet we feel that something savours well;
We note a dumb relief withheld before;
Our well-beloved is prisoner in the cell
    Of Time no more.

In this poem, as in a number of others, death promises release from the "cell of Time". In "Friends Beyond" the familiar ghosts of his past neighbours whisper contentedly to him that now they are "free of thought," and

"No more need we corn and clothing, feel of old terrestial
    stress;

Chill detraction stirs no sigh;
Fear of death has even bygone us; death gave all that we
    possess."

It appears again in a poem that could be by no-one but Thomas
Hardy.

JUBILATE

"The very last time I ever was here," he said
"I saw much less of the quick than I saw of the dead."
– He was a man I had met with somewhere before,
But how or when I now could recall no more.

"The hazy mazy moonlight at one in the morning
Spread out as a sea across the frozen snow,
Glazed to live sparkles like the great breastplate adorning
The priest of the Temple, with Urim and Thummim aglow.

"The yew-tree arms, glued hard to the stiff stark air,
Hung still in the village sky as theatre-scenes
When I came by the churchyard wall, and halted there
At a shut-in sound of fiddles and tambourines.

"And as I stood harkening, dulcimers, hautboys, and shawms,
And violoncellos, and a three-stringed double-bass,
Joined in, and were intermixed with a singing of psalms;
And I looked over at the dead men's dwelling-place.

"Through the shine of the slippery snow I now could see,
As it were through a crystal roof, a great company
Of the dead minueting in stately step underground
To the tune of the instrument I had before heard sound.

"It was 'Eden New', and dancing they sang in a chore,
'We are out of it all! – yea, in Little-Ease cramped no more!'
And their shrouded figures pacing with joy I could see
As you see the stage from the gallery. And they had no heed
    of me.

"And I lifted my head quite dazed from the churchyard wall
And I doubted not that it warned I should soon have my call,
But –"... Then in the ashes he emptied the dregs of his cup,
And onward he went, and the darkness swallowed him up.

(Though this must not obscure our main point, so much is characteristic and to be relished here: frost and moonlight and music, with the Biblical overtones carried by the glittering expanse and the musical instruments;[10] the theatrical and body imagery; the evidence of Hardy's cherished literary inheritance in the verbal and image echoes of Coleridge's "Kubla Khan"; the double meaning of "Eden New"; and above all the grotesque imagination that peoples a world beneath the turf with "the dead minueting in stately step underground." In fact Hardy's original version was even more grotesque in its detail, for he had the dead "allemanding without shoes.")

But we were thinking about claustrophobia and imprisonment in Time for the living. The caged bird is a recurrent image; and remembering the treadmill contraptions offered to other small caged animals, one is not far from a frequent image of modern life as "the rat-race". Hardy has it all there in his fixation on stairs.

> I am laughing by the brook with her,
>   Splashed in its tumbling stir;
> And then it is a blankness looms
>   As if I walked not there,
> Nor she, but found me in haggard rooms,
>   And treading a lonely stair.[11]

Even more clearly in the following poem (probably) about his father, he equates the daily treadmill of life with the pointless, uncreative shuttle up and down the stairs, which only seems to highlight the lack of purposeful movement in so many lives. (French slang encapsulates it neatly in the jingle: "Métro – boulot – dodo.")[12]

ON ONE WHO LIVED AND DIED WHERE HE WAS BORN

> When a night in November
>   Blew forth its bleared airs
> An infant descended
>   His birth-chamber stairs
> For the very first time,
>   At the still, midnight chime;

All unapprehended
His mission, his aim. –
Thus, first, one November,
An infant descended
    The stairs.

On a night in November
Of weariful cares,
A frail aged figure
    Ascended those stairs
    For the very last time:
    All gone his life's prime,
All vanished his vigour,
    And fine, forceful frame:
Thus, last, one November
Ascended that figure
    Upstairs.

On those nights in November –
    Apart eighty years –
The babe and the bent one
    Who traversed those stairs
    From the early first time
    To the last feeble climb –
That fresh and that spent one –
    Were even the same:
Yea, who passed in November
As infant, as bent one,
    Those stairs.

Wise child of November!
    From birth to blanched hairs
Descending, ascending,
    Wealth-wantless, those stairs;
    Who saw quick in time
    As a vain pantomime
Life's tending, its ending,
    The worth of its fame.
Wise child of November,
Descending, ascending
    Those stairs!

The same sense of fruitless repetition, almost of vertigo, is created in "The Clock-Winder". The parish clerk at his daily task begins shut in the trap of the dark church, and proceeds to the treadmill:

> Up, up from the ground
> Around and around
> In the turret stair
> He clambers, to where
> The wheelwork is,
> With its tick, click, whizz,
> Reposefully measuring
> Each day to its end
> That mortal men spend
> In sorrowing and pleasuring.
> Nightly thus does he climb
> To the trackway of Time.

The church and tower interior have become almost as suffocating, as limiting, as the domestic interiors with their doors, floors, encircling mirrors, and crowding furniture, or the "long dark gallery, Catacomb-lined," where people are waiting, waiting, "Who, motion past, were nevertheless not dead."[13] The stifling imprisonment and impossibility of movement is probably most explicit in "The Masked Face":

> I found me in a great surging space,
>   At either end a door,
> And I said: "What is this giddying place,
>   With no firm-fixéd floor,
>   That I knew not of before?"
> "It is Life," said a mask-clad face.
>
> I asked: "But how do I come here.
>   Who never wished to come;
> Can the light and air be made more clear,
>   The floor more quietsome,
>   And the doors set wide? They numb
> Fast-locked, and fill with fear."
>
> The mask put on a bleak smile then,
>   And said, "O vassal-wight,
> There once complained a goosequill pen

> To the scribe of the Infinite
> Of the words it had to write
> Because they were past its ken."

As in all Hardy's poems, he has used every poetic resource to reinforce the meaning. The picture is terrifying, with all the hallmarks of hideous modern methods of question and disorientation. The cruel masked face patronises its victim and by its refusal to explain leaves him even more shut in and "in the dark." By its place in the line, "They numb" has become almost a scream. The repetition of "f's" is like shivering lips or chattering teeth, with consonants that the fear-paralysed muscles can hardly say: "firm-fixéd floor", "mask-clad face", "fast-locked" are all part of the nightmare where our feet sway without foothold and we can neither speak nor move. In the last stanza Hardy has picked his words, particularly the archaisms, to foster a sense of unreality and disorientation in time. The old-fashioned goosequill pen, (a mere object, depersonalised,) and the scribe, the vassal-wight, and the crushing allusion to things "past its ken" combine to make him lose his place in time and any sense of real identity.

It is no accident that words in many of the last quotations have included *numb, bleak, bleared, blanched, chill, wan, ashes* and "all vanished his vigour." Many of these "neutral tones"[14] are important, recurrent symbols in Hardy's poetry. Reading on, one notices more linked "key" words and images like *fade, shrink, dwindle, sag, sink, dim*; and, in an excellent essay on "Hardy and the Cell of Time", Patricia Ingham, to whom I am much indebted, points out how this "human time" in which he lives is something which does not merely corrupt and deface, but actually "denature[s] things, removing the natural qualities of life, warmth, colour."[15] It is a theme explored by other poets. In his 1867 notebook Hardy had copied, with slight variation, a line from Swinburne – "Memory grey with many a flowerless year." There is a hint of Time's disconcerting fluidity and denaturing in one of Douglas Dunn's *Elegies*:

> Tonight, I shall look out at the dark trees,
> Writing this in the muddle of lost tenses
> At an o'clock of flowers turned colourless.

It was there at the start of this journey, in the wasted skin of "I

Look into my Glass". It is in the frozen desolation of "In
Tenebris I" where all life has gone (p 223); and in the "pale
corpse-like birth" of "A Commonplace Day", where the rain
slides "wanly upon the panes", "as have slid since morn my
colourless thoughts" (p 89). The stagnation of Hardy's time-cell
is the stagnation where living blood has ceased to course through
the veins; where, as he describes himself in "The Dead Man
Walking",

> I am but a shape that stands here,
> A pulseless mould,
> A pale past picture, screening
> Ashes gone cold.

Hardy was a "pale past picture" because his characteristic
glance was backward. The last of his line, with no children, (and
sadly disillusioned by the increasing barbarism of the 1914–18
war and its aftermaths), the future now held little for him.
Patricia Ingham goes on to discuss how Hardy was even trapped
by his heredity: in his fine poem "The Pedigree", the only
movement possible is "dwindling backward." It was a favourite
theme, developed in other poems and the later novels, and
closely connected with Darwin's evolutionary theories which
greatly influenced him.

THE PEDIGREE

I

> I bent in the deep of night
> Over a pedigree the chronicler gave
> As mine; and as I bent there, half-unrobed,
> The uncurtained panes of my window-square let in the
> watery light
> Of the moon in its old age:
> And green-rheumed clouds were hurrying past where
> mute and cold it globed
> Like a drifting dolphin's eye seen through a lapping
> wave.

II

> So, scanning my sire-sown tree,
> And the hieroglyphs of this spouse tied to that,
> With offspring mapped below in lineage,

Till the tangles troubled me,
The branches seemed to twist into a seared and cynic face
Which winked and tokened towards the window like a
    Mage
Enchanting me to gaze again thereat.

III

It was a mirror now,
And in it a long perspective I could trace
Of my begetters, dwindling backward each past each
    All with the kindred look,
Whose names had since been inked down in their
    place
On the recorder's book,
Generation and generation of my mien, and build, and
    brow.

IV

And then did I divine
That every heave and coil and move I made
Within my brain, and in my mood and speech,
    Was in the glass portrayed
As long forestalled by their so making it;
The first of them, the primest fuglemen of my line,
Being fogged in far antiqueness past surmise and reason's
    reach.

V

Said I then, sunk in tone,
"I am merest mimicker and counterfeit! –
    Though thinking, *I am I,*
And what I do I do myself alone."
– The cynic twist of the page thereat unknit
Back to its normal figure, having wrough its purport wry,
    The Mage's mirror left the window-square,
And the stained moon and drift retook their places
    there.

1916

Like the moon here Hardy was in his old age when he wrote this
poem. In others of his moon poems, the poet peering through the
pane at a human drama is often imaged as the moon; and here in
the second stanza the grammar does not help us to know for sure

whether it is the moon ("Like a . . . dolphin's eye") or the poet, or both as one, who is scanning the family tree – another typical instance of deliberate ambiguity. The face which wriggles from the maze of lines is one where experience has taken its toll; it magicks the watcher's gaze toward the window which, as it rapidly dissolves into a mirror, brings forth a line of shadowy faces, like the visions in "Old Furniture":

> Hands behind hands, growing paler and paler,
>   As a mirror in a candle-flame
> Shows images of itself, each frailer
>   As it recedes . . .

They are kindred faces, and faces of kindred; and as he watches the never-ending file he sees that they too are a kind of trap, a straitjacket within which he may writhe to no purpose, for all that he thought was individual to himself has been forestalled. All has been experienced, thought, written, done, by others of his "mien, and build, and brow." There is no escape, for all are entered in the book. There is no future, since he is merely a repetition of those who have gone before. Even the present is thus denuded of significance. The speaker, "sunk" in deep despair as in "the deep of the night", comes to believe that he is ruled by the past. As he admits this, the revelation unknits, untwists, back to the scene much as it was before[16] – and so in a way appears, as a bad dream might, perhaps only as a warning or a flash of insight, but not necessarily to be considered permanently true or valid. The whole thing, after all, is only one of Hardy's "moments of vision", his "fugitive impressions." Moreover, the poem has been interpreted as being an ingenious lifeline for the immortality of the poetry, even if the poet is mortal. Mary Jacobus picks out the ambiguity of the scanner's identity, moon or poet, and how "Hardy has granted independent existence to the eye, resourcefully evading the threat to the 'I' of the poem. . . . If the poet himself can't be thought to survive, his poetic vision – sufficiently detached or alienated from the poet, as moon or Mage – can at least be imagined as doing so."[17]

*   *   *   *   *   *

It is true that Hardy, despite sometimes feeling "upbraided" by his ancestors,[18] (let alone the critics), with a quiet persistence defends his own particular gift as a poet. The defences are scattered through the *Life*, in his Prefaces and the Apology to *Late Lyrics and Earlier*, and in some of his poems like "He Resolves to Say No More." This poem has a special connection with "The Pedigree", as its penultimate stanza shows:

> Let Time roll backward if it will;
> (Magians who drive the midnight quill
>   With brain aglow
>   Can see it so,)
> What I have learnt no man shall know.

It is Hardy's final farewell – the last poem of his last volume, prepared by him to be published on one of his next birthdays, but in the event published posthumously. It is the last in a series of farewells: for every volume of his verse (or of its principal title-giving group) ends in a valediction. The first is "I Look into my Glass", his adieu to youth; the last, "He Resolves to Say No More", follows the words: "We are getting near the end of dreams!" It was written probably in 1927 when his long-held hopes for humanity had been finally shattered.

It is not surprising that even in his first volume Hardy at 58 should be saying some farewells. What is interesting is that he is saying them in his mid-twenties. "Amabel", placed second in *Wessex Poems*, was written in 1865 or 1866, and already his characteristic backward look is evident. (I quote only selected stanzas.)

AMABEL

I marked her ruined hues,
Her custom-straitened views,
And asked, "Can there indwell
    My Amabel?"

I looked upon her gown,
Once rose, now earthen brown;
The change was like the knell
    Of Amabel.

Her step's mechanic ways
Had lost the life of May's;

Her laugh, once sweet in swell,
   Spoilt Amabel.

    . . . .

– I felt that I could creep
To some housetop, and weep
That Time the tyrant fell
   Ruled Amabel!

    . . . .

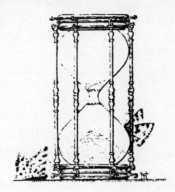

What Hardy shows first are the ruined hues, the dress now earthen brown – and only beyond them are seen Amabel's original state, her charming laugh and the rose-coloured dress. This kind of retrospective gaze is perhaps the most remarkable characteristic of his view of the past. He shows events when the development (sometimes the worst) has already happened – as in "The Ruined Maid", or "The Whitewashed Wall". If you look carefully at the hourglass illustration which he drew for "Amabel", you see that most of the sand has already run. He shows what things or people have become: the sunshade a "naked sheaf of wires", its happy bearer a probable ghost; the erstwhile home full of music and gaiety, a silent tomb; the sturdy young Dorset recruit, a hump in the arid *veldt*; the bird that trilled, now stuffed in a museum. Even when Hardy looks forward it is with an awareness that time will all too quickly make the future a has-been or a might-have-been. In "The Minute Before Meeting", a poem dating from his courtship days, he writes of the feeling we all know: the desire to put off the joy of meeting to prolong the delights of anticipation. He is already seeing that future moment when their time together will be a thing of the past.

    These – all too briefly – are some of the facets of Hardy's look at time and the past over his long career as a poet. Neither memory nor ghosts have been considered, though both have appeared in some of the poems read. Ghosts were always much in his mind. Indeed, considering his temperament, his training, and his penchant for Gothic art, it is surprising that he had to wait until he was 79 before he saw a ghost in, so to speak, the flesh. Nearly twenty years earlier, in 1901, he was commenting on his ghostlessness to William Archer, saying he would have given ten years of his life to see "an authentic, indubitable spectre."

For my part I say in all sincerity, 'Better be inconvenienced by visitants from beyond the grave than see none at all.' The material world is so uninteresting, human life is so miserably bounded, circumscribed, cabin'd, cribb'd, confined. I want another domain to expatiate in.[19]

Even as far back as 1888 a note had evinced Hardy's susceptibility to this "other domain."

March 9. British Museum Reading Room. Souls are gliding about here in a sort of dream – screened somewhat by their bodies, but imaginable behind them. Dissolution is gnawing at them all, slightly hampered by renovations. In the great circle of the library Time is looking into Space. Coughs are floating in the same great vault, mixing with the rustle of book-leaves risen from the dead, and the touches of footsteps on the floor.[20]

In the summer of the same year, only a month or two after his 48th birthday, Hardy wrote the following – "whimsically", according to his own account; but for the purpose of understanding both the importance to him of ghosts, and his peculiar retrospective glance, it's very revealing.

For my part, if there is any way of getting a melancholy satisfaction out of life it lies in dying, so to speak, before one is out of the flesh; by which I mean putting on the manners of ghosts, wandering in their haunts, and taking their views of surrounding things. To think of life as passing away is a sadness; to think of it as past is at least tolerable. Hence even when I enter into a room to pay a simple morning call I have unconsciously the habit of regarding the scene as if I were a spectre not solid enough to influence my environment; only fit to behold and say, as another spectre said: 'Peace be unto you!'[21]

(It is worth connecting this too with Hardy's remarkable powers of observation, and the ambivalent, low key tone of so many of his poems, where his attitude of "Here it is: I'm not saying any more, do what you will with it", declines to coerce the reader in any direction.)

On Christmas Eve 1919, however, the great thing happened. He saw a "real" ghost in Stinsford Churchyard, apparently that of his grandfather, on whose grave he had just put a sprig of holly.[22] His poetry had been full of ghosts for years. They appear constantly as images like "The day is turning ghost", or "When Frost was spectre-gray", or "Out of the past there rises a week". In "A Sign-Seeker", he longed for the reassurance of immortality that a "phantom parent, friend," might bring back from the grave – but lamented his own inability to discern such signs. In many other poems as he remembers the past the "upping ghosts press achefully" in "heavily-haunted harmony." In "A Christmas Ghost Story", (something of a companion piece to "Drummer Hodge",) the "puzzled phantom" of a young soldier questions why the message of the Prince of Peace has been rejected:

> And what of logic or of truth appears
> In tacking "Anno Domini" to the years?
> Near twenty-hundred liveried thus have hied,
> But tarries yet the cause for which He died.

We have noted the importance of Hardy's settings. Many of his ghosts are closely associated with places. The "Friends Beyond" who describe their peace in death seem to rise out of their surroundings in Mellstock Churchyard as they murmur to him through the drip of water or the cooling night's contractions:

> "Gone," I call them, gone for good, that group of local
>   hearts and heads,
>   Yet at mothy curfew-tide,
> And at midnight when the noon-heat breathes it back from
>   walls and leads,
>
> They've a way of whispering to me – fellow-wight who
>   yet abide –
>   In the muted, measured note
> Of a ripple under archways, or a lone cave's stillicide:

And in "Wessex Heights", a poem of great anguish written at about the same time as "In Tenebris I",[23] the haunting of the speaker's past is so tightly linked to specific places that it makes some of them no-go areas for him.

WESSEX HEIGHTS

(1896)

There are some heights in Wessex, shaped as if by a kindly
    hand
For thinking, dreaming, dying on, and at crises when I
    stand,
Say, on Ingpen Beacon eastward, or on Wylls-Neck
    westwardly,
I seem where I was before my birth, and after death may
    be.

In the lowlands I have no comrade, not even the lone man's
    friend –
Her who suffereth long and is kind; accepts what he is too
    weak to mend:
Down there they are dubious and askance; there nobody
    thinks as I,
But mind-chains do not clank where one's next neighbour
    is the sky.

In the towns I am tracked by phantoms having weird
    detective ways –
Shadows of beings who fellowed with myself of earlier
    days:
They hang about at places, and they say harsh heavy
    things –
Men with a wintry sneer, and women with tart
    disparagings.

Down there I seem to be false to myself, my simple self that
    was,
And is not now, and I see him watching, wondering what
    crass cause
Can have merged him into such a strange continuator as
    this,
Who yet has something in common with himself, my
    chrysalis.

I cannot go to the great grey Plain; there's a figure against
    the moon,
Nobody sees it but I, and it makes my breast beat out of
    tune;
I cannot go to the tall-spired town, being barred by the
    forms now passed
For everybody but me, in whose long vision they stand
    there fast.

There's a ghost at Yell'ham Bottom chiding loud at the fall
    of the night,
There's a ghost in Froom-side Vale, thin-lipped and vague,
    in a shroud of white,
There is one in the railway train whenever I do not want it
    near,
I see its profile against the pane, saying what I would not
    hear.

As for one rare fair woman, I am now but a thought of hers,
I enter her mind and another thought succeeds me that she
    prefers;
Yet my love for her in its fulness she herself even did not
    know;
Well, time cures hearts of tenderness, and now I can let her
    go.

So I am found on Ingpen Beacon, or on Wylls-Neck to the
    west,
Or else on homely Bulbarrow, or little Pilsdon Crest,
Where men have never cared to haunt, nor women have
    walked with me,
And ghosts then keep their distance; and I know some
    liberty.

The ghosts of Hardy's earlier poems are fairly traditional
haunters, often come back to teach or tell or reproach. But in
November 1912 there occurred a catastrophe which, in its
proper meaning, was to turn his poetry upside down: the death
of his first wife Emma.

After what seemed like a magical courtship in Cornwall, they
had married in 1874; but since the 1890s they had been
increasingly estranged, and by early 1899 Emma had decamped
to two attic rooms in Max Gate, living her own life where

possible and generally only meeting him at (often silent) meals. It is hard to understand his apparent neglect of her obvious pain in the last months and days; but their relationship is far too complex to analyse in a few lines. It needs to be studied in the accounts given by Gittings and Millgate: somewhere between these lies the elusive truth – or facets of it. The extraordinary result of Emma's death was to be not only the great *Poems of 1912-13*, but also subsequently something like a hundred poems about her which include some of the finest love-poetry in the English language. Not only this: after her death Hardy began to understand something about his own poetry which he had not seen before – and when this point in the journey is reached the traveller will have arrived at the heart of Hardy country.

After her death Emma, of course, joined her husband's gallery of ghosts. In "The Voice" and "After a Journey" and "The Phantom Horsewoman" she is at her most memorable; in "The Haunter" the agonising inability to get through to her living partner reflects the failure of communication in their lives.[24] Sometimes, too, when the dead leaves blow in on him asleep, or a moth taps at his window, he thinks it is she; but often she is in a strange way recognisably herself, though an unseen presence to be wondered at. It's not until after Emma's death that his ghosts become odder, more individual, more of an eccentric mixture of dead and living beings – in short, more grotesque. In one poem he sees a head alone, crowned with a hat and plume,

> Above the fog that sheets the mead...
> Moving along with spectre-speed;

In others, a row of ghosts comes back at night to sit – as if still incarnate – on a garden seat; and "old players' dead fingers" to a museum of musical instruments, to clutch and handle them.[25] The hands of "Old Furniture" return, with the fingers disconcertingly disembodied, to flicker over their past haunts. Memory-laden, he uses the past to explain the present.

OLD FURNITURE

> I know not how it may be with others
>   Who sit amid relics of householdry
> That date from the days of their mothers' mothers,

But well I know how it is with me
    Continually.

I see the hands of the generations
    That owned each shiny familiar thing
In play on its knobs and indentations,
    And with its ancient fashioning
        Still dallying:

Hands behind hands, growing paler and paler,
    As in a mirror a candle-flame
Shows images of itself, each frailer
    As it recedes, though the eye may frame
        Its shape the same.

On the clock's dull dial a foggy finger,
    Moving to set the minutes right
With tentative touches that lift and linger
    In the wont of a moth on a summer night,
        Creeps to my sight.

On this old viol, too, fingers are dancing –
    As whilom – just over the strings by the nut,
The tip of a bow receding, advancing
    In airy quivers, as if it would cut
        The plaintive gut.

And I see a face by that box for tinder,
    Glowing forth in fits from the dark,
And fading again, as the linten cinder
    Kindles to red at the flinty spark,
        Or goes out stark.

Well, well. It is best to be up and doing,
    The world has no use for one to-day
Who eyes things thus – no aim pursuing!
    He should not continue in this stay,
        But sink away.

This is surely one of Hardy's most beautiful and characteristic poems, with its nostalgic evocation of a past home and family; its rhythmic lilt suggesting the dancing note of the old violin "as whilom"; the choice of words that makes "quivers" echo in "plaintive", "linten" in "flinty", and "foggy" seem to follow from "the clock's dull dial"; and that makes the rhyming of every line appear so easy. Layers of meaning can be unwrapped one after the other – like the moth's presage of death in contemporary folklore,[26] or the uncertainties of reality betokened in the series of mirror images. The last stanza too brings that typical response from Hardy, the feeling that he himself is a ghost, one born out of due time – as usual with a body image, "one who eyes things thus" – and is fit only to fade and "sink away."

This blurring of the real distinctions between death and life, with ghosts who return to act in some ways as if still alive; ghosts who have grown up from their graves into strange composite creatures, the flowers and laurel and ivy that adorn the graveyard, and now have nerves and veins again, feeling the sun and rain[27] – this is part of Hardy's mismatch. It's a living in two worlds which don't synchronise, one of the places where his imagination, pushing always deeper and inward, reaches the grotesque. The inner vision of the mind and the outward reality of the world are at variance, and the confusion results in a kind of nightmare from which the poet cannot awake. As Dennis Taylor puts it in his study of Hardy and the grotesque, "The fusion of imagination and material world, like the fusion of ghostly spirit and material medium, results in the ominous distortion of each."[28]

Often in his novels he had explored the grotesque. In aesthetic theory, this concept had ranged from the idea of "distortion or unnatural combinations" – later somewhat despised by the rational eighteenth century – to being an important art form which the nineteenth-century Romantics tended to elevate as evidence of man's need and search for the supernatural, or even the sublime. In his poems, Hardy's little tragedies may often be called grotesque, (in the sense of being "ludicrous from incongruity"[29]) – like the following:

IN THE CEMETERY

"You see those mothers squabbling there?"
Remarks the man of the cemetery.
"One says in tears, ' '*Tis mine lies here!*'
Another, '*Nay, mine, you Pharisee!*'
Another, '*How dare you move my flowers*

And put your own on this grave of ours!'
But all their children were laid therein
At different times, like sprats in a tin.

"And then the main drain had to cross,
And we moved the lot some nights ago,
And packed them away in the general foss
With hundreds more. But their folks don't know,
And as well cry over a new-laid drain
As anything else, to ease your pain!"

As Emma's death is soon followed by the horrors of the 1914–18
war, the romantic dreams and memories of a happier past are
challenged by the nightmare of present reality – from which we
both cannot awake and yet do also awake too late, to find no
solution, but a world which has changed around us and where
our old images now only hopelessly confuse. The poem that
follows gives some flavour of Hardy's grotesque fantasies and of
his visions about the future.

A NEW YEAR'S EVE IN WAR TIME

I

Phantasmal fears,
And the flap of the flame,
And the throb of the clock,
And a loosened slate,
And the blind night's drone,
Which tiredly the spectral pines intone.

II

And the blood in my ears
Strumming always the same,
And the gable-clock
With its fitful grate,
And myself, alone.

III

The twelfth hour nears
Hand-hid, as in shame;
I undo the lock,
And listen, and wait
For the Young Unknown.

IV

In the dark there careers –
As if Death astride came
To numb all with his knock –
A horse at mad rate
Over rut and stone.

V

No figure appears,
No call of my name,
No sound but "Tic-toc"
Without check. Past the gate
It clatters – is gone.

VI

What rider it bears
There is none to proclaim;
And the Old Year has struck,
And, scarce animate,
The New makes moan.

VII

Maybe that "More Tears! –
More Famine and Flame –
More Severance and Shock!"
Is the order from Fate
That the Rider speeds on
To pale Europe; and tiredly the pines intone.

1915–16

It was inevitable that Hardy, with his philosophical cast of mind, his imaginative and emotional susceptibility, and moreover his training in Gothic architecture, should be irresistibly drawn to the grotesque. The coming of the war which destroyed all his hopes of man's gradual moral progress simply combined with his exploration of the grotesque: it led him, by way of contemplating the horrors of the human mind that could create such wars, to a fearful vision of the future. In "A New Year's Eve in War Time" one is left with no answer but the dissolution of civilisation.[30]

We may, by this all-too-hasty reference to the grotesque as it is seen in his ghosts, have appeared to stray from a survey of Hardy and time. But the two are connected, not only through the imagination, but through the function of memory. Memory makes us what we are – as one realises when an aged person's loss of memory completely dislocates his sense of his (or her) own reality, and his or her own actual link with it. Hardy from his earliest poems is fascinated to see how many of his characters are ruled by memories; and as his poetry and understanding develop, he comes to see that a memory buried within himself can be the source of a new realisation, and a new experience when it is articulated in a poem.

Notes

1   *Lit. Notes* Entry 2448

2   *The New Dawn's Business*

3   *Rome: On the Palatine; A Kiss*

4   Ronald Marken, "'As Rhyme Meets Rhyme'" in *PTH*, 19. See also page 291

5   See *A Light Snowfall after Frost*, page 232

6   *Embarcation*

7   *Hap* – see page 194; *She, to Him I*

8   *At the Piano; In a Eweleaze near Weatherbury*

9   *Life*, 377

10 See Exodus XXVIII, 15–21, 30; and Daniel, III,5.

11 *The Dream is – Which?*

12 It seems impossible to render into equally pithy rhyming English this definition of people's lives today being bounded by "Tube – work – sleep".

13 *Fragment*

14 See the poem *Neutral Tones* dated 1867

15 *PTH* 123

16 Though the moon is now "stained" – some typical Hardy symbolism.

17 Mary Jacobus, "Hardy's Magian Retrospect", *Essays in Criticism* vol 32

18 *Night in the Old Home*

19 William Archer, *Real Conversations*, (London 1904) 45

20 *Life*, 206

21 *Life*, 209

22 Letter from Florence Hardy to S.C. Cockerell, 27 Dec 1919, Friends of a Lifetime, ed Meynell (London 1940)

23 See pp 49 and 223

24 For these poems see Chapter VI

25 *The Head above the Fog; The Garden Seat; Haunting Fingers*

26 See eg my *Figures in a Wessex Landscape* (London 1987) 50–51, and the poems *The Moth-Signal* and *Something Tapped*

27 *Transformations*

28 *Dennis Taylor*, 110

29 Both definitions from the Oxford English Dictionary

30 *Dennis Taylor* discusses this theme and poem more widely, 127–9

4

SAY YOU REMEMBER!

'*Memory is the faculty of poetry*' – Stephen Spender
'*All our perceiving is a memory . . . All our memory is a perceiving.*' –
Norman Nicholson

FORMER BEAUTIES

These market-dames, mid-aged, with lips thin-drawn,
    And tissues sere,
Are they the ones we loved in years agone,
    And courted here?

Are these the muslined pink young things to whom
    We vowed and swore
In nooks on summer Sundays by the Froom,
    Or Budmouth shore?

Do they remember those gay tunes we trod
    Clasped on the green;
Aye; trod till moonlight set on the beaten sod
    A satin sheen?

They must forget, forget! They cannot know
    What once they were,
Or memory would transfigure them, and show
    Them always fair.

In the relaxed tone of this poem's opening, there is a hint of
amused incredulity as the speaker wonders if the "muslined pink
young things" of his past can possibly have come to this. The
"lips thin-drawn,/And tissues sere" make an unpleasant picture;
it combines with some of the ideas unfortunately associated with
"market-women" to contrast strongly with the scenes that
follow. So carefree and buoyant were these summer Sundays of
youth, the inexhaustible and single-minded energies of the

moonlight dance, and the throb of passion.

As he remembers them, savours them, the passion gathers and explodes.

> They must forget, forget! They cannot know
> What once they were....

The cry is almost intolerably plangent and poignant, a vehement cry of loss. Memory, the all-powerful, the part of us which often rules our lives, which transforms what we see and understand, memory has somehow failed them – as it has not failed him, for in his memory their beauty still, tragically, lives on.

Memory, for Hardy, is the one force strong enough to resist Time. It is also a vital constituent of each person's individuality and life. It helps to make up each different self. Without it we begin to die, to wither. He seems to have been surprisingly aware of this even at the age of 26, when he wrote in implied pity for the

> souls of Now, who would disjoint
> The mind from memory.[1]

Thirty-five years later he published "Tess's Lament", a poem exquisitely understanding of that character he had created, who often seemed to him actually to have lived. In its repeated, remorseful phrases, its echoing rhymes, the nature and crucial importance of memory come home.

TESS'S LAMENT

I

> I would that folk forgot me quite,
>   Forgot me quite!
> I would that I could shrink from sight,
>   And no more see the sun.
> Would it were time to say farewell,
> To claim my nook, to need my knell,
> Time for them all to stand and tell
>   Of my day's work as done.

II

> Ah! dairy where I lived so long,

I lived so long;
Where I would rise up staunch and strong,
And lie down hopefully.
'Twas there within the chimney-seat
He watched me to the clock's slow beat –
Loved me, and learnt to call me Sweet,
And whispered words to me.

III
And now he's gone; and now he's gone; ...
And now he's gone!
The flowers we potted perhaps are thrown
To rot upon the farm.
And where we had our supper-fire
May now grow nettle, dock, and briar,
And all the place be mould and mire
So cozy once and warm.

Further memories twist the knife in her heart. She ends:

IV
It wears me out to think of it,
To think of it;
I cannot bear my fate as writ,
I'd have my life unbe;
Would turn my memory to a blot,
Make every relic of me rot,
My doings be as they were not,
And gone all trace of me!

The conjunction of the two lines beginning "I'd have my life unbe" is no accident: to blot out her memory (in both senses of the phrase) would be to begin the process of undoing herself and her life.

In another poem, it is Memory that the speaker questions when he wants to know what has happened to him: "O Memory, where is now my truth/my joy/my hope", and so on. And when he thinks of his own life, his two wives and his beloved sister, Hardy ends:

With how strange aspect would there creep
The dawn, the night, the daytime,

> If memory were not what it is
>   In song-time, toil, or pray-time. –
> O were it else than this,
>   I'd pass to pulseless sleep![2]

(In many poems, those who have "passed to pulseless sleep" assert that their only hope of immortality lies in their being remembered by those who loved them.[3] So memory is vital too for those poor ghosts who wander through Hardy's poems.)

Memory is not only an essential part of being alive and being our particular selves: it is our inevitable companion, and it fills our minds. From birth to death we are "in memories nurst" and with "mindsight memory-laden." We have seen the intensity of Hardy's memory in "Silences" and "On a Discovered Curl of Hair"; but even rather trivial incidents which provoked a poem show its power. "How I remember him!" he says of the sick stranger encountered only once on the road; or of the blind giant led at a country fair by a "shrewd-eyed" dwarf:

> Various sights in various climes
> I have seen, and more I may see yet,
> But that sight never shall I forget,
> And have thought it the sorriest of pantomimes,
>   If once, a hundred times![4]

If he thought of that scene so often, how much more was his mind filled by the deeper emotions of remembered love. Probably the finest examples are in the *Poems of 1912–13* (look, for example, at the third stanza of "The Phantom Horsewoman" on page 151); but so many of his most beautiful poems are those which spring from a "memoried passion."

THE OLD GOWN

(Song)

> I have seen her in gowns the brightest,
>   Of azure, green, and red,
> And in the simplest, whitest,
>   Muslined from heel to head;
> I have watched her walking, riding,
>   Shade-flecked by a leafy tree,

Or in fixed thought abiding
By the foam-fingered sea.

In woodlands I have known her,
When boughs were mourning loud,
In the rain-reek she has shown her
Wild-haired and watery-browed.
And once or twice she has cast me
As she pomped along the street
Court-clad, ere quite she had passed me,
A glance from her chariot-seat.

But in my memoried passion
For evermore stands she
In the gown of fading fashion
She wore that night when we,
Doomed long to part, assembled
In the snug small room; yea, when
She sang with lips that trembled,
"Shall I see his face again?"

So often the memories that "prick on, ceaselessly" are those, particularly, of remorse. Remorse is of the essence of human life, since one of Hardy's most important themes is that one awakes to understanding too late. People only recognise their full desire or need when it can no longer be fulfilled; they only realise how they have hurt someone when it is too late to make amends.

O the regrettings infinite
When the night-processions flit
Through the mind![5]

Like "Tess's Lament", another of Hardy's most evocative lyrics is about remorse and mental pain.

THE BALLAD-SINGER

Sing, Ballad-singer, raise a hearty tune;
Make me forget that there was ever a one
I walked with in the meek light of the moon
When the day's work was done.

Rhyme, Ballad-rhymer, start a country song;

> Make me forget that she whom I loved well
> Swore she would love me dearly, love me long,
> Then – what I cannot tell!
>
> Sing, Ballad-singer, from your little book;
> Make me forget those heart-breaks, achings, fears;
> Make me forget her name, her sweet sweet look –
> Make me forget her tears.

The speaker begins sturdily, calling for a "hearty tune". He does not make much of his first "Make me forget", and it looks as if he has shrugged his shoulders and put it behind him. Even the moon, unlike so many of Hardy's moons, is deceptively meek and trite and seems to bear no ominous portents. But with the second insistent call to the singer – only now he is called a rhymer – we begin to feel uneasy: does the speaker protest too much? Is the hurt deeper than it seemed and needing a louder cry? There is an almost violent disjunction beween what he calls for and what is happening, for something is out of step. He calls for rhyming, to help him forget; yet as everyone knows ("Remember, remember, the Fifth of November"), it is rhyming that helps one to recall. The hurt is savage, magnified by the poet's ironical juxtaposition of these two irreconcilables: and in the last stanza the defences are down and the floodgates opened, for the misery is too strong to be contained. Not just once, as in earlier stanzas, but three times here are we caught up in the endless ring of those unhappy phrases "Make me forget";[6] and, as in "Tess's Lament", the very repetitions are how people speak in remorse and unsalved regret. Then, the poem's intensity, set in motion with "Swore she would love me dearly, love me long," and wound tighter by "the heartbreaks, aching, fears," begins to run painfully slow to concentrate our gaze on the precise indelible picture, the picture from which memory will not release his eyes:

> her sweet sweet look –
> Make me forget her tears.

This man's memories fill his mind. They may obsess him so much that they govern his life. Many Hardy characters, as we have seen, are ruled by their memories. There is one who is oblivious of the changing seasons on the down, never hears what the thorn tree whispers as it comments to each passer-by on the pain of frost or the sweetness of summer – for when he walks on the down he is wrapped/rapt in his own memories, and to him the thorn speaks only one theme:

> But by day or by night,
> And in winter or summer,
> Should I be the comer
> Along that lone height,   *
> In its voicing to me
> Only one speech is spoken:
> "Here once was nigh broken
> A heart, and by thee."[7]

The ballad of "The Trampwoman's Tragedy" shows her haunting the moor where the world seemed to come to an end for her. The widow in "Bereft" relives the stages of each single day, bound fast by memory to her dead husband and their past life together:

> When the supper crock's steaming
> And the time is the time of his tread,
> I shall sit by the fire and wait dreaming
> In a silence as of the dead.
> > Leave the door unbarred,
> > The clock unwound,
> > Make my lone bed hard –
> > Would 'twere underground!

Often the one who is thus memory-impelled would prefer to be in the remembered world rather than in the present. Particularly after Emma's death, as Hardy increasingly drew on the store of his own memories to fund a poem and to re-evaluate his experience, it was often the joys of memory, not just its pain, that he savoured – and this in his own life as well as in his fictional characters'. "In the Small Hours" is typical of his ability to bring alive the nostalgia of a cherished past world in a lyrical ballad:

IN THE SMALL HOURS

I lay in my bed and fiddled

With a dreamland viol and bow,
And the tunes flew back to my fingers
I had melodied years ago.
It was two or three in the morning
When I fancy-fiddled so
Long reels and country dances,
And hornpipes swift and slow.

And soon anon came crossing
The chamber in the gray
Figures of jogging field-folk –
Saviours of corn and hay –
To the air of "Haste to the Wedding",
As after a wedding-day;
Yea, up and down the middle
In windless whirls went they!

There danced the bride and bridegroom,
And couples in a train,
Gay partners time and travail
Had longwhiles stilled amain!...
It seemed a thing for weeping
To find, at slumber's wane
And morning's sly increeping,
That Now, not Then, held reign.

Yet in another poem the pain is stilled into a repose that is also
characteristic of Hardy:

JOYS OF MEMORY

When the spring comes round, and a certain day
Looks out from the brume by the eastern copsetrees
And says, Remember,
I begin again, as if it were new,
A day of like date I once lived through,
Whiling it hour by hour away;
So shall I do till my December,
When spring comes round.

I take my holiday then and my rest
Away from the dun life here about me,
Old hours re-greeting

With the quiet sense that bring they must
Such throbs as at first, till I house with dust,
And in the numbness my heartsome zest
For things that were, be past repeating
When spring comes round.

Here he has come to terms with this experience – expressing it in the rounded form, the completed circle, of the poem, and the suggestion that he and his memories are part of the endlessly renewed cycle of life.

In it too is the recognition, repeated in so many poems, that memory is activated by external factors, like dates and places, and by the perceptions of the senses. (Proust was discovering the same thing in that famous involuntary evocation of his childhood when he dipped a madeleine in his tea.)

So the map revives her words, the spot, the time...[8]

The lowlands of "Wessex Heights" are forbidding because of his memories; and

When I see the room it hurts me
As with a prickling blade,
Those women being the memoried reason why my cheer
deserts me.[9]

Dates act like places. "An Anniversary" begins:

It was at the very date to which we have come,
In the month of the matching name,
When, at a like minute, the sun had upswum,
Its couch-time at night being the same...

Glowing embers always raise memories – "spent flames limning ghosts"; and the midnight scents of "Shut Out That Moon" (page 268) are redolent of the "sweet sentiments" of the past.

So many experiences are revived by sounds, particularly music. Hardy felt it in his own life as, for example, he wrote about his wife's past duets with her sister:

Since every sound moves memories,

... how shall I bear
Such heavily-haunted harmony?[10]

His poetic characters also feel it most powerfully. Old Norbert
is brought to tears by the street-fiddler outside, for he plays the
very tune Norbert's mother used to sing.

"And as I grew up, again and again
    She'd tell, after trilling that air,
Of her youth, and the battles on Leipzig plain
    And of all that was suffered there! ...
          . . . . .
And whenever those notes in the street begin,
    I recall her, and that far scene,
And her acting of how the Allies marched in,
    And her tap of the tambourine!"

Often the foundations of a shaky marriage are rocked by the
meddlesome throb of a particular air – as in the story *The Fiddler
of the Reels*, and several poems like this:

IN THE NUPTIAL CHAMBER

"O that mastering tune!" And up in the bed
Like a lace-robed phantom springs the bride;
"And why?" asks the man she had that day wed,
With a start, as the band plays on outside.

"It's the townsfolk's cheery compliment
Because of our marriage, my Innocent."

"O but you don't know! 'Tis the passionate air
To which my old Love waltzed with me,
And I swore as we spun that none should share
My home, my kisses, till death, save he!
And he dominates me and thrills me through,
And it's he I embrace while embracing you!"

Perhaps Hardy's most charming evocation of the senses' bond with memory is in "Under the Waterfall', the poem he put immediately before the *Poems of 1912-13* – a haunting premonition of loss.

UNDER THE WATERFALL

"Whenever I plunge my arm, like this,
In a basin of water, I never miss
The sweet sharp sense of a fugitive day
Fetched back from its thickening shroud of gray.
      Hence the only prime
      And real love-rhyme
      That I know by heart,
      And that leaves no smart,
Is the purl of a little valley fall
About three spans wide and two spans tall
Over a table of solid rock,
And into a scoop of the self-same block;
The purl of a runlet that never ceases
In stir of kingdoms, in wars, in peaces;
With a hollow boiling voice it speaks
And has spoken since hills were turfless peaks."

"And why gives this the only prime
Idea to you of a real love-rhyme?
And why does plunging your arm in a bowl
Full of spring water, bring throbs to your soul?"
"Well, under the fall, in a crease of the stone,
Though where precisely none ever has known,
Jammed darkly, nothing to show how prized,
And by now with its smoothness opalized,
      Is a drinking-glass:

> For, down that pass
> My lover and I
> Walked under a sky
> Of blue with a leaf-wove awning of green,
> In the burn of August, to paint the scene,
> And we placed our basket of fruit and wine
> By the runlet's rim, where we sat to dine;
> And when we had drunk from the glass together,
> Arched by the oak-copse from the weather,
> I held the vessel to rinse in the fall,
> Where it slipped, and sank, and was past recall,
> Though we stooped and plumbed the little abyss
> With long bared arms. There the glass still is.
> And, as said, if I thrust my arm below
> Cold water in basin or bowl, a throe
> From the past awakens a sense of that time,
> And the glass we used, and the cascade's rhyme.
> The basin seems the pool, and its edge
> The hard smooth face of the brook-side ledge,
> And the leafy pattern of china-ware
> The hanging plants that were bathing there.
>
> "By night, by day, when it shines or lours,
> There lies intact that chalice of ours,
> And its presence adds to the rhyme of love
> Persistently sung by the fall above.
> No lip has touched it since his and mine
> In turns therefrom sipped lovers' wine."

There is a fairy-tale quality about this poem, a sense of the lovers being enclosed, as lovers are, in a world and time of their own. The typesetting shows it in the four short lines round "My lover and I". Their companion is the incessant ripple of the waterfall which links them with all ages and all humanity – and which Hardy four times describes as the "rhyme", three times more specifically as the "rhyme of love": the thing which makes one remember. The narrative is too precise to be sentimental, too much aware of the ironies of life with its prosaic and poetic contrasts; so that, as Ronald Marken says in his admirable discussion of this poem, "there is even gentle mockery in the rhyming of 'bowl' with 'soul'."[11] Other contrasts strengthen the meaning and the atmosphere. The simple colloquial questions –

"And why does plunging your arm in a bowl...?" - and the
opening statement and demonstration - "Whenever I plunge my
arm, like this..." - are at variance with the hint of dread, the
images of death and the irrecoverable, in

> The sweet sharp sense of a fugitive day
> Fetched back from its thickening shroud of gray.

The last stanza leans on the passing of time, "By night, by day";
on the eternity of the "rhyme of love/Persistently sung by the
fall above"; and on the sanctity of love celebrated in "that
chalice of ours". It ends as if with Hardy's favourite filmy gauze
hung between us and the secret mysterious preserve where

> No lip has touched it since his and mine
> In turns therefrom sipped lovers' wine.

So it is that
> as said, if I thrust my arm below
> Cold water in basin or bowl, a throe
> From the past awakens a sense of that time:

memory is stirred by the action of the senses. This means that the
seen, and the scene, will vary for each person according to what
his inner sight and his sensory perception does with it. This was a
frequent theme of Hardy's. "We colour according to our moods
the objects we survey." "The poetry of a scene varies with the
minds of the perceivers..." "The beauty of association is
entirely superior to the beauty of aspect, and a beloved relative's
old battered tankard to the finest Greek vase."[12]

Since memory is so powerful, since it can fill our minds and
control our lives, it can also shape what we see; and sometimes
what we see "before the intenser/Stare of the mind" becomes
more real than what we see with our eyes. Past scenes, alive in
our memory,

> Have a savour that scenes in being lack,
> And a presence more than the actual brings.

They can be more real than the present and the outer world,
more real than "fact" and the change going on around us.

> Foremost in my vision
> Everywhere goes she;
> Change dissolves the landscapes,
> She abides with me.[13]

When his old friend the poet William Barnes was Rector of Winterborne Came, Hardy used often to walk across the field that separated their houses to visit him. In a beautiful, and technically unusual, poem called "The Last Signal", Hardy describes how when Barnes died, he watched from a distance the coffin being carried to the church, and how the sunlight suddenly glinting on it seemed like a farewell wave of Barnes' hand. Later Hardy paid a duty call on the new Rector; but time and his memory transformed the occasion.

THE OLD NEIGHBOUR AND THE NEW

> 'Twas to greet the new rector I called here,
>   But in the arm-chair I see
> My old friend, for long years installed here,
>   Who palely nods to me.
>
> The new man explains what he's planning
>   In a smart and cheerful tone,
> And I listen, the while that I'm scanning
>   The figure behind his own.
>
> The newcomer urges things on me;
>   I return a vague smile thereto,
> The olden face gazing upon me
>   Just as it used to do!
>
> And on leaving I scarcely remember
>   Which neighbour to-day I have seen,
> The one carried out in September,
>   Or him who but entered yestreen.

This blurring of the vision between what is and what was, between the story and the current fact, shows most clearly in Hardy's poem about his beloved grandmother, who lived with her son's family until her death in 1857. Here one can see how the child who had listened, rapt, grew up into the social historian who noted and remembered, and the poet who saw.

ONE WE KNEW

(M.H. 1772–1857)

She told how they used to form for the country dances –
"The Triumph", "The New-Rigged Ship" –
To the light of the guttering wax in the panelled manses,
And in cots to the blink of a dip.

She spoke of the wild "poussetting" and "allemanding"
On carpet, on oak, and on sod;
And the two long rows of ladies and gentlemen standing,
And the figures the couples trod.

She showed us the spot where the maypole was yearly
planted,
And where the bandsmen stood
While breeched and kerchiefed partners whirled, and
panted
To choose each other for good.

She told of that far-back day when they learnt astounded
Of the death of the King of France:
Of the Terror; and then of Bonaparte's unbounded
Ambition and arrogance.

Of how his threats woke warlike preparations
Along the southern strand,
And how each night brought tremors and trepidations
Lest morning should see him land.

She said she had often heard the gibbet creaking
As it swayed in the lightning flash,
Had caught from the neighbouring town a small child's
shrieking
At the cart-tail under the lash. . . .

With cap-framed face and long gaze into the embers –
We seated around her knees –
She would dwell on such dead themes, not as one who
remembers,
But rather as one who sees.

She seemed one left behind of a band gone distant
So far that no tongue could hail:

Past things retold were to her as things existent,
　　Things present but as a tale.

20 May 1902

Here again "ember" rhymes with "remember", as it was to do
(metaphorically) more than a dozen years later when Hardy
watched the logs burning on his hearth – and remembered his
past life with them in another form.

LOGS ON THE HEARTH

A Memory of a Sister

The fire advances along the log
　　Of the tree we felled,
Which bloomed and bore striped apples by the peck
　　Till its last hour of bearing knelled.

The fork that first my hand would reach
　　And then my foot
In climbings upward inch by inch, lies now
　　Sawn, sapless, darkening with soot.

Where the bark chars is where, one year,
　　It was pruned, and bled –
Then overgrow the wound. But now, at last,
　　Its growings all have stagnated.

My fellow-climber rises dim
　　From her chilly grave –
Just as she was, her foot near mine on the bending limb,
　　Laughing, her young brown hand awave.

December 1915

Hardy first published this with a refrain, "That time, O! –" after
the second line of each stanza. I think he was right to remove it.
It leaves one of those extraordinarily simple poems, apparently,
which seems as if it had written itself. "There is a latent music in
the sincere utterance of deep emotion," Hardy had noted in the
Life;[14] and it is part of his genius to allow it to be heard without
rhetoric or sentimentality. The poem is rich: every moment,
every nuance is clear. The reader glimpses the one-time
abundance of bloom and fruit, only to hear its knell – a knell

which it soon appears has sounded for the girl who was almost part of the tree. One shares the climber's hard-won progress up the tree, "first my hand... then my foot... inch by inch," only to drop suddenly to where the wood lies now in all its helpless immobility, hissing in the flames,

> Sawn, sapless, darkening with soot.

"Darkening" is a word which often carries messages of anger or pain or finality; the image continues in "where the bark chars". Reading on, there could even be an echo in the mind of that blackness tinged with purple which is found in "prunes", the tinge reflected in the stagnated blood of a purple wound – the wound of a brother, too, who has lost the sister to whom he was always unusually close. This is the end, he knows. And yet, more real than the logs on the fire, and vividly enshrined in the present tense,

> My fellow-climber rises dim...
> Just as she was, her foot near mine on the bending limb,
> Laughing, her young brown hand awave.

Her youth, her joy, her supple limbs matching the tree's, have recovered substance; memory has brought another equally valid kind of reality.

There are many fine poems in which Hardy's "mindsight" or vision grows with such force that it is more real than the actual scene. Despite all his years of married unhappiness, all his fulminations against the irksomeness of the dead marriage-bond, he could still write this in the aftermath of Emma's death:

"THE CURTAINS NOW ARE DRAWN"

(Song)

I

> The curtains now are drawn,
> And the spindrift strikes the glass,
> Blown up the jaggèd pass
> By the surly salt sou'-west,
> And the sneering glare is gone
> Behind the yonder crest,

While she sings to me:
"O the dream that thou art my Love, be it thine,
And the dream that I am thy Love, be it mine,
And death may come, but loving is divine."

II

I stand here in the rain,
With its smite upon her stone,
And the grasses that have grown
Over women, children, men,
And their texts that "Life is vain";
But I hear the notes as when
    Once she sang to me:
"O the dream that thou art my Love, be it thine,
And the dream that I am thy Love, be it mine,
And death may come, but loving is divine."

1913

All the fragmented, jagged, surly, sneering images of the first
stanza, and the drenching, smiting, smothering images of the
second cannot obliterate what is reality for the man who stands
by the grave:

But I hear the notes as when
    Once she sang to me.

And if one reads again "On a Discovered Curl of Hair" on page
10, (a curl found after Emma's death in a locket of 1870), one is
brought at once from what might have been a rather
commonplace post-mortem situation to an intensity of focus, a
sensation of sun, and air, and movement, of living colour and
substance, which on one level convinces us of its reality.

It is not surprising, with memories like these, that Hardy
himself and his characters sometimes prefer the memoried
world to the actual. He comes nearest, perhaps, to surrender in
the moment he describes in "The Shadow on the Stone". In a
letter to an old friend he wrote how after Emma's death

the saddest moments of all are when I go into the garden and
to that long straight walk at the top that you know, where she
used to walk every evening just before dusk, the cat trotting

faithfully behind her; and at times when I almost expect to see her as usual coming in from the flower-beds with a little trowel in her hand.[15]

These moments, when Hardy stood like the Druid Stone brooding and alone under the trees in his garden, were shaped into a poem – as with his memory he shaped the shadows into a vision of the departed Emma:

THE SHADOW ON THE STONE

I went by the Druid stone
That broods in the garden white and lone,
And I stopped and looked at the shifting shadows
That at some moments fall thereon
From the tree hard by with a rhythmic swing,
And they shaped in my imagining
To the shade that a well-known head and shoulders
Threw there when she was gardening.

I thought her behind my back,
Yea, her I long had learned to lack,
And I said: "I am sure you are standing behind me,
Though how do you get into this old track?"
And there was no sound but the fall of a leaf
As a sad response; and to keep down grief
I would not turn my head to discover
That there was nothing in my belief.

Yet I wanted to look and see
That nobody stood at the back of me;
But I thought once more: "Nay, I'll not unvision
A shape which, somehow, there may be."
So I went on softly from the glade,
And left her behind me throwing her shade,
As she were indeed an apparition –
My head unturned lest my dream should fade.

Begun 1913: Finished 1916

The strength of the vision is such that he can hardly disbelieve. He walks on blindly, his head unturned, with a determination to preserve it that is doomed by a sad echo of the old tale of Orpheus and his loss.

What happens when a past memory dominates the actual scene is another disjunction: we become positively dislocated from the present while we are only tenuously joined to the past. Hardy explored this problem – this dislocation and confusion involving time and change and the nature of reality, memory and vision – in greatest depth during the last ten years or so of his long life. It led him into the realm of the grotesque and a kind of prophetic insight into the workings of the human mind and imagination. Through this and the events in the world about him he saw the kinds of perversion, obsession and illusion that led to the "dark madness... of war"; the nightmare, the phantasmal fears, the "Famine and Flame – /More Severance and Shock!" of "A New Year's Eve in War Time". Dennis Taylor's study of "Hardy's Apocalypse" traces in some detail the development of his war poetry; how he and other contemporary writers saw the war as the annihilation of the romantic dream of continual betterment too comfortably enjoyed by the Victorians; and how the awakening from this dream – into the nightmare of actuality – is a part of his constant search into the "too late" theme and the visionary powers of the human mind.

Those visionary powers belong particularly to poets,

> The visioning powers of souls who dare
> To pierce the material screen.

The poem from which those lines come links the memories that fill the poet's mind – "a mind with sight" – with the long experience of humanity, and with the threads of understanding that he spins from it.

THE HOUSE OF SILENCE

> "That is a quiet place –
> That house in the trees with the shady lawn."
> "– If, child, you knew what there goes on
> You would not call it a quiet place.
> Why, a phantom abides there, the last of its race,
> And a brain spins there till dawn."
>
> "But I see nobody there, –
> Nobody moves about the green,
> Or wanders the heavy trees between."

"– Ah, that's because you do not bear
The visioning powers of souls who dare
    To pierce the material screen.

"Morning, noon, and night,
Mid those funereal shades that seem
    The uncanny scenery of a dream,
Figures dance to a mind with sight,
And music and laughter like floods of light
    Make all the precincts gleam.

"It is a poet's bower,
Through which there pass, in fleet arrays,
Long teams of all the years and days,
Of joys and sorrows, of earth and heaven,
That meet mankind in its ages seven,
    An aeon in an hour."

Spinning and weaving are important images for Hardy, as is the idea of "shaping". Memory does both. It weaves the people of the past into grey ghosts in an old woman's mind; and as Hardy muses on his father's violin (page 203), his memories "shape [its] olden story". One sees often in his poems how "memory shaped old times anew"; how this mental activity can create something fresh out of an old experience. In "Thoughts of Phena" he remembers a favourite cousin, Tryphena Sparks; when she dies unexpectedly he finds he has not a single memento of her.[16] Yet memory comes into its own. Lacking tangible and visible supports, it can even create something better, a more faithful picture "fined in my brain... the more". This beautiful lyric, written in March 1890 before Hardy had given up novel-writing, shows what skill he had achieved years before he published his first volume of verse.

THOUGHTS OF PHENA

At News of Her Death

Not a line of her writing have I,
    Not a thread of her hair,
No mark of her late time as dame in her dwelling, whereby
    I may picture her there;
And in vain do I urge my unsight

> To conceive my lost prize
> At her close, whom I knew when her dreams were
>   upbrimming with light,
> And with laughter her eyes.
>
> What scenes spread around her last days,
>   Sad, shining, or dim?
> Did her gifts and compassions enray and enarch her sweet
>   ways
>   With an aureate nimb?
> Or did life-light decline from her years,
>   And mischances control
> Her full day-star; unease, or regret, or forebodings, or fears
>   Disennoble her soul?
>
> Thus I do but the phantom retain
>   Of the maiden of yore
> As my relic; yet haply the best of her – fined in my brain
>   It may be the more
> That no line of her writing have I,
>   Nor a thread of her hair,
> No mark of her late time as dame in her dwelling, whereby
>   I may picture her there.

March 1890

Unless he was present at Tryphena's wedding to Charles Gale in 1877 Hardy may not have seen her for nearly twenty years. Yet it was typical of him to carry a memory or emotion buried deep within him for a long time before creating a poem from it. Of several other girls whom he regarded as a "lost prize" of his youth, Louisa Harding was to prove, poetically, of great longevity. Since class differences prevented their friendship, he could only gaze at her from afar, and once murmured "Good evening", as they met in the lane. He records seeing her only "down to his twenty-third or twenty-fourth year", and she died in 1913; yet he wrote three poems about her, the first not published until 1922, and the last – "To Louisa in the Lane" – actually written "not many months before his death".[17] Its refrain is "Ah, I remember."

*   *   *   *   *   *

The "buried emotion" which Hardy found could remain in his memory like an unpolished nugget became a priceless asset.

Forty years after an experience he could draw it out again, the gleam scarcely tarnished, and bring all those years of maturing understanding to refining it – "fined in my brain" – and creating art from it. But it was not until he himself had been through the refiner's fire of suffering, and spent many years working at poetry, that the full implications for it of the buried emotion became clear to him. During those years, beginning with the early poems of the 1860s, and particularly when he was able to concentrate on poetry from the late 1890s, he was meticulously yet adventurously exploring every thoroughfare in the art. Not only was he experimenting all the time in numerous and varied metres and rhyme schemes. Probably more significantly, he was reconnoitring the relations between matter and manner – different themes and frameworks, or, in turn, a single theme in different guises; and particularly how a theme and its framework (or setting) could be made so organically one that each could complete the other, and the poem become a satisfying unity. He was also coming to see how the development shown taking place in a poem could mirror the development of a day or a life – and so be a kind of re-enactment of reality.

So far this exploration has been a brief look at the ground, picking out some of Hardy's preoccupations and the main features of his world throughout his career – the importance of places and people, of time and memory. But it was many years before all his experimenting and understanding came together: when it did, it was the peak of his achievement. Let's start towards the peak, and see how he reached it.

Notes

1   *She, to Him III*

2   *Memory and I; Conjecture*

3   Eg *Her Immortality, His Immortality, The To-be-Forgotten*

4   *At a Country Fair*

5   *The Face at the Casement; The Peace-Offering*

6   John Freeman's poem *Caterpillars* ends similarly:
        Over and over and over and over again
        The same hungry thoughts and the hopeless same regrets,

> Over and over the same truths, again and again
> In a heaving ring returning the same regrets.

7   *The Voice of the Thorn*

8   Proust: *A la Recherche du Temps Perdu/Remembrance of Things Past:*
    I Swann's Way, Overture. Proust describes too the flood of
    recollection caused by the smell of the varnished stairs up which
    he went in grief as a child to bed – a grief which "when it
    assumed this olfactory guise, my intellect was powerless to
    resist..." (Tr. Scott-Moncrieff and Kilmartin, Penguin
    Modern Classics, p 30.) There are many interesting connections
    between Hardy and Proust – see also pp 109, 272
    The Place on the Map

9   *A Musical Incident*

10 *A Duettist to her Pianoforte*

11 *PTH* 28

12 *A Pair of Blue Eyes*, ch XXII; *Life*, 50, 120

13 *In the Mind's Eye*

14 *Life*, 311

15 Letter to Florence Henniker, 17 December 1912

16 *Life,* 224. In view of the controversy about this relationship, see
    Millgate, 105–7

17 *Life*, 26; *Life*, cancelled typescript, *Notebooks*, 217

5

HOW IT HAPPENED:

Integrating poetry and life

In 1901 Hardy published "A Commonplace Day". In a score of ways it brings us straight into his world – a world where the ordinary, the commonplace, is deliberately used to show the extraordinary; a world often of drab greyness, kindled into warmth by the glow of a fire, and the glow of a passionate feeling for people and the world's potential.

A COMMONPLACE DAY

The day is turning ghost,
And scuttles from the kalendar in fits and furtively,
To join the anonymous host
Of those that throng oblivion; ceding his place, maybe,
To one of like degree.

I part the fire-gnawed logs,
Rake forth the embers, spoil the busy flames, and lay the ends
Upon the shining dogs;
Further and further from the nooks the twilight's stride
extends,
And beamless black impends.

Nothing of tiniest worth
Have I wrought, pondered, planned; no one thing asking
blame or praise,
Since the pale corpse-like birth
Of this diurnal unit, bearing blanks in all its rays –
Dullest of dull-hued Days!

Wanly upon the panes
The rain slides as have slid since morn my colourless
thoughts; and yet

Here, while Day's presence wanes,
And over him the sepulchre-lid is slowly lowered and set,
He wakens my regret.

Regret – though nothing dear
That I wot of, was toward in the wide world at his prime,
Or bloomed elsewhere than here,
To die with his decease, and leave a memory sweet, sublime,
Or mark him out in Time....

– Yet, maybe, in some soul,
In some spot undiscerned on sea or land, some impulse rose,
Or some intent upstole
Of that enkindling ardency from whose maturer glows
The world's amendment flows;

But which, benumbed at birth
By momentary chance or wile, has missed its hope to be
Embodied on the earth;
And undervoicings of this loss to man's futurity
May wake regret in me.

One needs to read this poem several times to see the pattern, and
perhaps to overcome a dull, negative droop of the mind which it
may at first induce. The man is in a twilight world, a twilight of
the mind too at the end of a wasted day. The time has passed
since morning in the way it often passes for Hardy – wan and
colourless, draining vigour and life. We see the last wavering of
the day partnered by the last waverings of the fire, the "scuttle"
of the retreating day's fluctuating light echoed in the crackle and
scrape as the ashy logs are parted and the busy flames die down.
As the daylight fades into darkness the glow of the fire is for a
time enhanced; and so is the man's meditation as he gazes into
the embers. The end of the day and the consequent rise of the fire
act together, and waken his regret.

    On this line the poem turns, as his meditation turns. His
reflections, which have been colourless like his setting, the
"dull-hued Day", are warmed at the thought of the
"blooming," the "memory sweet, sublime" that might have
been. The "enkindling ardency" and its "maturer glows" pick
up the fire in metaphor, so that the subject of the poem and its
setting are closely linked; and the new idea is lit up in the last
flare of the fire. This swell and fall in his thinking, and in the

firelight, are reflected in the swell and fall of the language. Muted until the regret is awakened, in stanzas five and six it expands with the warmth of his hope, in more eager, musical, unconstrained phrases.

But the day must die, and the fire must die, and the hope of some lovely act that may have redeemed the day is chilled and numbed by the workings of chance in the world. In the unusual word "undervoicings" is heard the last flare of the fire, like the flare of his inner voice of regret – the final unifying element in Hardy's masterly construction of the whole poem. In it, setting and subject are grafted into one growth. We know the feel of a wasted day and a useless self, which spreads to a contemplation of the universal: the all too familiar recognition that it is only as something nears its end that we begin to realise what we ought to have done with it. The whole poem is an integrated experience through the mutual illumination of its form and theme.

"A Commonplace Day" is probably the first poem in which Hardy, after many experiments, succeeds in fusing the theme so completely with its setting: by which I mean not just the scene of the poem, but its form and structure, its setting as a jewel is set. In the poems that follow, he continues to develop this fusion, and to express through it some of his deepest convictions about life and poetry.

We have seen how one of Hardy's preoccupations is the growing discrepancy between the human mind and the world it lives in; between what is real to us and what is actually happening in the world; between our too-late realisations and our vanished opportunities. In a large number of his most significant poems he uses the setting to dramatise this theme. A character muses while she is engaged in some occupation or in some particular place; and as she (or he) meditates, she increasingly parts company with the "real" world, penetrating deeper and deeper into the world of her reverie – until a sudden interruption from the real world breaks it. Brought sharply back to awareness, she finds that time has passed and the world has changed, leaving her behind. (This happens to many of the characters in Hardy's novels. One has only to think, for example, of the young Tess driving her hives to market in the small dark hours, and brooding on the planet Earth until she falls asleep – to the terrible awakening of the collision with the postcart.)

In "A Commonplace Day" Hardy is just beginning to glimpse the poetic possibilities of a character's meditation, in a setting which in some way both affects and reflects his meditation. There is too a hint of an idea which he was to develop as his expertise grew: that the movement of thought in a poem can be an imitation of the movement of thought during a day – or even during a lifetime. So his brooding by the fire – which is deepened and quickened by the passing of the day – also brings him the realisation that a day has passed with nothing to show for it; and the way he has sat in the few minutes of the poem's meditation is like the way he has sat through the day. There will be other days, he says, "of like degree", so perhaps the unproductive minutes of this poem are representative not just of a day but of a whole lifetime. The idea is barely recognised here; Hardy was to develop it later.

If we want to see how he did this, we have to take a leap in time to that later period, and look at a poem which was not published until 1917. It is probably the clearest example of how skilfully Hardy's understanding grew: how a character, musing within his setting, can be jolted back to awareness of the real, but now discordant world; and how the poem can be an imitation of a whole life, or even of the pattern of human history.

COPYING ARCHITECTURE IN AN OLD MINSTER

(Wimborne)

How smartly the quarters of the hour march by
    That the jack-o'-clock never forgets;
        Ding-dong; and before I have traced a cusp's eye,
Or got the true twist of the ogee over,
        A double ding-dong ricochetts.

Just so did he clang here before I came,
    And so will he clang when I'm gone
        Through the Minster's cavernous hollows – the same
Tale of hours never more to be will he deliver
        To the speechless midnight and dawn!

I grow to conceive it a call to ghosts,

Whose mould lies below and around.
Yes; the next "Come, come," draws them out from
    their posts,
And they gather, and one shade appears, and another,
    As the eve-damps creep from the ground.

See – a Courtenay stands by his quatrefoiled tomb,
    And a Duke and his Duchess near;
And one Sir Edmund in columned gloom,
And a Saxon king by the presbytery chamber;
    And shapes unknown in the rear.

Maybe they have met for a parle on some plan
    To better ail-stricken mankind;
I catch their cheepings, though thinner than
The overhead creak of a passager's pinion
    When leaving land behind.

Or perhaps they speak to the yet unborn,
    And caution them not to come
To a world so ancient and trouble-torn,
Of foiled intents, vain lovingkindness,
    And ardours chilled and numb.

They waste to fog as I stir and stand,
    And move from the arched recess,
And pick up the drawing that slipped from my hand,
And feel for the pencil I dropped in the cranny
    In a moment's forgetfulness.

This poem may not be familiar since, astonishingly, it hardly
ever appears even in selections of Hardy's poetry, let alone in
any general anthology. Read it two or three times awarely, and
you will probably find it draws you ineluctably into its shifting,
shadowy world. With the brisk opening and fast speed of the
first stanza, the speaker and reader both begin firmly in the
time-marshalled "real" world – Ding-dong! We feel, rather as
he does, that he has hardly settled in his corner and established
the pad comfortably on his knee and assessed his sketching
subject before – ding-dong, there it goes again. And again! We
hear the echo; so does the speaker. It echoes other things than the
actual sound, reverberations into the past as the cavernous
hollows, the ancient atmosphere, take hold of him and dwarf his

frail humanity in a succession of frail humans. And then we stumble incapably over the "tale of hours never more to be will he deliver", blundering headlong into "the speechless midnight and dawn!" We seem to be out of control here, our tongue unable to get round its syllables before the next boom, and mocked by the majestic silent eloquence of the great world's steady roll through darkness to light. As we try to catch up with ourselves we are drawn on before we can, drawn on powerlessly by a force represented in the stressed, suggestive phrase "I grow to conceive it a call to ghosts"; and by the next inexorable clang, which has become an invitation – "Come, come," – that we now eagerly look for, as it calls the shades of the past out of their hidden places. There are two possible meanings to "As the eve-damps creep from the ground"; and the ambiguity, like the obstructiveness of the earlier stumbling line, is deliberate. Are the shades misty *like* the eve-damps, or is it just that they creep out of their settings *at the same time*? (Hardy's holograph version was "Creeping like damps from the ground"; but he saw how he could thicken the cloud of unknowing, and make the setting and the idea mutually inextricable.) He beckons us: "See –," taking us into the past, further and further through time to the unknown of prehistory. Those he names are staunchly individual, this Duke and his Duchess, the impressive Courtenay, Sir Edmund and the Saxon king; and as they become real to him, he wonders how their lives connect with his own in the unchanging story of "ail-stricken mankind". Could it have been a subliminal echo of the French "aile" that brought his next image, the evocative "overhead creak of a passager's pinion/ When leaving land behind"? It both reminds us of the outer setting, the natural world overarching us (like the speechless midnight and dawn), and also increases our sense of distance from the real world, as we move – leaving land behind – deeper into the abstract world of the poet's reverie.

Here we drift not only in the shadowy gloom of the Minster or the darkening sky, but in the mists of words from the past, like "parle" and "passager", and words from the common stock, the inherited clichés, of human experience. The world of Hardy is still as it was for the shades, "a world so ancient and trouble-torn." He moves from his thought of them to a contemplation of this world, in well-worn abstractions that link him to the people of the past, that express the human limitations that bounded them, as they now bound him. The abstractions end with the "ardours chilled and numb" which surely reflect the physical state of the thinker as he stirs from his cramped position and comes back to the "real" world where we began. What does he find? That the eve-damps have become the night-fogs; that the wash of time which has passed over him has swept him up to the concrete present, the moment of now against which he dashes after his centuries-old experience of the last hour.

Time is; Time was; Time takes us unaware; "Thee, too, the years shall cover."[1]

> Ding-dong; and before I have traced a cusp's eye,
>   Or got the true twist of the ogee over
>   A double ding-dong ricochetts.

As in life so in the poem: the theme of the poem is perfectly embodied in its structure. The poem itself is a microcosm of life.

* * * * * *

With "Copying Architecture" Hardy had come a long way from the early poems published in 1898, in which his experiments with settings and themes and imagery had not yet found a perfect balance. To my mind the best exposition of his development is Dennis Taylor's *Hardy's Poetry, 1860–1928*. I have already referred to his discussions of "Hardy's Apocalypse" and his war poetry. Professor Taylor's map of Hardy's poetry is on a scale where the details and the evolution of the landscape can be examined; and anyone who wishes to explore it in greater depth than this introductory journey can allow is strongly recommended to read his book. Here is how he summarises the development of Hardy's meditative lyric:

The story begins with poems Hardy wrote in the nineteenth century and published in *Wessex Poems* (1898). He establishes his characteristic meditative speaker within a natural setting. But the meditative frame of the poem, the interaction of mind and setting, is not yet made fully consistent with the subject of the speaker's thoughts. At the turn of the century, in poems published in *Poems of the Past and Present* (1902), Hardy develops the implications of the meditative frame and explores (a) how the setting conditions the speaker's thoughts in complex ways, (b) how a meditation lasting a few minutes can become the model of how an entire day is spent. In the following decade, in poems written c 1904–12 and published in *Time's Laughingstocks* (1909) or *Satires of Circumstance* (1914), Hardy begins (a) to relate the subject of his philosophical speculations to the meditative frame of his poem, and (b) to link these meditative poems with another series of developing poems, those containing a lover's journey. This connection becomes an extremely fruitful one. A more ambitious analogy begins to develop: the way a man pursues a vision of the years is like the way a man pursues his thoughts during a meditation. The changing world of the lover's journey is like the changing setting of the lyric speaker. In 1912 the full implications of this analogy become clear to Hardy in a very direct and personal way. His wife dies and the *Poems of 1912–13* which follow include some of his greatest achievements.

    ... With the crisis of 1912 the elements of Hardy's poetry come together in a mature and definitive way. The poem becomes the model of a man's life. The way the poem grows and develops in the mind recapitulates the way the mind has developed over a lifetime.[2]

We shall look briefly in another chapter at some of Hardy's "philosophical speculations." The natural progression here is to his poems of a lover's journey; for they lead to the *Poems of 1912–13* which, as Taylor suggests, is where the strands we have been disentangling begin to weave together.

    Hardy's favourite pilgrimage image has been noted. A glance at about the first 35 poems of *Wessex Poems* shows how many of them concern movement and journeying. "Her Immortality" begins

> Upon a noon I pilgrimed through
>   A pasture, mile by mile,
> Unto the place where last I saw
>   My dead love's living smile.

In the rather tedious poem before it, "My Cicely," a young man journeys to the burial, as he thinks, of his former love – only to find the dead woman had the same name but was another person altogether. His own lady, with cruel irony, he has already unknowingly met in a roadside tavern, so changed, with "her liquor-fired face, her thick accents", that he did not recognise her. The landscape (or setting) in these and other poems about lovers' journeys is no mute backdrop. It can express Hardy's criticism of his character; it can foster the character's illusions; it can remind us, with its man-made relics, of past generations who have faced similar crises.

By the time Hardy came to write the long poem "The Revisitation," (published in 1904) he was using the setting even more significantly to change the course of the story and the lives. The first nine stanzas tell how the lover, stimulated by his return to the place and the anniversary of a previous betrayal and parting, sets off on a journey in quest of the lost love. He finds her as night falls, haunting her father's downland where they used to meet.

[X]

Round about me bulged the barrows
As before, in antique silence – immemorial funeral piles –
Where the sleek herds trampled daily the remains of flint-tipt
    arrows
Mid the thyme and chamomiles;

[XI]

And the Sarsen stone there, dateless,
On whose breast we had sat and told the zephyrs many a
    tender vow,
Held the heat of yester sun, as sank thereon one fated mateless
From those far fond hours till now.

[XII]

Maybe flustered by my presence
Rose the peewits, just as all those years back, wailing soft and
    loud,
And revealing their pale pinions like a fitful phosphorescence
Up against the cope of cloud,

[XIII]

Where their dolesome exclamations
Seemed the voicings of the self-same throats I had heard when
    life was green,

Though since that day uncounted frail forgotten generations
    Of their kind had flecked the scene. –

[XIV]
    And so, living long and longer
In a past that lived no more, my eyes discerned there,
    suddenly,
That a figure broke the skyline – first in vague contour, then
    stronger,
    And was crossing near to me.

[XV]
    Some long-missed familiar gesture,
Something wonted, struck me in the figure's pause to list and
    heed,
Till I fancied from its handling of its loosely wrapping vesture
    That it might be She indeed.

[XVI]
    'Twas not reasonless: below there
In the vale, had been her home; the nook might hold her even
    yet,
And the downlands were her father's fief; she still might come
    and go there; –
    So I rose, and said, "Agnette!"

[XVII]
    With a little leap, half-frightened,
She withdrew some steps; then letting intuition smother fear
In a place so long-accustomed, and as one whom thought
    enlightened,
    She replied: "What – *that* voice? – here!"

[XVIII]
    "Yes, Agnette! – And did the occasion
Of our marching hither make you think I *might* walk where
    we two –"
"O, I often come", she murmured with a moment's coy
    evasion,
    "('Tis not far), – and – think of you."

[XIX]
    Then I took her hand, and led her
To the ancient people's stone whereon I had sat. There now
    sat we;

And together talked, until the first reluctant shyness fled her,
And she spoke confidingly.

[XX]

    "It is *just* as ere we parted!"
Said she, brimming high with joy – "And when, then, came
    you here, and why?"
"– Dear, I could not sleep for thinking of our trystings when
    twin-hearted."
She responded, "Nor could I.

[XXI]

    "There are few things I would rather
Than be wandering at this spirit-hour – lone-lived, my
    kindred dead –
On this world of well-known feature I inherit from my
    father:
Night or day, I have no dread....

[XXII]

    "O I wonder, wonder whether
Any heartstring bore a signal-thrill between us twain or no? –
Some such influence can, at times, they say, draw severed
    souls together."
I said, "Dear, we'll dream it so."

They are lost in their dream, in a fantasy where he almost thinks
the peewits are the identical birds that flapped around him long
ago. The landscape seeks to remind him, though ambivalently,
of the passing of time and the death of love; but, longing to
preserve the dream, he is blind to its message,

            living long and longer
    In a past that lived no more.

Sitting together on the stone, they fall asleep. It is only when
the morning breaks that the revealing sun harshly blazes reality
out of fantasy: as it was to do increasingly in the meditative
lyrics, the setting interrupts both the dream cherished over the
years, and the dream indulged through this night.

[XXV]

How long I slept I knew not,

But the brief warm summer night had slid when, to my swift
    surprise,
A red upedging sun, of glory chambered mortals view not,
    Was blazing on my eyes,

[XXVI]

    From the Milton Woods to Dole-Hill
All the spacious landscape lighting, and around about my feet
Flinging tall thin tapering shadows from the meanest mound
    and mole-hill,
    And on trails the ewes had beat.

[XXVII]

    She was sitting still beside me,
Dozing likewise; and I turned to her, to take her hanging
    hand,
When, the more regarding, that which like a spectre shook
    and tried me
    In her image then I scanned;

[XXVIII]

    That which Time's transforming chisel
Had been tooling night and day for twenty years, and tooled
    too well,
In its rendering of crease where curve was, where was raven,
    grizzle –
    Pits, where peonies once did dwell.

[XXIX]

    She had wakened, and perceiving
(I surmise) my sigh and shock, my quite involuntary dismay,
Up she started, and – her wasted figure all throughout it
    heaving –
    Said, "Ah, yes: I am *thus* by day!

[XXX]

    "Can you really wince and wonder
That the sunlight should reveal you such a thing of skin and
    bone,
As if unaware a Death's-head must of need lie not far under
    Flesh whose years out-count your own?

[XXXI]

'Yes: that movement was a warning
Of the worth of man's devotion! – Yes, Sir, I am *old*," said she,
"And the thing which should increase love turns it quickly
    into scorning –
And your new-won heart from me!"

[XXXII]
    Then she went, ere I could call her,
With the too proud temper ruling that had parted us before,
And I saw her form descend the slopes, and smaller grow and
    smaller,
    Till I caught its course no more....

[XXXIII]
    True; I might have dogged her downward;
– But it *may* be (though I know not) that this trick on us of
    Time
Disconcerted and confused me. – Soon I bent my footsteps
    townward,
    Like to one who had watched a crime.

[XXXIV]
    Well I knew my native weakness,
Well I know it still. I cherished her reproach like physic-
    wine,
For I saw in that emaciate shape of bitterness and bleakness
    A nobler soul than mine.

[XXXV]
    Did I not return then, ever? –
Did we meet again? – mend all? – Alas, what greyhead
    perseveres! –
Soon I got the Route elsewhither. – Since that hour I have seen
    her never:
    Love is lame at fifty years.

What the setting has precipitated, the woman's pride and
realism and his own emergent disillusion complete. (In "My
Cicely", the lover chooses to keep the illusion and pretend it was
the dead woman, after all, who was his love; and the landscape is
shown to be at variance with him.)[3]
    In "The Revisitation", Hardy makes the changing setting as

important to the travelling lover as to the daydreamer; in fact here the traveller is also the dreamer. As Taylor points out in his analysis, Hardy comes to see similarities between these two types of poem. Both the journeying lover and the meditating man or woman are following a vision in their minds, usually a vision deriving from the past; and both are set in a world which affects them as it changes round them.

The biggest change for forty years was about to happen in Hardy's personal life: the sudden death of his wife. He, like everyone who knew him, was totally unprepared for its effect on him. He discovered then that he had been living an illusion: cherishing in his mind a vision of his wife that was forty years out of date; like the lover of his poems pursuing a mirage, or the meditating character following his mind's eye deeper and deeper into a fantasy that clashed with what the world calls real. The theme of his poetry had caught up with his own life.

Notes

1   *Life*, 287

2   *Dennis Taylor*, 7-8. A new book by Professor Taylor on Hardy's metres is due to be published as I prepare these notes (autumn 1988)

3   See pp 96, 228

6

TRACES OF AN OLD FIRE:

The Poems of 1912–13

I

It was before dawn, by starlight, that Hardy set out on 7 March 1870 from the cottage at Bockhampton where he had been born – and was again temporarily living with his parents – to make the awkward journey to Cornwall. The church at St Juliot, near Boscastle, was in need of restoration, and Hardy was sent by Mr Crickmay the architect to begin the business. The journey involved some changing of trains between Dorchester and Launceston, in "a sort of cross-jump journey, like a chess-knight's move," as Emma herself was vividly to describe it many years later. At Launceston Hardy hired a pony and trap to cover the last eighteen miles, and finally arrived, again by starlight, at the door of St Juliot rectory. Readers of *A Pair of Blue Eyes* will find the story largely familiar. Hardy found that the rector, Caddell Holder, was in bed with gout, and his wife was attending him upstairs; it fell to her sister to open the door and welcome the slight, bearded stranger who stood diffidently on the doorstep. For them both, this was a fateful moment they never forgot – for him, the unexpected sight of a young woman in brown with long bright hair; for her, in her rural isolation, a rather mysterious visitor with a piece of paper sticking out of his pocket which she later found out was not a blueprint but a poem. Many years later she described it in *Some Recollections*, and he wrote a poem which captured the moment as she might have seen it.

"A MAN WAS DRAWING NEAR TO ME"

> On that gray night of mournful drone,
> Apart from aught to hear, to see,
> I dreamt not that from shires unknown

> In gloom, alone,
> By Halworthy,
> A man was drawing near to me.
>
> I'd no concern at anything,
> No sense of coming pull-heart play;
> Yet, under the silent outspreading
> Of even's wing
> Where Otterham lay,
> A man was riding up my way.
>
> I thought of nobody – not of one,
> But only of trifles – legends, ghosts –
> Though, on the moorland dim and dun
> That travellers shun
> About these coasts,
> The man had passed Tresparret Posts.
>
> There was no light at all inland,
> Only the seaward pharos-fire,
> Nothing to let me understand
> That hard at hand
> By Hennett Byre
> The man was getting nigh and nigher.
>
> There was a rumble at the door,
> A draught disturbed the drapery,
> And but a minute passed before,
> With gaze that bore
> My destiny,
> The man revealed himself to me.

It was Hardy's first visit to the wild coast of Cornwall, and to a man of his visual and aesthetic sensibility it could not fail to speak with tremendous power. This must partially explain the spell under which he fell. Emma Gifford was not in the first bloom of youth, and had not been admitting to more than 25 years for the last five. She had, however, a vivacity and a playfulness which enchanted Hardy, and a fearlessness on horseback as she clattered down the steep hillsides, her bright hair streaming in the wind, which called out all his admiration. It was a new world, and an enclosed one, which for the next few days they shared. By the time he had to return to Dorset, magic had taken hold of him.

WHEN I SET OUT FOR LYONNESSE

(1870)

When I set out for Lyonnesse
A hundred miles away,
The rime was on the spray,
And starlight lit my lonesomeness
When I set out for Lyonnesse
A hundred miles away.

What would bechance at Lyonnesse
While I should sojourn there
No prophet durst declare,
Nor did the wisest wizard guess
What would bechance at Lyonnesse
While I should sojourn there.

When I came back from Lyonnesse
With magic in my eyes,
All marked with mute surmise
My radiance rare and fathomless,
When I came back from Lyonnesse
With magic in my eyes!

Hardy and Emma corresponded, and in August of the same year he returned for a week to St Juliot. It was a time of pure enchantment when they walked or rode, picnicked and explored together in a way that "Under the Waterfall" and many other poems delightfully record. If Hardy was reticent about his background, he was seemingly a respectable architect; and the elderly rector and his young wife (whose days did not always pass without sisterly friction) must have been glad to watch the romance develop. An understanding was reached between the two which enabled them to face the four ensuing years before they could marry; for Hardy was at a crucial point in his career, hovering between novel-writing and architecture. That summer he was in fact serialising *A Pair of Blue Eyes* in *Tinsley's Magazine*, and (bv an exemplary postal service) he hustled the next instalment from Cornwall back to London. The proofs were to be sent to him at Bodmin: for he and Emma had gone together to seek her father's acceptance of their engagement. It was a disastrous visit. A retired, perhaps failed, solicitor with alcoholic tendencies, Mr Gifford despised Hardy's social background. Nor was Hardy's proud, possessive mother in favour of his marrying at all, let alone marrying a strange woman of unknown stock who probably gave herself airs. It was a measure of this double opposition that when, with the success of *Far from the Madding Crowd*, Thomas and Emma eventually married on 17 September, 1874, the ceremony took place in London and was attended only by her uncle as celebrant, her brother, and another statutory witness. Hardy wrote laconically to tell his brother Henry that the marriage was made, explaining that he and Emma were going to Paris "for materials for my next story."

For the next few years whenever possible Hardy kept his wife and his parents apart. Before they finally settled at Max Gate in June 1885, the couple lived in a succession of rented homes in Surbiton, Paddington, Swanage, Yeovil, Sturminster Newton, Tooting, and Wimborne, from most of which we have a legacy of poems (such as "Copying Architecture in an Old Minster"). Of Sturminster Newton, where they lived at Riverside Villa from 1876–8, Hardy wrote: "It was their first house and, though small, probably that in which they spent their happiest days."[1]

> Lifelong to be
> Seemed the fair colour of the time

he wrote in "The Musical Box", one of three poems about Sturminster that appeared in *Moments of Vision*; and in 1922 he published "A Two-Years' Idyll," a cancelled version of whose opening line was: "Never such joy was."

A TWO-YEARS' IDYLL

> Yes; such it was;
> Just those two seasons unsought,
> Sweeping like summertide wind on our ways;
> Moving, as straws,
> Hearts quick as ours in those days;
> Going like wind, too, and rated as nought

Save as the prelude to plays
    Soon to come – larger, life-fraught:
        Yes; such it was.

    "Nought" it was called,
        Even by ourselves – that which springs
Out of the years for all flesh, first or last,
        Commonplace, scrawled
    Dully on days that go past.
Yet, all the while, it upbore us like wings
    Even in hours overcast:
        Aye, though this best thing of things,
        "Nought" it was called!

    What seems it now?
        Lost: such beginning was all;
Nothing came after: romance straight forsook
        Quickly somehow
    Life when we sped from our nook,
Primed for new scenes with designs smart and tall....
    – A preface without any book,
    A trumpet uplipped, but no call;
        That seems it now.

As early as July 1875 they had had a significant quarrel while
visiting Bournemouth; and it was of Tooting, where they
moved, still childless, in March 1878, that Hardy later wrote in
The Life that there "they seemed to begin to feel that 'there had
past away a glory from the earth.' And it was in this house that
their troubles began."

* * * * *

The story of Thomas and Emma Hardy's estrangement can be
read in full elsewhere. I have briefly referred to it, and to the
puzzle or scandal of how Hardy, thought by his friends to be a
man of humane and high principles, could have so ignored his
wife's suffering before her death. "Truth lies at the bottom of
the well." What chiefly concerns the reader in this exploration
of his poetry is the effect of that death, and the courtship which
was the guiding light of their life together. It was not until after
Emma died that Hardy realised how he had depended on it.
    For Hardy, that Cornish courtship was luminous. It was a

time of "radiance rare and fathomless," bathed in what Gray had called (and Hardy had already copied in his notebook) "the purple light of love." We should linger a little on this word "purple." Hardy had grown up with it in a rather special way, for before he was ten his mother had given him a copy of Dryden's translation of Virgil's *Aeneid*. (The effect of this reading matter on him as a future poet may be incalculable.) In fairly wide use among Latin poets, the word *purpureus* in Virgil's time could include "red, pink, violet, blackish etc" and when used poetically had the general sense of "bright, brilliant, beautiful," or "glowing."[2] For Hardy, the word "purple" had a particular significance – strong spiritual and emotional resonances, many of which derived from Virgil as well as Gray. It recurs in many poems:

> Out of the past there rises a week
> Enringed with a purple zone.[3]

It was what Grace Melbury, in *The Woodlanders*, imagined as the necessary aura that should surround her progress to the altar, "flushed by the purple light and bloom of her own passion." It occurs significantly in *Desperate Remedies*; and in *A Pair of Blue Eyes* it describes the burgeoning love of Stephen Smith for Elfride. "She looked so intensely *living* and full of movement as she came into the old silent place that young Smith's world began to be lit by 'the purple light' in all its definiteness."

In *The Life*, Hardy described Emma in almost identical terms.[4] He wrote *A Pair of Blue Eyes* while courting Emma; its setting is Emma's Cornwall where they met in March 1870, and it reflects their relationship and characters in many particulars. In March 1895 Hardy (always sensitive to dates and places) wrote a new preface for the novel of more than twenty years before. It included these words:

> The place is pre-eminently (for one person at least) the region of dream and mystery. The ghostly birds, the pall-like sea, the frothy wind, the eternal soliloquy of the waters, the bloom of dark purple cast that seems to exhale from the shoreward precipices in themselves lend to the scene an atmosphere like the twilight of a night vision.

The grip of this dream and vision upon Hardy in 1895 is apparent. Yet this was at a time when he and his wife were hardly speaking, living separate existences with major differences of opinion, their life constantly grating with "their wedlock's aftergrinds."[5]

When Emma died, Hardy discovered that the vision and the dream, the encircling memory of their first love, and the purple light, had never left him. It was the evolving reality of their relationship which had never taken hold of his inner sight. Like Pierston in *The Well-Beloved*, and to some extent in ways that Proust clearly understood,[6] Hardy had been nursing a romantic image of his love, which had not changed with the years either of his own ageing, or the fading of love, or the transformations of the world. At Emma's death he found he was still on a lover's journey, still tracking a vision which had governed the life of his imagination for forty years. At her death he set his desk calendar to March 7 [1870] and kept it so until he died.

Like the flooding sunrise revealing Agnette's worn features in "The Revisitation", the death of Emma shocked Hardy into recognising the chasm that lay between his vision and the reality of their world and their relationship. His favourite theme, the discrepancy between the human mind and the world it lives in, had become exemplified in his own life.

Not only had the Hardys' marriage been in several senses sterile; his succession of short-lived fantasies with other women had, for about five years before Emma's death, settled upon one younger woman, Florence Dugdale, who had called out the tenderness and protectiveness in Hardy which should have been devoted to his wife. Florence had inspired two or three beautiful poems, like "On the Departure Platform" and "After the Visit", in which Hardy had raised

> The eternal question of what Life was,
> And why we were there, and by whose strange laws
> That which mattered most could not be.

Emma's death in November 1912 at first seemed an unlooked for release from those laws. By early March 1913 Florence reported to Edward Clodd that Hardy had even reserved a place for her among the Hardy family graves at Stinsford – his highest accolade. They married in February 1914. Yet Florence, who had witnessed the unhappy marriage and felt deep sympathy for both protagonists, was dismayed to find that, far from the way being clear now that Emma was dead, Hardy on the contrary was now obsessed with her memory. In the year after her death he wrote, astonishingly, about fifty poems about her; and the number was, in the years to come, nearly to treble that.

That Hardy was enthralled by a past vision of Emma had early been suggested in the card he wrote for her funeral wreath: "From her Lonely Husband, with the Old Affection." After the initial shock, bewilderment, and guilt attendant on her death, the next imperative gradually became clear. Within three months he had resolved to make his own last lover's journey, retracing his steps to Cornwall to revisit all the old haunts of their courtship on the anniversaries of their first meetings. After he had left, Florence wrote to Edward Clodd:

> He says that he is going down for the sake of the girl he married, and who died more than twenty years ago. His family say *that* girl never existed, but she did exist to him, no doubt.

So Hardy tried to reconcile what was happening in his "mindsight" with what actually happened in real life. He called the *Poems of 1912–13* (subtitled "*Veteris vestigia flammae*", "the traces of an old fire") an "expiation."[7] In them he created the final expression, the final experience, of his love for the woman he had met forty years before.

II

Legends or lives of star-crossed lovers have always made popular entertainment. Marilyn Monroe and even the Browning love-letters are in a line stretching through time to a dozen famous lamented couples (like those Hardy enumerated in "The Clasped Skeletons.") Of these Orpheus and Eurydice, Dido and Aeneas, Tristan and Iseult, Dante and Beatrice, should be remembered now.

As one reads the "Poems of 1912–13" attentively it becomes clear that at the back of much of Hardy's thinking were some of the myths about lovers which have long gripped the minds of men and women. Tristan and Iseult, with their Cornish setting, were an obvious one. In 1916 Hardy wrote: "Alas, I fear your hopes of a poem on Iseult – the English, or British, Helen – will be disappointed. I visited the place forty-four years ago with an Iseult of my own, and of course she was mixed in the vision of the other."[8] We have noticed too in "The Shadow on the Stone" an echo of the story of Orpheus, who broke his agreement with the King of the Underworld not to look round at his wife Eurydice as she followed him back to earth – and so lost her for ever. The Orpheus theme can be seen elsewhere in Hardy. But there are other echoes. One is of Dante's *Divina Commedia*, well thumbed and copied by Hardy and quoted in the novels.[9] (Emma, in August 1870, was reading it.) Without pressing connections too hard, one can even hear as echoes of Dante favourite Hardy phrases like "without blame, without praise." But the clearest echo comes through Dante's own echo of Virgil, whose spirit Dante imagines as his companion on his visit to Hell. Canto XXX of the *Purgatorio* reads, in D.L. Sayers' translation:

> I turned to leftward – full of confidence
> As any little boy who ever came
> Running to mother with his fears and pains
>
> To say to Virgil: "There is scarce a dram
> That does not hammer and throb in all my blood;
> I know the embers of the ancient flame."

"*Conosco i segni dell' antica fiamma*": Dante's almost straight quotation from the very line in Book IV of *The Aeneid* which Hardy chose as his epigraph to *The Poems of 1912-13* – "*veteris vestigia flammae*", "the traces of an old fire."

In this book Dido, widowed Queen of Carthage, recognises in herself again the symptoms of love. In Dryden's words, "She fed within her veins a flame unseen." He continues, (incidentally introducing the word "purple" where Virgil doesn't):

> Now, when the purple morn had chas'd away
> The dewy shadows, and restored the day...

– now, Dido confesses to her sister that since her first husband was killed, she has felt for nobody what she now feels for the Trojan hero Aeneas:

Agnosco veteris vestigia flammae,

I recognise the sparks of an old fire.

We know how much Virgil's *Aeneid* meant to Hardy, not only from the frequent references and quotations in many of his novels (including, for example, the choice of the names Cytherea and Aeneas in *Desperate Remedies*), but also in *The Life*. He acknowledges there that he re-read "Virgil's *Aeneid* (of which he never wearied.)"[10] It is clear that the story of Dido had a particular significance for him after Emma's death. Aeneas, wrecked at Carthage after the fall of Troy, dallies in a form of marriage with Dido, until the gods remind him of his destiny as founder of Rome. He leaves her and Carthage, and, unknown to him, the despairing Dido takes her own life. After some adventures, Aeneas descends to the Underworld to visit the ghost of his father. On the way to Elysium, (lucky ghost), Aeneas glimpses, half hidden in the shades, –

> Doubtful as he who runs, through dusky night,
> Or thinks he sees, the moon's uncertain light –

a silent and bitter Dido, who turns away from him with disdain. Sadly he bids her farewell. Other suicides, lovers, children, and unburied dead in torment he sees; and then he comes out into a haven of peace and light and joy, the Fields of the Blessed. The difference between the rest of the Underworld and Elysium is very clear:

> Fortunate groves, where happy souls repair,
> And lawns of green, the dwellings of the blest.
> A purple light, a more abundant air
> Invest the meadows. Sun and stars are there,
> Known but to them.[11]

> *Devenere locos laetos et amoena virecta*
> *Fortunatorum memorum sedesque beatas*
> *Largior hic campos aether et lumine vestit*
> *Purpureo, solemque suum, sua sidera norunt.*

We see, even if we have no Latin, the pre-eminent position of the word "*purpureo*"; we feel the quality of light and air, sun and stars, which are unique to Paradise. It is this context above all, Donald Davie argues in his essay on "Hardy's Virgilian Purples", that shows Hardy's purple light to have a spiritual connotation. Virgil was in his mind with the "traces of an old fire," and the betrayal of love – for Dido, for Emma, for all men and women. But he was there also because of Aeneas' quest for the beloved dead in the Underworld, his attempts at reconciliation, and his location of "'the purple light' in all its definiteness" uniquely in that part of it where the spirits dwelt in happiness after death.

Davie suggests that among all the complex factors in the writing of the *Poems of 1912–13* was Hardy's urgent need to know whether or how Emma had survived, whether there was any existence for her in the purple light among the blessed.[12]

> Where drives she now? It may be where
> No mortal horses are,
> But in a chariot of the air
> Towards some radiant star.[13]

* * * * * *

Hardy to Edward Clodd, 13 December 1912:

> One forgets all the recent years and differences, and the mind goes back to the early times when each was much to the other – in her case and mine intensely much.

Hardy to A.C. Benson, as quoted in Benson's diary, 2 November 1913:

> The verses came; it was quite natural; one looked through the years and saw some pictures; a loss like that just makes one's old brain vocal!

Hardy to Florence Henniker, 17 July 1914:

> Some of them I rather shrink from printing – those I wrote just after Emma died, when I looked back at her as she had originally been, and when I felt miserable lest I had not treated her considerately in her latter life. However I shall publish them as the only amends I can make, if it were so.

POEMS OF 1912-13

Veteris vestigia flammae

THE GOING

Why did you give no hint that night
That quickly after the morrow's dawn,
And calmly, as if indifferent quite,
You would close your term here, up and be gone
    Where I could not follow
    With wing of swallow
To gain one glimpse of you ever anon!

    Never to bid good-bye,
    Or lip me the softest call,
Or utter a wish for a word, while I
Saw morning harden upon the wall,
    Unmoved, unknowing
    That your great going
Had place that moment, and altered all.

Why do you make me leave the house
And think for a breath it is you I see
At the end of the alley of bending boughs
Where so often at dusk you used to be;
    Till in darkening dankness
    The yawning blankness
Of the perspective sickens me!

    You were she who abode
    By those red-veined rocks far West,
You were the swan-necked one who rode
Along the beetling Beeny Crest,
    And, reining nigh me,
    Would muse and eye me,
While Life unrolled us its very best.

Why, then, latterly did we not speak,
Did we not think of those days long dead,
And ere your vanishing strive to seek
That time's renewal? We might have said,
    "In this bright spring weather

We'll visit together
Those places that once we visited."

Well, well! All's past amend,
Unchangeable. It must go.
I seem but a dead man held on end
To sink down soon.... O you could not know
That such swift fleeing
No soul foreseeing –
Not even I – would undo me so!

December 1912

From the title alone of this opening poem, with its quiet
solemnity, there is a sense of the curtain rising on a drama that
will engage all our human faculties. Hardy's customary low-key
reticence, his lack of rhetoric, seems to allow the intensity of his
emotion to burn through white-hot. In the last stanza that
reticence, the refusal to allow the reader to go any further with
him, tries to take over again; but the emotion bursts out in the
broken snatches, revealing the shock and disarray caused by that
"great going" which "altered all." It was a disarray which took
Hardy by surprise and by storm.

Like most bereaved people, Hardy finds himself asking
"Why? Why? Why?" Despite this urgent questioning, despite
the misery admitted at the end, the organising of his emotion
into poetry has done its work: the earlier stanzas seem to be
more controlled, more meditative, a little more detached than
the last, as if the speaker, like an artist, were standing back to
view his work and take the perspective. The evocation of the
past, and the romantic distance of the "red-veined rocks far
West" add length to that perspective. As always with Hardy,
the poem is full of contrasts – night and dawn, going and staying,
soft and hard, knowledge and ignorance, solid house and dusky
mirage, blankness and vividness, darkness and brightness, seeing
and not seeing, present and past, long time and moments, here
and there, intimacy and declamation, the thought of amelioration
and the reality of hopelessness, lyrical lines and flat, interrupted
lines of very ordinary speech. We have found ourselves before
now on this journey in the glade with the shadows and the falling
leaf, near that "alley of bending boughs" where the poet would

not turn his head lest his dream should fade. Again there is a hint of Orpheus, a fellow lyric poet, and of the shadowy Dido in the underworld, as he thinks "for a breath it is you I see.... Where so often at dusk you used to be."

William Buckler, concentrating on the subtexts, or ideas that underlie these poems, has suggested that the theme of poetry itself is obliquely introduced in the rather unexpected "wing of swallow" image, which takes any reader who, like Hardy, is familiar with Swinburne, to his poem "Itylus." Two Greek myth versions here seem to be mingled, concerning the death of a child and the transformation of his mother and aunt into swallow and nightingale. Philomel, lover of song, can never forget the departed one though her sister swallow will; nor can she follow her to sunnier realms of oblivion.

> O sweet stray sister, O shifting swallow,
>   The heart's division divideth us.
>   Thy heart is light as a leaf of a tree;
> But mine goes forth among sea-gulfs hollow
>   To the place of the slaying of Itylus,
>   The feast of Daulis, the Thracian sea.
>   . . . . .
>   Thou hast forgotten, O summer swallow,
>   But the world shall end when I forget.

The differing responses of nightingale and swallow to death and tragedy reflect the inevitable differences in life; and Hardy's complex analysis in "The Going" of a tragic moment and a tragic division between himself and Emma may imply, suggests Buckler, that "poetic expression rather than poetic silence is the chief hope for spiritual renewal."[14] It is clear that this is a fundamental principle of the sequence: Hardy needs to review and recreate the whole experience in poetry.

Certainly the poetic vision plays upon reality, and brings a shifting scatter of scenes and perspectives sometimes far removed from it. The myth that Emma's death was "calm" and without forewarning is promoted also in the poem "Best Times" (page 240), where Hardy's earlier version is nearer the truth than his later amended one. The phantom Emma who vanished (like Eurydice) beyond the bending boughs gives way to another romantic vision of her as "the swan-necked one."

Perhaps it is the hint of an unresolved hostility in the words "Would muse and eye me" which prepares one for the questions that follow. "Why, then, latterly, did we not speak...?" Why, indeed; perhaps because only the unattainable was desirable? Their earlier "going" from each other, their total lack of communication, had been a kind of death, (like Eurydice's time in the underworld). It is repeated (like her second death) in their final and perpetual inability to communicate now. Did Hardy feel the pangs of guilt as he postulated here the conversations they never had, the visits they *might* have made – which in life he had so often refused Emma? The conditional tense is a skilful way of evading the issue and continuing the fantasy. The broken lines of the last stanza close that fantasy, leaving the reader no space for probing or further answer. "All's past amend... It must go."

Every reader will find his or her own way into the deep places of this great poem, as of each one in the series. As the first of the elegies it points the way to the themes of those that follow. The next poem repeats the eye imagery of "The Going" (which meant so much to Hardy), and recalls another going, a November day only a week before her death, when Emma went out by taxi to visit some friends beyond Puddletown. On her journey she passed the Stinsford churchyard where all the Hardys were buried. "That night," writes Millgate, "she had a violent attack of what Hardy persuaded himself was dyspepsia."[15] Millgate's and Gittings' accounts of the next few days differ only in the degree of blame they attach to Hardy's behaviour; but not long after nine o'clock on the morning of 27 November Emma died.

YOUR LAST DRIVE

Here by the moorway you returned,
And saw the borough lights ahead
That lit your face – all undiscerned
To be in a week the face of the dead,
And you told of the charm of that haloed view
That never again would beam on you.

And on your left you passed the spot
Where eight days later you were to lie,
And be spoken of as one who was not;

Beholding it with a heedless eye
As alien from you, though under its tree
You soon would halt everlastingly.

I drove not with you.... Yet had I sat
At your side that eve I should not have seen
That the countenance I was glancing at
Had a last-time look in the flickering sheen,
Nor have read the writing upon your face,
"I go hence soon to my resting-place;

"You may miss me then. But I shall not know
How many times you visit me there,
Or what your thoughts are, or if you go
There never at all. And I shall not care.
Should you censure me I shall take no heed
And even your praises no more shall need."

True: never you'll know. And you will not mind.
But shall I then slight you because of such?
Dear ghost, in the past did you ever find
The thought "What profit," move me much?
Yet abides the fact, indeed, the same, –
You are past love, praise, indifference, blame.

December 1912

So often seeing a figure set up against a background, Hardy in
the opening word suggests himself standing on the road outside
Max Gate, retracing Emma's return that November night – as
he was to stand on an October night many years later, waiting
for his second wife's return from a London nursing home
("Nobody Comes", page 278). Both times he was isolated and
alone; but while the later poem reveals his loneliness, "Your Last
Drive" is bitter. It reflects more of those days when they did not
speak; a defiant independence in Emma, an edgy self-
justification in him. Her indifference *now* is the mirror of his to
her when she was alive. The ellipsis after "I drove not with
you..." implies the reason for his defensiveness, that he secretly
blames himself for his neglect. The praise and blame motif
which recurs elsewhere suggests their continual sparring. Yet
Hardy is not remembering a conversation that really happened:
as in "The Going", he is creating one that never did happen,

cleverly divorcing us (and himself) from reality by the conditional tenses and the run over at the first stanza's end:

> And you told of the charm of that haloed view
> That never again would beam on you.

Though the first line is Emma's, it was only Hardy who could later have known about the second. The whole conversation is a confusion: Emma's words (but not Hardy's) are in quotation marks though they were never spoken. What she is reported as saying she could never have known. Despite the unreality the picture is compelling; and it is the concocted conversation that is the most memorable part of the poem.

In the next poem, the wrestling with conscience, guilt, and hostility is put aside; so are the fantasies of its two predecessors. It gives a poignant picture of the small but devastating real incidents associated with loss.

THE WALK

> You did not walk with me
> Of late to the hill-top tree
>   By the gated ways,
>   As in earlier days;
>   You were weak and lame,
>   So you never came,
> And I went alone, and I did not mind,
> Not thinking of you as left behind.
>
> I walked up there to-day
> Just in the former way;
>   Surveyed around
>   The familiar ground
>   By myself again:
>   What difference, then?
> Only that underlying sense
> Of the look of a room on returning thence.

Harold Nicolson, in his diaries, uses a family phrase, "the coffee cups," which for them were a symbol of that feeling of loss on return, after a parting, to the last evidences of the loved one's presence. "The Walk" may be a trivial incident; but it is part of

universal human experience, compressed with the utmost
simplicity into a mere sixteen lines. These bare lines, so like
prose, are adorned only with a sincerity and an emotion that
totally convinces. There is no phantom, no need for histrionics:

> Only that underlying sense
> Of the look of a room on returning thence.

I have mentioned the eye imagery – the heedless eye, the
"turning to eye me", the darkening glimpse, the perspective –
that links the first two poems of this elegy sequence. The visual
was probably Hardy's most developed sense: the look of a room
tells all. The poem reflects the life: with characteristic restraint
Hardy is trying to come to terms with the shock of the new daily
situation. This included a reliving, a redefining in poetry, of
small moments – like "The Last Performance", Emma's
apparently prescient farewell to her piano. (Though written in
December 1912 this poem was, like others, not selected for this
sequence.) During that month and the early part of 1913 Hardy
wrote "more [poems] than he had ever written before in the
same space of time."[16] They all explore the new present; the
past, both recent and distant, which had created it; his own
future; and the relation of his art to his life.

By the end of January 1913, when he wrote "Rain on a
Grave," it seems as if Hardy was able to focus realistically on
Emma as dead and buried.

RAIN ON A GRAVE

> Clouds spout upon her
>   Their waters amain
>   In ruthless disdain, –
> Her who but lately
>   Had shivered with pain
> As at touch of dishonour
> If there had lit on her
> So coldly, so straightly
>   Such arrows of rain.
>
> One who to shelter
>   Her delicate head

Would quicken and quicken
Each tentative tread
If drops chanced to pelt her
That summertime spills
In dust-paven rills
When thunder-clouds thicken
And birds close their bills.

Would that I lay there
And she were housed here!
Or better, together
Were folded away there
Exposed to one weather
We both, – who would stray there
When sunny the day there,
   Or evening was clear
   At the prime of the year.

Soon will be growing
   Green blades from her mound,
And daisies be showing
   Like stars on the ground,
Till she form part of them –
Ay – the sweet heart of them,
Loved beyond measure
With a child's pleasure
   All her life's round.

31 January 1913

Perhaps this beginning recalls the grotesque gargoyle incident in *Far from the Madding Crowd*. It may start from reality, but the delicate attention Hardy now pays to Emma's exaggerated weaknesses seems hardly to be a true account of his actual behaviour (even if the reference to their frequent, and her unwilling, visits to Stinsford churchyard to moon over her in-laws' graves is part of the irony of their life.) It is the first of this sequence which fixes Emma in "a loamy cell"; the first to concentrate on physical separation, and the first of several in this group which associate Emma with flowers. The idea that death provided new life is one that we have met before in Hardy; he knew it too in other elegies such as Tennyson's "In Memoriam",

Arnold's "Thyrsis", and Shelley's "Adonais" – a poem, and a poet, he loved. It is more than likely that "Adonais", with its recurrent star imagery and lines like "He is made one with Nature," was in the background of his mind, conscious or subconscious, as he wrote this poem. The daisies appear in later Hardy poems as straight symbols of the grave; here, in addition, they are used to emphasise the new picture he is drawing of Emma as the childlike one.

It is a theme that links "Rain on a Grave" with the poem that follows.

"I FOUND HER OUT THERE"

I found her out there
On a slope few see,
That falls westwardly
To the salt-edged air,
Where the ocean breaks
On the purple strand,
And the hurricane shakes
The solid land.

I brought her here,
And have laid her to rest
In a noiseless nest
No sea beats near.
She will never be stirred
In her loamy cell
By the waves long heard
And loved so well.

So she does not sleep
By those haunted heights
The Atlantic smites
And the blind gales sweep,
Whence she often would gaze
At Dundagel's famed head,
While the dipping blaze
Dyed her face fire-red;

And would sigh at the tale
Of sunk Lyonnesse,
As a wind-tugged tress

Flapped her cheek like a flail;
Or listen at whiles
With a thought-bound brow
To the murmuring miles
She is far from now.

Yet her shade, maybe,
Will creep underground
Till it catch the sound
Of that western sea
As it swells and sobs
Where she once domiciled,
And joy in its throbs
With the heart of a child.

December 1912

After the claustrophobic setting of the grave one is suddenly in
the freedom and freshness of the salt-aired edge of the world. It
is a scene to which Hardy turned even in the shock of "The
Going", a perspective of charm when the one nearer home only
filled him with blank despair. Although this poem was actually
written in December 1912, before the preceding one, Hardy's
transposition of it in the sequence suggests not only that the first
healing may have begun, but also the springing of a new, wider
thought from the sight of Emma's grave. Though "She will
never be stirred/In her loamy cell", though

she does not sleep
By those haunted heights,

yet paradoxically the picture he evokes in such detail, with its
roar and colour and throb, suggests that somehow she *will* return
there; that the heights forever haunted for him by her memoried
presence (and probably by the aura of Tristan and Iseult) will be
haunted again. So one is prepared for the last stanza, with its
almost grotesque image of her shade tunnelling under the turf,
leaving behind the wretched associations of Dorchester to find
the magical region of Cornwall where their happiness had been
unalloyed.

Hardy's writing of these poems was fuelled by what he found
in Emma's papers after her death. Among them was a charming

fragment of autobiography in about 15,000 words called *Some Recollections*, which she had finished not long before her death. It was a description of her life until her marriage, including vivid pictures of her time in Cornwall – "this very remote spot, with beautiful sea-coast, and the wild Atlantic Ocean rolling in with its magnificent waves and spray, its white gulls and black choughs and grey puffins, its cliffs and rocks and gorgeous sunsettings sparkling redness in a track widening from the horizon to the shore." It deeply affected Hardy, and he published some (rather pedantically corrected) extracts in *The Life*. It is clear from a comparison with his poems that Emma's pages reminded him of incidents (like the daisies of "Rain on a Grave"), or actually suggested wording.

Other papers, however, were far less agreeable. For the last twenty years of her marriage Emma's diaries, which Hardy now read for the first time, were frank in their criticisms and dislike of her husband. We have no record of these parts (though his second wife later called them "diabolical"), since he was quick to destroy them; but reading them cannot but have shaken him. It is possible that they contributed to the bitterness of the next poem, the sixth in the sequence.

WITHOUT CEREMONY

It was your way, my dear,
To vanish without a word
When callers, friends, or kin
Had left, and I hastened in
To rejoin you, as I inferred.

And when you'd a mind to career
Off anywhere – say to town –
You were all on a sudden gone
Before I had thought thereon,
Or noticed your trunks were down.

So now that you disappear
For ever in that swift style,
Your meaning seems to me
Just as it used to be:
Goodbye is not worth while!

One critic has characterised this poem as "so gentle and

natural."[17] To me any gentleness here is that of the tiger. If "natural" refers to the style, I agree that much of it is colloquial and prosaic; but the very sound and positioning of the term "my dear" seems to me barbed. Such, however, was their life together: she because of his indifference needing to forge an independence of her own, he as a result finding her unpredictable. The poem has its vivid moments, with its impression of modern slang in her "career[ing] off" somewhere, and the sudden pile-up of trunks in the hall; but its prevailing note is of that smarting exploration of small incidents, contained in an obsessive one-sided conversation with her to whom he seldom spoke in later life, and now could not reach when he would.

In the next poem, "Lament", the tone changes, as it does often throughout the sequence: as if Hardy were turning and twisting in every direction to catch any echo or glimpse, to pursue any track that would bring her nearer – like his own description in "After a Journey":

> Where you will next be there's no knowing,
> Facing round about me everywhere.

Bright and tight-lipped by turns, the contrasting tones of "Lament" repeat Hardy's state of mind: shining with memories or fancies, shadowed by the darker reality of the present.

LAMENT

> How she would have loved
> A party to-day –
> Bright-hatted and gloved,
> With table and tray
> And chairs on the lawn
> Her smiles would have shone
> With welcomings ... But
> She is shut, she is shut
>   From friendship's spell
>   In the jailing shell
>   Of her tiny cell.
>
> Or she would have reigned

At a dinner to-night
With ardours unfeigned,
And a generous delight;
All in her abode
She'd have freely bestowed
On her guests... But alas,
She is shut under grass
    Where no cups flow,
    Powerless to know
    That it might be so.

And she would have sought
With a child's eager glance
The shy snowdrops brought
By the new year's advance,
And peered in the rime
Of Candlemas-time
For crocuses... chanced
It that she were not tranced
    From sights she loved best;
    Wholly possessed
    By an infinite rest!

And we are here staying
Amid these stale things
Who care not for gaying,
And those junketings
That used so to joy her,
And never to cloy her
As us they cloy!... But
She is shut, she is shut
    From the cheer of them, dead
    To all done and said
    In her yew-arched bed.

"Never to be forgotten parties!" wrote Emma of her young life in Plymouth.

The military and navy usually present, *tarlatine* dresses and book-muslin the most frequent kind of dress worn, with ribbons and flowers – and very graceful and light and airy we all looked in them. Splendid sashes and stockings and shoes also adorned us, and our hair floated about in the rush of air made by our whirlings.[18]

Emma's artless self-portrait is of one who thrived on gaiety and social contact. She continued to do so, still dressed in a white frock and blue sash, until her last summer and her last garden party. The implication here in the last stanza, that such junketings only now cloy Hardy since her death, is again a poetic manipulation: temperamentally, his sociability took other forms. But his vivid evocation of Emma's, even if exaggerated, provides sobering contrasts with the reiterated toll of "She is shut, she is shut..."

These contrasts are carefully structured. In the first stanza the house furniture brought out into the open is set against the "jailing shell," and it is from the friendship provided by her guests that Emma is separated. The friendship theme links it to the second stanza. The dinner party gives way to the grave "where no cups flow", and her reign at table, her conscious and active generosity, becomes, in contrast, her powerlessness. Powerlessness leads, in the third stanza, to the thought of childhood, mirrored, perhaps, in the "shy" snowdrops; but the eager restlessness of a child contrasts with Emma's own trance in "an infinite rest", shut away blind beneath a hard wintry sod, in a new year not of her own choosing.

If the picture of Emma in "Lament" is "of one who is not", one "dead/To all done and said", "The Haunter", with Hardy's characteristic irony, seems to say that that's all *he* knows about it.

THE HAUNTER

He does not think that I haunt here nightly:
    How shall I let him know
That whither his fancy sets him wandering
    I, too, alertly go? –
Hover and hover a few feet from him
    Just as I used to do,
But cannot answer the words he lifts me –
    Only listen thereto!

When I could answer he did not say them:
    When I could let him know

How I would like to join in his journeys
   Seldom he wished to go.
Now that he goes and wants me with him
   More than he used to do,
Never he sees my faithful phantom
   Though he speaks thereto.

Yes, I companion him to places
   Only dreamers know,
Where the shy hares print long paces,
   Where the night rooks go;
Into old aisles where the past is all to him,
   Close as his shade can do,
Always lacking the power to call to him,
   Near as I reach thereto!

What a good haunter I am, O tell him!
   Quickly make him know
If he but sigh since my loss befell him
   Straight to his side I go.
Tell him a faithful one is doing
   All that love can do
Still that his path may be worth pursuing,
   And to bring peace thereto.

Emma's imagined tenderness is as affecting as her inability
to be heard is tragic: it matches their life. Hardy is too honest
to avoid it; their lack of communication and the memories of
his many visits without her, often in more congenial feminine
company, must have been gall and wormwood.

When I could answer he did not say them:
   When I could let him know
How I would like to join in his journeys
   Seldom he wished to go.

Their separation is complete. She can speak, as it seems to us,
convincingly, but not be heard; he can speak, but never see or
hear her. Yet the dear ghost (twice, "faithful") persists in her
loving care for him; and one wonders if he is even secretly
admitting her to the world of his poetry, the "places only
dreamers know", from which in later life he had excluded

her.[19] In that idyllic natural setting, and in the cherished land
of his past, (much of it with ecclesiastical overtones like the
"old aisles") she is at his side. It needs to be said that Hardy
did not achieve the last four lines of this poem, with their
loving reconciliation, at the first publication in 1914. Then
those lines had read:

> And if it be that at night I am stronger,
> Go, too, by day I do:
> Please, then, keep him in gloom no longer
> Even ghosts tend thereto!

The changes were part not only of Hardy's maturing as a poet,
but also of the fanciful creation, the Emma-who-might-have-
been, which he built up as he came to his own terms with her
death.

The metre, with its gentle ebb and flow, and its
predominantly feminine rhymes, surely contributes to the
poignancy of the poem. It may even blind the reader, for a
time, to the poet's feat in maintaining the identical double
rhymes throughout the four stanzas. Just as the theme was
foreshadowed in "The Going", so these double rhymes and
this lyrical rhythm – "all to him," "call to him", – take us
forward now to the next poem, "The Voice": one of his
greatest.

THE VOICE

> Woman much missed, how you call to me, call to me,
> Saying that now you are not as you were
> When you had changed from the one who was all to me,
> But as at first, when our day was fair.
>
> Can it be you that I hear? Let me view you, then,
> Standing as when I drew near to the town
> Where you would wait for me: yes, as I knew you then,
> Even to the original air-blue gown!
>
> Or is it only the breeze, in its listlessness
> Travelling across the wet mead to me here,
> You being ever dissolved to wan wistlessness,
> Heard no more again far or near?

Thus I; faltering forward,
Leaves around me falling,
Wind oozing thin through the thorn from norward
And the woman calling.

December 1912

"They hear a voice in every wind
And snatch a fearful joy",[20]

Hardy had copied in a notebook dated as far back as 1867, in
which he wrote particularly valued phrases or lines from
other poets. In later notebooks and papers he copied more
than one version of Goethe's line: "In this world there are
few voices and many echoes." His favourite lesson in church
was that about the "still, small voice;" and in his own Bible he
marked the following verse (I Corinthians XIV, 10, Authorised
Version 1611): "There are, it may be, so many kinds of voices in
the world, and none of these is without signification." With
Hardy's aural sensitivity it is no surprise either that he favoured
such lines or that he should have heard, or thought he heard, the
voice of Emma calling on the wind.

Poets and critics are unanimous in their acclaim of this
poem. "It is an exceptional poem by any standards, a real
invention." (Thom Gunn). "As beautiful and as musical as any
other love-poem in English; but it has a peculiar authentic-
ity..." (David Cecil). "The very summit of its author's
achievement." (F.R. Leavis). "The most powerful of all his
lyrics", says Douglas Brown, and he concludes: "Such
moments do not happen often in the history of a language."[21]
Some would place the summit elsewhere, perhaps with
"After a Journey", "At Castle Boterel", or "During Wind
and Rain." Every reader finds his or her own understanding of
such a poem, and as always each reading brings new
discoveries.

At a first reading one may be tempted to dismiss the
opening triple rhymes, and a phrase like "when our day was
fair", as inadmissible clichés. But as we re-read, and stumble,
as the poet does, against the obstacles of cold reality, the harsh
present which breaks into, and overpowers, the faint echo of
the woman's fading voice, we realise that they are there by

precise choice. At first the intensity of his feeling, of his inner vision and hearing, makes that world far more real than the cheerless sodden landscape where he stands. The falling dactyls "call to me, call to me," not only have the quality of echo, but as they recede, they image the receding voice with its whisper on the wind, and we know that the distance between the couple is lengthening. Even in this blur between two worlds the truth is distinct. She had changed and was different from the woman he had first loved; but that time of first love had a quality we recognise at once: our day was fair. After holding our breath in the single lone sentence of this stanza we breathe out the phrase in a sweeping, comprehensive understanding.

Then the music's rhythm stutters with the question: the pause after "Can it be you that I hear?" makes us insecure. The first "then" is unstressed, less important than the overriding desire to *see*; the second "then" is stressed, a heartfelt cry for the past. The difference of stress gives life and body to the dactyls, lest we should settle too easily into a conventional *tum-ti-ti*. And for a moment we do see: we see the woman in her air-blue gown, focused against a background as Hardy had always learnt to focus his visual memory, statue-like perhaps, but with the only colour in the poem, and the sea air of Cornwall blowing round her.

But the vision fades as the voice fades. In the third stanza one hears only what's left of the voice, the sibilants, hissing in the wind which blows stronger and drowns it. And as the voice is dissolved, the speaker's morale and the calling, echoing rhythm break down into monosyllabic, awkward, prose: "Heard no more again far or near."

The desolation of the last stanza is one that Hardy bears alone, compressed into a "Thus I" which allows the reader to come not one step nearer. The repeated sad vowel of "or" and "all" seems to reinforce this desolation. The rhythm has become heavy and stumbling, with its alliteration of uncertain "f's" and the trochees *forward, falling*, which dominate the stanza. Only in the third line do a few dactyls try to return in

Wínd oŏziňg | thin thrŏugh the | thorn

as the final echo of her voice evaporates in those repeated

"th's," overborne by the glacial wind's threnody. Hardy's favourite image of himself as a bare tree, leaves around me falling, is complete.

After "The Voice", almost any poem would be a drop to earth. In fact it is a characteristic of these *Poems of 1912-13* that they ebb and flow in what J. Hillis Miller calls a "wave-like pulsation of recovery and loss."[22] It is evident already that, after "The Going" stakes out the ground, they fall into groups or pairs which pivot on a number of different factors. One is how the speaker talks to, and of, the dead woman: sometimes as "you", sometimes as "she"; sometimes irrevocably dead, sometimes elusively heard or glimpsed, as a ghost or as she was when they first met.

Another factor is the part played by time and tenses. We shuttled between the far past, the present, and the recent past as Hardy relives, and re-examines, and recreates the time of courtship (Cornwall), the time of estrangement (Dorchester), and the time now, when Emma is no more – but when he is trying to re-evaluate the whole experience and create a new understanding of it. The death of Emma is experienced both emotionally, as grief, remorse and sense of loss; and also intellectually, with all the pain of analysis and questions needing to be resolved – or to be recognised as unanswerable. So it is on both levels that resolution must be attempted by the poet. William Morgan suggests that, in each poem and in the cycle as a whole, Hardy is using time as a structure to interpret, explain, and delimit the total experience. It is a mark of his integrity that he never loses sight of the present reality, even when he recreates the past at its happiest; yet a proper understanding, both intellectual and emotional, of the past – far and recent – is the only consolation for the present.[23]

The distress of this present is perhaps most poignantly conveyed in "The Voice" and, in different ways, it is also conveyed in the two poems that follow it. "His Visitor", like "The Haunter", is in the imagined voice of Emma; but its tone and its message are quite dissimilar to the earlier poem.

HIS VISITOR

I come across from Mellstock while the moon wastes weaker

To behold where I lived with you for twenty years and
      more:
I shall go in the gray, at the passing of the mail-train,
And need no setting open of the long familiar door
      As before.

The change I notice in my once own quarters!
A formal-fashioned border where the daisies used to be,
The rooms new painted, and the pictures altered,
And other cups and saucers, and no cozy nook for tea
      As with me.

I discern the dim faces of the sleep-wrapt servants;
They are not those who tended me through feeble hours
      and strong,
But strangers quite, who never knew my rule here,
Who never saw me painting, never heard my softling song
      Float along.

So I don't want to linger in this re-decked dwelling,
I feel too uneasy at the contrasts I behold,
And I make again for Mellstock to return here never,
And rejoin the roomy silence, and the mute and manifold
      Souls of old.

1913

The reader moves between Hardy's typical contrasts: the
temporal and geographical precision of the first stanza – Max
Gate stands about a quarter of a mile above the London-
Dorchester railway line – and the dreamlike fantasy of the
sleeping household; the ordinary, conversational tone and
rhythm, with trite words like "cozy nook" – and the
extraordinarily evocative, rather fey, picture of the late
mistress wandering about the house warbling her "softling
song"; the contrast between past and present made explicit in
the domestic changes and the loss of the daisies; the sounds of
the living, and the silence – the roomy silence – of that vast
congregation underground. The pain is in her resolve to
return there "never", her implied criticism that he has
forgotten her; and for Hardy in this pain (who often suggested
that death was a release and, at least in the grave, a reunion
with those he loved), it is also in the hint that Emma might be

having the best of the bargain.

The next poem is a puncturing let-down.

A CIRCULAR

As "legal representative"
I read a missive not my own,
On new designs the senders give
    For clothes, in tints as shown.

Here figure blouses, gowns for tea,
And presentation-trains of state,
Charming ball-dresses, millinery,
    Warranted up to date.

And this gay-pictured, spring-time shout
Of Fashion, hails what lady proud?
Her who before last year ebbed out
    Was costumed in a shroud.

The difference between these two poems could hardly be greater. The clipped lines begin as near-doggerel – reflecting the tone of the catalogue, as well as the exhausted poet, who is drained by his attempts (apparently so far unsuccessful) to order in his mind the past and present of this catastrophic experience. Temperamentally, Hardy could not have failed to see the fashions ending in a shroud, or the ironies of a vernal recall of the dead. If he was being ghoulish over small incidents it was because this is what bereavement includes. (Millgate tells how, had he not been dissuaded, Hardy would have published a poem called "The Sound of Her" – or rather, of the screws being driven into her coffin.[24]) It may surprise us that he included this poem in the sequence: but it accurately reflects some of the aridity and pain he was experiencing. Moreover, anyone who reads through the Lock Collection of Hardyana in Dorchester County Library will see how Hardy has the last laugh – and also convinces us of the realism of his banal vision. There in the box among the many newspaper obituaries of him in January 1928 – literally feet of columns – is that of the *Morning Post*. The cutting is so long that the sheet has to be folded up from the bottom, showing the page's reverse side. "Nation's Homage to Thomas Hardy..." intone the headlines in large capitals; but underneath, covering the main part of the article, is a large sketched advertisement from the back fold. Two fashionable 1920s figures, in cloche hats and stylish poses, meet the eye. And the letter press? *"Smart travelling coat in fine quality novelty tweed, 49/6d."* *"New Spring Frock in satin-backed crêpe, £5.18.6d."* No irony could be more appropriate or more instructive.

After this trough, the next poem shows Hardy beginning to lift his head and take new bearings. The tang of salt air, and the memory of a girl in a green valley were beginning to work a spell on him – and to make him form a resolve. He would go to Cornwall and revisit the old haunts.

A DREAM OR NO

Why go to Saint-Juliot? What's Juliot to me?
  Some strange necromancy
  But charmed me to fancy
That much of my life claims the spot as its key.

Yes. I have had dreams of that place in the West,
  And a maiden abiding
  Thereat as in hiding;
Fair-eyed and white-shouldered, broad-browed and brown-
   tressed,

And of how, coastward bound on a night long ago,
  There lonely I found her,
  The sea-birds around her,
And other than nigh things uncaring to know.

So sweet her life there (in my thought has it seemed)
  That quickly she drew me
  To take her unto me,
And lodge her long years with me. Such have I dreamed.

But nought of that maid from Saint-Juliot I see;
  Can she ever have been here,
  And shed her life's sheen here,
The woman I thought a long housemate with me?

Does there even a place like Saint-Juliot exist?
  Or a Vallency Valley

With stream and leafed alley,
Or Beeny, or Bos with its flounce flinging mist?

February 1913

The barked, monosyllabic first line, representing Hardy's
rational self, as it does in the later questions, gives way at once
to the other self of feeling, light of rhythm and rhyme, which
is spellbound and dream-driven towards that place in the
West. Even without the word "key", it is plain that Hardy is
in a puzzle: did the places, the girl, or the past ever exist? This
poem is dated February 1913: by the end of that month he had
made the decision to visit Cornwall. The possibility of
actually seeing these places both vividly revives his memories
and also confronts him, in his absorbed introspection, with
panic and doubts: since the magical time forty years before, he
had never, incredibly, set foot on that coast.

The poem is a watershed in the sequence. It turns its back
on the unhappy preceding Dorset poems, and like a breath of
wind blowing away a fog, it clears the mist from the sketchy
pictures of "I Found Her Out There" and impels us on a
journey to follow the travelling shade. We are then
imaginatively prepared for one of the most superb poems that
Hardy ever wrote.

AFTER A JOURNEY

Hereto I come to view a voiceless ghost;   a
    Whither, O whither will its whim now draw me?   b
Up the cliff, down, till I'm lonely, lost,   a
    And the unseen waters' ejaculations awe me.   b
Where you will next be there's no knowing,   c
    Facing round about me everywhere,   g
        With your nut-coloured hair,   g
And gray eyes, and rose-flush coming and going.   c

Yes: I have re-entered your olden haunts at last;   a
    Through the years, through the dead scenes I have tracked   b
      you;   a
What have you now found to say of our past –   b
    Scanned across the dark space wherein I have lacked you?   b
Summer gave us sweets, but autumn wrought division?   c
    Things were not lastly as firstly well   d

With us twain, you tell?
But all's closed now, despite Time's derision.

I see what you are doing: you are leading me on
     To the spots we knew when we haunted here together,
The waterfall, above which the mist-bow shone
     At the then fair hour in the then fair weather,
And the cave just under, with a voice still so hollow
     That it seems to call out to me from forty years ago,
          When you were all aglow,
And not the thin ghost that I now frailly follow!

Ignorant of what there is flitting here to see,
     The waked birds preen and the seals flop lazily;
Soon you will have, Dear, to vanish from me,
     For the stars close their shutters and the dawn whitens
          hazily.
Trust me, I mind not, though Life lours,
     The bringing me here; nay, bring me here again!
          I am just the same as when
Our days were a joy, and our paths through flowers.

Pentargan Bay

This poem brings one in on the crest of a wave of recovery;
yet it does so with a tenderness, an intimacy, and a
vulnerability that are set in a flint-like realism. Hardy, on his
lover's journey, finds that the voice that leads him now is not
the woman's travelling on the breeze, but the soliloquies of
the waters and the hollow plash of the cascade in the darkness
– the darkness which is both in the real scene and in the
landscape of his mind. Though the ghost is voiceless, it is the
clearest he has felt her yet: astonishingly vivid, and as if in the
flesh, mistress in her own place. He has to attend her in that
place and unflinchingly face the questions that must be asked –
but are barely answered. As so often, Hardy expresses in
his broken lines and awkward inversions the inner distress of
his heart. He knows that the questions are unanswerable;
indeed, he evades the answers by putting them as questions
in the voiceless Emma's mouth, with remote archaisms like
"wrought" and "twain" to distance them. All is closed and he
cannot go back. Time laughs wryly; but it does not necessarily
laugh last.

For just as Hardy originally wrote "soothed" instead of "closed", one senses a healing beginning in the third stanza. "I see what you are doing": he begins to understand. The experience is set in the cradle of time: "Hereto I come...." "Through the years, through the dead scenes..." "... it seems to call out to me from forty years ago...";[25] and he can see her, in one sentence, as the girl who was "all aglow", but who is now, like him, becoming "thin" and "frail". From his vantage point he can see the reality and quality of their love as it was (or as he feels it was) which not even the tragic later years can destroy. It was the core of his life, the central and sovereign moment which has ruled it ever since. So as the horizon lightens, his darkness and his burden lighten. "How marvellously," writes Douglas Brown, "the preening and the flopping of bird and seal dismiss the evasive phantom!"[26] (The seals are remembered by Emma in her *Recollections*: in evoking them here Hardy must have felt a new closeness and a renewed sharing of the experience.) His supremely sure touch is not afraid to introduce the relaxed, colloquial "flop lazily" into a moment of high poetic tension. He then combines with it the domestic intimacy of closing down at the end of the day; and the tender familiarity of "Soon you will have, Dear, to vanish from me," – so different from the acid "my dear" which accompanied the vanishing of "Without Ceremony." There is no declamation or rhetoric, but the everyday, ordinary moments of life are where he finds truth and repose.

Hardy has come a long way since "The Going." Then, he was "undone", "a dead man held on end/To sink down soon." By the end of this poem he is almost sprightly, fully in command; and he makes the tremendous claim that he is

.... just the same as when
Our days were a joy, and our paths through flowers.

Can this really be so? And were the young couple really aware, in that summer of forty years gone, of the "rareness, ripeness, richness" of those moments, as he sees them now looking back? He thinks of them now as "the then fair hour in the then fair weather"; but on other pages he draws Emma in the rain, in the words that became a catchphrase with them: "It never looks like summer."[27] With that great chasm of married misery between then and now, it seems as if Hardy all through these poems is creating a phantom Emma who companions him "to places/Only dreamers know;" an Emma who might have been, but was not – "his family say *that* girl never existed, but she did to him, no doubt..."; an Emma whom he could only see in visions when it was impossible to see her in the flesh. Like Knight and Elfride: "Not till they were parted, and she had become sublimated in his memory, could he be said to have even attentively regarded her."[28] And as there are two Emmas, the real and the phantom, so there could similarly be two Hardys speaking in these poems: the husband who was at first "undone", and the poet who is now creating in art a new experience from this critical moment of his life.

In saying that he is "just the same" after more than forty years, (an assertion frequently contradicted in other poems), Hardy seems to be doing two things. On the one hand, he is full of joy at this recovery of love; he has reached an awareness and a view of Emma that is happier than any in the cycle so far, and he wants to identify himself with it. On the other hand, he has brought his guilt and remorse across the dark space and faced the fact that all's past amend, all's closed now; yet he has gone on to give the memories of their good time a kind of curative continuance. This is complex and delicate; and in order to preserve it, like "Thus I; ..." he closes the door on his readers, and to some extent on himself and Emma, with this categorical statement which inhibits further query.

We are left with a sense of repose – a sense that all's closed, but not now entirely past amend. The pain is accepted; a new understanding has been achieved out of the wreck, and a new work of art both discovers and celebrates it. It is the beloved ghost who has led him to this understanding – as both Virgil and Beatrice guided Dante on his journey. Orpheus, lonely husband and poet of the backward glance, may stir again here in the depths of consciousness; and an underworld which allows its denizens escape until the dawn.

* * * * *

"After a Journey" is in the gentle, meditative tone that befits the calm of nightfall. The next poem is altogether brisker.

A DEATH-DAY RECALLED

Beeny did not quiver,
    Juliot grew not gray,
Thin Valency's river
    Held its wonted way.
Bos seemed not to utter
    Dimmest note of dirge,
Targan mouth a mutter
    To its creamy surge.

Yet though these, unheeding,
    Listless, passed the hour
Of her spirit's speeding,
    She had, in her flower,
Sought and loved the places –
    Much and often pined
For their lonely faces
    When in towns confined.

Why did not Valency
    In his purl deplore
One whose haunts were whence he
    Drew his limpid store?
Why did Bos not thunder,
    Targan apprehend
Body and breath were sunder
    Of their former friend?

In "After a Journey" we were in a dream world of shifting
darkness and the steady fall of water; but apart from the final
place-ascription we might have been on almost any Western
Atlantic coast. "A Death-Day Recalled", in contrast, continues
the geographical precision of "A Dream or No". Pentargan
Bay, north of Boscastle, was one of Emma and Tom's favourite
picnic places. The cliff forming its northern wall is black and
sheer and has been identified as the Cliff-Without-a-Name of *A
Pair of Blue Eyes*, with the extra attribution of the height of Beeny
Cliff, which itself stretches farther north again from Pentargan
Bay, covering the whole headland towards the Gull Rock.[29] The
little stream which Elfride follows in the novel "was smaller
than that in her own valley, and flowed altogether at a higher
level."

I am going to the shore by tracking the stream, [she tells Knight.] I believe it empties itself not far off, in a silver thread of water, over a cascade of great height.

This waterfall, soon dissolved into spray on its 250ft descent, is the one "above which the mist-bow shone", the waterfall of "After a Journey." (It was another waterfall, in the Vallency valley, under which Tom and Emma lost their picnic glass. Incidentally, Hardy's two spellings of "Val[l]ency" follow local custom, which was ambivalent; but *his* choices were deliberate, to ensure the correct scansion stress.)

What is the effect of this geographical exactitude? Twice before in this sequence, after shrouds and graves, it has given openness and freedom. The reader has come a distance from the unhappiness of Max Gate and Stinsford churchyard, to Arcadian places where great happiness was experienced; where those little incidents and jokes of love and companionship were closely associated with the actual landscape – it is drenched with memories and emotion. Yet, in a strange way, although it is so personal to the story of Thomas and Emma, the fixed, named points of that landscape form a framework which seems to give the story objectivity, and so universality. It is as if we were, in "A Death-Day Recalled", looking down from a great height – perhaps with the "hawk's vision" which Auden so admired in Hardy[30] – on to the foamy sonorous shore and the black cliffs towering over the winding river; and it is with this detachment that we are able to contemplate the deeper questions that beset Hardy – and all human beings – in our attempt to evaluate experience and memory.

One of these questions is the relationship of the external world to human suffering – what is often loosely called the pathetic fallacy, the attribution of human feelings to Nature. Though Hardy's poems are full of it,[31] here he directly contradicts it – and adds another "Why?" to the questions of the bereaved. He appears to be blaming the landscape Emma loved so much for not reciprocating that love or showing due respect when she died. This seems to reflect one of Hardy's most constant attitudes to nature, expressed in a number of poems: that Nature, so-called Mother Nature, is, in terrible irony, statuesque and blind, "unknowing and unheeding" the plight of human beings or the havoc she creates.[32] It is all the more ironical that he should again in this poem link Emma with flowers. Where Wordsworth wreathed his Lucy in flower images and felt a deep communion with "kind Nature", Hardy only emphasises the gulf between an uncaring Nature and struggling humanity.

This poem has other links besides flower imagery with preceding poems in the sequence. One cannot fail to hear again the note of guilt, sounded in "The Going" and "The Haunter", that Emma had never been able to revisit the places she loved. It also leads naturally forward to the next poem, where in a characteristic Hardy movement we home in from the general view of "A Death-Day Recalled" to focus on a particular point: Beeny Cliff.

BEENY CLIFF

March 1870–March 1913

I

O the opal and the sapphire of that wandering western sea,
And the woman riding high above with bright hair flapping free –
The woman whom I loved so, and who loyally loved me.

II

The pale mews plained below us, and the waves seemed far away
In a nether sky, engrossed in saying their ceaseless babbling say,
As we laughed light-heartedly aloft on that clear-sunned March day.

III

A little cloud then cloaked us, and there flew an irised rain,
And the Atlantic dyed its levels with a dull misfeatured stain,
And then the sun burst out again, and purples prinked the main.

IV

– Still in all its chasmal beauty bulks old Beeny to the sky,
And shall she and I not go there once again now March is nigh,
And the sweet things said in that March say anew there by and by?

V

> What if still in chasmal beauty looms that wild weird
> western shore,
> The woman now is – elsewhere – whom the ambling pony
> bore,
> And nor knows nor cares for Beeny, and will laugh there
> nevermore.

The spontaneous, lyrical happiness of the first stanzas may be
surprising, even exaggerated; but it is after all the remembering
of a time of joy in reciprocated love. The parallel phrases of
"The woman whom I loved so, and who loyally loved me," seem
to reassure with harmony and security. The jewelled sparkle of
the opening, the alliteration and the assonance of the second
stanza all combine with that heady feeling of the heights to
drench the reader in the actual scene, in all its shifting light and
sound. Even the sudden cloud and shower are flashed away by
the return of sun and colour, in a line,

> And then the sun burst out again, and purples prinked
> the main,

which, with its internal rhyme, its poised halfway caesura and its
iambic dance, recalls the satisfying balance of line three. Hardy's
words are vivid and idiosyncratic: an "irised" rain, a
"misfeatured stain", the "plaining" of the seagulls with all its
root meaning of bewailing and lament, its cross-reference to the
wheeling of the French "planer". There is the extraordinarily
sprightly "prink", of which Donald Davie writes:

> It is characteristic audacity: from the imperial splendour of
> "purples" we are required, with "prinks", to sidle through a
> boudoir or an aviary on our way to the no less imperial
> vastness of "the main". Such strenuousness is typical of
> Hardy.[33]

I have referred briefly to Davie's article and to the "purple
light of love" which colours much of Hardy's writing and
his lover's journey through the underworld in pursuit of Emma.
Yet there is hardly a hint of the pain behind this poem until the
fourth stanza. Here the versification continues to tell more
than the poet explicitly will. The initial dash is one of
only two remaining in the *Poems of 1912–13* (which shows its

importance, since so many final or opening dashes were altered in earlier or later editions.) Joined with the solemn accent on "– Still", it brings a warning. The reader is slowed too by the heavy alliteration of "in . . . beauty bulks old Beeny . . ."; and given a particular impression – of gulfs, finality, and separation – by the word "chasmal". Hardy's repetition of "chasmal beauty" turns it into something of an intended cliché, to be disregarded, just as he says in "What if still . . .": for no beauty can bring back the woman. With this the suppressed grief breaks like the pounding of waves in those mostly alliterative stresses – "that wíld wéird wéstern shóre" – the long reiterated "ore" sound also carrying its measure of sorrow. The bright, confident picture of woman and horse is sadly diminished, broken by the delayed euphemism "– elsewhere –" like "a catch in the voice," as Paulin puts it:[34] a catch which the reader has to interpret, since nowhere does the speaker say that the woman is dead. (This making the reader work to fill in gaps is central to Hardy.) In the last line the echoing parallelism, rocked by the repeated "nors" and "ands", seems to mock the happy certainty of its predecessors. Hardy's understatement is all the more powerful for being conveyed through metre and rhyme.

*   *   *   *   *   *

We have looked at how Hardy began, in poems like "A Commonplace Day", to glimpse what he only later learnt to develop with more skill – to bind his matter and manner, his theme and his setting, in one whole; and to show how the setting could condition a person's thought and meditation. The way such a meditation goes can be in miniature like the way a day or even a lifetime goes. The man or woman who sits and thinks can insensibly retreat further and further into his or her own world, and when an interruption brings him back to consciousness he finds time has passed, things have changed: and he experiences a new understanding. So does the lover on his journey. The image he has been pursuing, in his mind and as he travels, is long out of date: the loved one has grown old or vanished beyond time.

When Emma vanished, Hardy awoke to the truth about their marriage, and about life. Slowly, almost imperceptibly over the years, it had deteriorated and gone sour in a way that probably neither fully understood. The shadows had gathered steadily, but not until the storm broke had the lightning lit up the scene and shown it as it was. It was only then, it seemed, as with so many bereavements, that Hardy understood how life works: that often we awake to understanding only when it's too late.

Emma's death precipitated not only this realisation, but also a new recognition of how a poem, urged out of a person's life, actually completes and sharpens the understanding of experience. "The scales had not fallen from my eyes," wrote Hardy of some poems he had first published in 1911, "and when I reprinted them [in 1914] they had."[35]

When the scales fell, one of the results of Hardy's illumination was to be the great poem "At Castle Boterel".

AT CASTLE BOTEREL

As I drive to the junction of lane and highway,
　　And the drizzle bedrenches the waggonette,
I look behind at the fading byway,
　　And see on its slope, now glistening wet,
　　　　Distinctly yet

Myself and a girlish form benighted
　　In dry March weather. We climb the road
Beside a chaise. We had just alighted
　　To ease the sturdy pony's load
　　　　When he sighed and slowed.

What we did as we climbed, and what we talked of
　　Matters not much, nor to what it led, –
Something that life will not be balked of
　　Without rude reason till hope is dead,
　　　　And feeling fled.

It filled but a minute. But was there ever
　　A time of such quality, since or before,
In that hill's story? To one mind never,
　　Though it has been climbed, foot-swift, foot-sore,
　　　　By thousands more.

Primaeval rocks form the road's steep border,
　　And much have they faced there, first and last,
Of the transitory in Earth's long order;

But what they record in colour and cast
Is – that we two passed.

And to me, though Time's unflinching rigour,
In mindless rote, has ruled from sight
The substance now, one phantom figure
Remains on the slope, as when that night
Saw us alight.

I look and see it there, shrinking, shrinking,
I look back at it amid the rain
For the very last time; for my sand is sinking,
And I shall traverse old love's domain
Never again.

March 1913

After the flowing rhythm, the lush images and the colour of
"Beeny Cliff", this poem, with its matter-of-fact conversational opening and its terse sentences, may seem a flat anti-
climax. Yet if ever a poem repaid closer acquaintance it is this
one. It begins with that most characteristic act: the clear
visualising of a person silhouetted against the landscape. From
the time of his daily lunch-hour visits to the National Gallery as
an apprentice architect, Hardy had trained himself to remember
pictures in this way. He came to know well many painters' work
and his novels are full of descriptions related to different artists'
styles. In *Desperate Remedies*, when Cytherea turned her head:
"Those who remember Greuze's 'Head of a Girl' have an idea of
Cytherea's look askance at the turning."[36] In *The Woodlanders*
Grace watches Fitzpiers on Darling gradually disappearing
along the ridge: "The sky behind him being deep violet she could
still see white Darling in relief upon it – a mere speck now – a
Wouvermans eccentricity reduced to microscopic dimensions."[37]
As Fitzpiers first moved off she had seen "his plodding steed
rendering him distinctly visible yet." This last phrase recurs in
other novels as well as in "At Castle Boterel". (We'll look again
at Hardy's predilection for shapes and outlines.) In this poem the
phrase leads without a break into the second stanza, which
begins to parallel the journey he is taking now, in the rain, with
the journey of forty years before, "in dry March weather."
Cleverly the present and the past are bonded together, the
spatial and the temporal, in phrases with double meanings like "I

look behind," "I look back." What he sees "distinctly yet" is seen not with his physical sight, but with his mind. Like many of the poems in this cycle, what comes across as most real is what Hardy envisioned, not what he actually saw. Yet there is no confusion between these two journeys: the wetness of the present one is emphasised in contrast to the first, the ascent on foot forty years ago, allowed a longer savouring time than he now has climbing in the sodden waggonette. We start with the second visit, but the focus narrows to the first; and in the third stanza Hardy's habitual progression begins from the personal to the general and philosophical: the focus bores into the meaning, not just the fact, of that time together. It becomes a matter of life and death. Then:

> It filled but a minute. But was there ever
> A time of such quality, since or before,
> In that hill's story?

"A time of such quality." This is the memorable, the eternal, which remains, held in the scene and the rocks in perpetuity. Quality cannot be quantified. The sweep of human and prehuman history is viewed, but this moment stands supreme. Time, naturally, does its worst; but it is not all destructive: it has a double function. Although on the one hand it is Time that has taken Emma's "substance" from him, yet on the other it is that forty-year-old perspective which now, because he is looking and seeking to understand, reveals and clarifies all.

> I look and see it there, shrinking, shrinking,
> I look back at it amid the rain
> For the very last time.

Here the artistry becomes particularly apparent. The rain and the evening, and the lengthening perspective as he is carried further from the place, are the physical and actual partners of the action of Time in his life. If Time has both blocked and enhanced his vision of the substance of his old love, so does the rain both block and enhance his vision of the "phantom figure." We see why from the beginning the "glistening wet" has been a kind of backcloth which has both shown up and also, inevitably, partly misted the vision. For with the help of Time, and thought, and contemplation – one could say, reflection – the picture, the meaning, of his forty-year-long "mindsight" has been clarified; but because of Time and rain and the final achievement of understanding it must go;

> for my sand is sinking,
> And I shall traverse old love's domain
> Never again.

The reader, experiencing the completeness of this poem's bonding of life and art, knows why Dennis Taylor writes: "This is a great moment in English poetry."[38] "At Castle Boterel" is a perfect imitation of life. The poem's journey to an understanding and assessment of his love – substance and phantom – is the pattern of his life's journey of forty years to that same assessment. Like a photographer sorting his negatives, he has superimposed over the picture of the first journey the experience of the second. Out of that experience he has created a final, new, whole understanding of the life's long pursuit; and when we achieve such an understanding of experience we no longer need to worry at it – it can lie down in peace. In the poem, as in his life, Hardy reaches the final sharp clarity of that moment before it fades away.

"At Castle Boterel" shows Hardy's distinction as a poet whose poetry springs directly and deeply out of life. It also shows something of the secret of his appeal. He makes no attempt to lure one to read with great flourishes. He begins in a situation where any human may be, using as his tools the speech of everyday life.

> We climb the road
> Beside a chaise. We had just alighted
> To ease the sturdy pony's load
> When he sighed and slowed.

But the picture unfolds, as the words and the thought, the sounds and the insight, the rhythm of reason and emotion, grow in power. The everyday lifts to the everlasting as we watch two figures on a sloping road and join in a journey of understanding.

*   *   *   *   *   *

In *Some Recollections* Emma Hardy, writing of her Plymouth childhood, described the bells of St Andrew's church playing their regular carillon of the tune called The Old Hundred-and-Thirteenth.

> I have good reason to remember it – as we lived for five years not far away, and that tune with its haltings and runs plays up in my head often even now . . .[39]

On his way back from St Juliot in March 1913 Hardy stopped in Plymouth to complete the Emma pilgrimage. Of several poems written or begun there, "Places" was included in the *Poems of 1912–13*.

PLACES

Nobody says: Ah, that is the place
Where chanced, in the hollow of years ago,
What none of the Three Towns cared to know –
The birth of a little girl of grace –
The sweetest the house saw, first or last:
      Yet it was so
      On that day long past.

Nobody thinks: There, there she lay
In a room by the Hoe, like the bud of a flower,
And listened, just after the bedtime hour,
To the stammering chimes that used to play
The quaint Old Hundred-and-Thirteenth tune
      In Saint Andrew's tower
      Night, morn, and noon.

Nobody calls to mind that here
Upon Boterel Hill, where the waggoners skid,
With cheeks whose airy flush outbid
Fresh fruit in bloom, and free of fear,
She cantered down, as if she must fall
      (Though she never did),
      To the charm of all.

Nay: one there is to whom these things,
That nobody else's mind calls back,

Have a savour that scenes in being lack,
And a presence more than the actual brings;
To whom to-day is beneaped and stale,
    And its urgent clack
    But a vapid tale.

Plymouth, March 1913

By now the reader is familiar with what often happens in this sequence. What nobody actually says, thinks, or remembers is what Hardy plays up and what remains in the mind as the poem's core. In the last stanza the "one" who is contrasted with "nobody else" is in fact one who never did see the little girl in these places. This stanza also makes plain what has been mentioned in the survey of Hardy and memory: how much more real to the speaker is the world of his imagination than "scenes in being" or "the actual", which are dismissed as "a vapid tale."

Stanza three, however, is what leads to this assertion. It is more vivid even than the "stammering chimes" and the flower-like child. The evocation of Emma on horseback is no Plymouth scene, but an interpolation of something Hardy actually did see; and though he writes it in Plymouth (or back in Dorset), he talks of Boterel Hill as "here". The reader has felt the intensity of his emotion at Boscastle and Pentargan: there is no doubt that the St Juliot area is, as he says, the "key" to the deepest springs within him. Though it has not been generally noted, this is borne out by his inscription on Emma's tombstone in Stinsford churchyard (made in April 1913.) His design for his parents' and his sister Mary's inscriptions had simply included the places and dates of their births and deaths; there is no mention, for example, of the places away from Dorchester where Mary had studied or taught. Yet Emma's inscription reads:

Here lies Emma Lavinia, wife of Thomas Hardy, O.M. and daughter of John Attersoll Gifford. She was born at Plymouth, Nov. 24, 1840 * Lived at St. Juliot, Cornwall, 1868–1873 * Died at Max Gate, Dorchester, Nov. 27, 1912. This for remembrance.

Increasingly Hardy's "remembrance" of her turned upon her as "ghost-girl-rider." Her own simple descriptions of her joy on horseback are clearly reflected in these poems:

Riding about on my Fanny I enjoyed the place immensely...
The splendid air made me strong and healthy, with red
cheeks... An unforgettable experience to me, scampering up
and down the hills on my beloved mare alone, wanting no
protection, the rain going down my back often and my hair
floating on the wind... Fanny and I were one creature, and
very happy both of us... The Villagers stopped to gaze when
I rushed down the hills. A butterman laid down his basket
once to exclaim loudly for no one dared except myself to ride
in such wild fearless fashion.

When Hardy came to visit her,

I rode my pretty mare Fanny and he walked by my side and I
showed him some of the neighbourhood – the cliffs, along the
road, and through the scattered hamlets, sometimes gazing
down at the solemn small shores where the seals lived, coming
out of great caverns very occasionally.[40]

Those seals came out on their "solemn small shores" in "After a
Journey". "The Phantom Horsewoman" is the next poem; and
in the first edition it was with this poem that the sequence ended.

THE PHANTOM HORSEWOMAN

I

Queer are the ways of a man I know:
     He comes and stands
     In a careworn craze,
     And looks at the sands
     And the seaward haze,
     With moveless hands
     And face and gaze,
     Then turns to go...
And what does he see when he gazes so?

II

They say he see as an instant thing
     More clear than to-day,
     A sweet soft scene
     That was once in play
     By that briny green;
     Yes, notes alway

Warm, real, and keen,
What his back years bring –
A phantom of his own figuring.

III

Of this vision of his they might say more:
Not only there
Does he see this sight,
But everywhere
In his brain – day, night,
As if on the air
It were drawn rose bright –
Yea, far from that shore
Does he carry this vision of heretofore:

IV

A ghost-girl-rider. And though, toil-tried,
He withers daily,
Time touches her not,
But she still rides gaily
In his rapt thought
On that shagged and shaly
Atlantic spot,
And as when first eyed
Draws rein and sings to the swing of the tide.

1913

The phantom rider is a creature of Hardy's imaginative power and vigour. Though the poem begins with an apparently detached bystander recording a man's strange actions, the emotional pitch intensifies through the short cantering lines with their close-knit rhymes, until in a kind of trance the reader too is caught in the swing of the tide. The poem is a natural development from the last stanzas of "Places": the most "warm, real, and keen" is "what his back years bring – a phantom of his own figuring." His memory has caught fire, set alight by this inner vision which is so fundamental to Hardy. The scene is brilliantly communicated: first, mutedly like the seaward haze, but with inspired choice of words like "moveless";[41] then giving texture, light, warmth, colour and scent in the "sweet soft scene" – "More clear than to-day" –

That was once in play
By that briny green.

The vision becomes obsessive; and the image is the one that made
the picture of Tryphena "fined in my brain" – the pattern
drawn, engraved, printed or etched on the mind as he carries this
"rose bright", "airy flush" vision within him wherever he goes.
The rider is inseparable from the place, which has a Shangri-la
effect of keeping her young and immortal, just as the rocks of
Boterel Hill contain within them the everlasting record of her
presence. In this poem we share in the intense focus with which
Hardy clarifies the vision he has been assembling, accumulating,
through this sequence – and perhaps through his lifelong,
hardly-aware harbouring of that vision of the girl by the shore.
As in the poem the vision has clarified, so in the life he has
journeyed a long way, like his other poetic lovers, to reach this
moment of articulation, this new creation of his experience.

It seems clear that after the revisiting of Cornwall Hardy
achieved through his poetry a way of managing the complex
emotions aroused by Emma's death. On its tenth anniversary, as
an old man of 82, he was still writing poems about her.[42] It looks
however as if the "glad confident morning" of his imagined or
recreated love, which climaxed in "After a Journey", "At
Castle Boterel", and "The Phantom Horsewoman", suffered
diminishment in the years after they were first published in 1914.
This appears to be why he deposed "The Phantom Horsewoman"
from its triumphant end position and tacked on the three poems
that in later editions he chose to end the series.

THE SPELL OF THE ROSE

I mean to build a hall anon,
    And shape two turrets there,
    And a broad newelled stair,
And a cool well for crystal water;
    Yes; I will build a hall anon,
    Plant roses love shall feed upon,
    And apple trees and pear."

He set to build the manor-hall,
    And shaped the turrets there,
    And the broad newelled stair,

And the cool well for crystal water;
   He built for me that manor-hall,
   And planted many trees withal,
   But no rose anywhere.

   And as he planted never a rose
   That bears the flower of love,
   Though other flowers throve
Some heart-bane moved our souls to sever
   Since he had planted never a rose;
   And misconceits raised horror shows,
   And agonies came thereof.

   "I'll ment these miseries," then said I,
   And so, at dead of night,
   I went and, screened from sight,
That nought should keep our souls in severance,
   I set a rose-bush. "This", said I,
   "May end divisions dire and wry,
   And long-drawn days of blight."

   But I was called from earth – yea, called
   Before my rose-bush grew;
   And would that now I knew
What feels he of the tree I planted,
   And whether, after I was called
   To be a ghost, he, as of old,
   Gave me his heart anew!

   Perhaps now blooms that queen of trees
   I set but saw not grow,
   And he, beside its glow –
Eyes couched of the mis-vision that blurred me –
   Ay, there beside that queen of trees
   He sees me as I was, though sees
   Too late to tell me so!

ST LAUNCE'S REVISITED

   Slip back, Time!
   Yet again I am nearing
   Castle and keep, uprearing
   Gray, as in my prime.

At the inn
Smiling nigh, why is it
Not as on my visit
   When hope and I were twin?

Groom and jade
Whom I found here, moulder;
Strange the tavern-holder
   Strange the tap-maid.

Here I hired
Horse and man for bearing
Me on my wayfaring
   To the door desired.

Evening gloomed
As I journeyed forward
To the faces shoreward,
   Till their dwelling loomed.

If again
Towards the Atlantic sea there
I should speed, they'd be there
   Surely now as then?...

Why waste thought,
When I know them vanished
Under earth; yea, banished
   Ever into nought!

WHERE THE PICNIC WAS

Where we made the fire
In the summer time
Of branch and briar
On the hill to the sea,
I slowly climb
Through winter mire,
And scan and trace
The forsaken place
Quite readily.

Now a cold wind blows,
And the grass is gray,
But the spot still shows

As a burnt circle – aye,
And stick-ends, charred,
Still strew the sward
Whereon I stand,
Last relic of the band
Who came that day!

Yes, I am here
Just as last year,
And the sea breathes brine
From its strange straight line
Up hither, the same
As when we four came.

– But two have wandered far
From this grassy rise
Into urban roar
Where no picnics are,
And one – has shut her eyes
For evermore.

"The Spell of the Rose", by its formality and abstract language, is far removed from the other *Poems of 1912–13*. The "cool well for crystal water" bubbles no rhyme of love; the man is preoccupied with the stony details of architecture rather than living horticulture; and it is full of heart-bane, misconceits, horrid shows, miseries, severance, divisions dire and wry, and days of blight. Did the return to Max Gate raise all these phantoms, which had been transfigured and blown away by the fresh winds of Cornwall into the rose flush of the woman riding – now only an ironical twist to the planting of the flower of love? The saddest falling-off from that vision is the complete uncertainty with which the poem ends. It is clear that any reconciliation was, inevitably, too late; but there is no indication that their severance was ever healed in spirit after her death, or that his "mis-vision" was ever "couched". After the gaze that brought him a view of her, seen

as an instant thing
More clear than to-day

and the vision when she,

> as when first eyed
> Draws rein, and sings to the swing of the tide,

this image of blindness and eye disease withers and blights.

One is not reassured by "St Launce's Revisited", a poem of grayness, mouldering, and gloom, which banishes that immortal vision in the conviction that earth covers all, all is closed now.

"Where the Picnic Was" reasserts the baleful influence of Max Gate. Bailey suggests[43] that the picnic was not in Cornwall, but during Hardy's birthday weekend in June 1912 ("last year" to the poem's holograph date of 1913), when W.B. Yeats and Henry Newbolt came to Dorset from the "urban roar" of London to present Hardy with the Gold Medal of the Royal Society of Literature, and with Emma they all went for a picnic. Though the short lines are of similar length to "The Phantom Horsewoman"'s, their vigour and élan are diminished. All the images are Hardy's symbols of misery: a gray, wintry, forsaken place with the charred fire remains, and himself a "relic" too – one who, he feels so often, has no business to be still alive. ("I travel as a phantom now...")[44] Though the sea is visible, it is muted and unfamiliar. The trite jangle and rhythm of "Yes, I am here/Just as last year," is in mocking contrast to the end of "After a Journey":

> I am just the same as when
> Our days were a joy, and our paths through flowers.

It is another irony that where, in this ebb and flow of recovery and loss, some of the most positive poems end with the negatives "Nevermore" or "Never again", yet here in this sad farewell to Emma the negative is twisted into a false positive – "evermore" – a word which still sounds a dolorous knell.

The lover's journey to St Juliot had at the time ended with the most vivid evocation of Emma as the phantom horsewoman. The mention of St Juliot on her tombstone was Hardy's last clinging to the magical Lyonnesse where she seemed, even as a phantom, to be most herself. But the exaltation could not last, and he knew that to make the *Poems of 1912–13* a true echo of his life the last three poems must be added. Although an inveterate meddler with his own work, he never moved them again.

"Where the Picnic Was" ends with the stated fact of Emma's death. Hardy always believed in facing facts squarely and in one sense there is no other possible end to the cycle. Artistically and realistically, however, this poem fits perfectly as the last. In the charred remains of the picnic fire are seen, burnt through, "veteris vestigia flammae", the ashes of an old flame.

In the *Poems of 1912-13* Hardy came to a new understanding of his own life and poetry. They reflect the varied reactions to Emma's death which succeeded each other during those months of November to April. Beginning with shock and miseries, they move from that recent past in Dorchester to the distant past of the Cornish idyll, where the rosy vision of Emma grows like the dawn light taking over the sky. It is only when he becomes aware that it is a phantom figure he sees – one which, while he withers daily, has not been touched by the years – that his eyes are opened. He realises that the experience of these months replicates the experience of his forty-year-long marriage: that over the years he has been, imaginatively, blind to the truth, nursing his mindsight, pursuing an inner vision while ignoring the reality which is changing around him. With Emma's death, and his strenuous efforts to understand it and to re-orientate himself, he came to see exemplified in himself the tragic themes he had already identified in his novels and earlier poems: the too-late awakening, and the human consciousness at odds with the world around it. He also saw how, working out his memories in his poems, articulating in them the final understanding of the experience – creating what John Middleton Murry called "not the record but the consummation of an experience"[45] – how this could rivet human life and poetry together, making the one grow out of the other like the transformations of the things growing in the country churchyard. Now, at 72, he had enough poetic material for the rest of his life; and behind him, a lifetime of buried emotions only waiting to be "exhumed" and transformed.

Notes

1 *Life*, 111

2 Smith's *Smaller Latin-English Dictionary*

3 *The Change*

4 *The Woodlanders*, ch XXIV; *Desperate Remedies*, Ch III,2 – a quotation from Gray's *Progress of Poesy*, "on Cytherea's day"; *A Pair of Blue Eyes,* ch IV; *Life*, 73

5 *Honeymoon Time at an Inn*

6 *Life*, 432. (The second quotation is Saurat's paraphrase of Proust: see *Dennis Taylor*, 162, n 23)

7 R.L. Purdy, *Thomas Hardy: A Bibliographical Study* (London 1954), 166

8 Letter to S.C. Cockerell, 20 September 1916

9 Eg *Desperate Remedies*, VIII,5; *The Return of the Native*, I, ch 3

10 *Life*, 5, and see also *Life*, 397

11 Virgil, *Aeneid*, Bk VI, lines 638–41, tr E Fairfax-Taylor (1903) (Virgil's lines 767–71)

12 Donald Davie, "Hardy's Virgilian Purples", *Agenda*, 138–56

13 *A Woman Driving*

14 William Buckler, "The Dark Space Illumined: A Reading of Hardy's *Poems of 1912–13*", *Victorian Poetry*, vol 17, (1979), 101

15 *Life*, 359; *Millgate*, 484; Hardy's letter of 17 December 1912 to Mrs Henniker.

16 *Life*, 361

17 Douglas Brown, *Hardy's Elegiac Power*, quoted *Casebook*, 163. *Dennis Taylor*, 29, finds it full of "bitter recriminations."

18 E.L. Hardy, *Some Recollections*, ed E. Hardy and R. Gittings (London 1961) 6

19 Eg at the presentation to Hardy on 2 June 1912 of the Royal Society of Literature's Gold Medal (by Henry Newbolt and W.B. Yeats) in the drawing-room at Max Gate – from which he insisted that Emma be excluded (*Millgate*, 477). She was similarly forbidden his study. (R. Gittings, *The Older Hardy*, 193, 196.)

20 Gray, *Ode on a Distant Prospect of Eton College*, Lit. Notes 1867, entry 86

21 Gunn, *"Hardy and the Ballads"*, *Agenda*, 43; Cecil, "The Hardy

Mood", *Casebook*, 238; Leavis, *New Bearings in English Poetry*, 56; Douglas Brown, *Thomas Hardy*, quoted *Casebook* 167-8.

22 J. Hillis Miller, *Thomas Hardy: Distance and Desire*, (Cambridge, Mass 1970) 249.

23 William Morgan, "Form, Tradition, and Consolation in Hardy's *Poems of 1912-13*". Proceedings of the Modern Language Association, (1974) 89

24 *The Sound of Her*, previously uncollected, is in *The Complete Poetical Works of Thomas Hardy*, ed S. Hynes, vol III, 304 (Oxford 1985)

25 Hardy is sometimes criticised for clichés in words like "all aglow" (although the word "aglow" does not feature in the index of the *Oxford Dictionary of Quotations*; in Bartlett's *Familiar Quotations* (1979) the only entry is, interestingly enough, a translation of Virgil's *Georgics*, IV, 1.169, "All aglow is the work".) Rather, perhaps a similar use by eg Jerome Kern in a particularly simple lyric like "The way you look to-night" testifies to such a word's universal appeal.

26 *Thomas Hardy*, quoted *Casebook*, 166

27 Two sketches by Hardy in the Dorset County Museum and a poem are so entitled. See also *Desperate Remedies*, XV, 3, and the poem *The Figure in the Scene*.

28 *A Pair of Blue Eyes*, chapter XX

29 Denys Kay-Robinson, *Hardy's Wessex Re-appraised*, 249-50 (David & Charles 1972)

30 W.H. Auden, "A Literary Transference", originally in the *Southern Review*, VI, 1940, reprinted in *Hardy: A Collection of Criticial Essays*, ed A.J.Guérard (New Jersey, 1963). "For more than a year I read no one else", wrote Auden, and added that what he most valued in Hardy was "his hawk's vision, his way of looking at life from a very great height" – pp 136, 139.

31 Eg *The Seasons of Her Year, The Wind's Prophecy, A Backward Spring* etc

32 Eg *The Bullfinches, The Sleep-Worker, Doom and She, The Lacking Sense*; and see Chapter VIII

33 Donald Davie, *op cit*, *Agenda*, 139

34 Tom Paulin, *Thomas Hardy: The Poetry of Perception* (London 1975), 74

35 Letter to Edmund Gosse, 16 April 1918

36 *Desperate Remedies*, IV, 2. See Alastair Smart, "Pictorial Imagery in the Novels of Thomas Hardy", *Review of English Studies* New Series, vol XII, no 47 (1961). (Smart points out that this painting in the National Gallery has since been re-attributed to one of Greuze's followers.)

37 *The Woodlanders*, ch XXVIII

38 *Dennis Taylor*, 27

39 *Some Recollections*, 6–7. The tune is to be found in the (old) *Ancient and Modern* Standard version hymnbook, no 171.

40 *Some Recollections*, 30, 31, 35.

41 See pp 171 and 198

42 *Ten Years Since*

43 J.O. Bailey, *The Poetry of Thomas Hardy: A Handbook and Commentary*. (Chapel Hill, N.C., 1970)

44 Both title and first line of a poem. See also page 55.

45 John Middleton Murry, *op cit*, *Casebook* 85.

7

BURIED EMOTION AND NEW LIFE

It has been said that when all the long-explored experiments of Hardy's poetry came together, it was the peak of his achievement. The *Poems of 1912–13* show for the first time how he made connections between the reverie of a person caught in a changing setting, or the pilgrim lover pursuing an obsolete reverie in a changing setting, and the poem being a structured pattern, a recapitulation, of those reveries and journeys of the mind over a lifetime. It was after this that he was able to write "Copying Architecture in an Old Minster" and other poems like it,[1] published, particularly, in *Moments of Vision* (1917).

At this time (and even ten years later in the obituary notices already mentioned), Hardy's achievement as a poet was still minimised by readers, still overshadowed in many minds by his corpus of novels. Hardy, who had always preferred poetry to prose, was deeply hurt. Only two or three critics of the time (and indeed for many years after) stand out as putting a proper valuation on his poetry, and beginning to understand what he was doing. John Middleton Murry's essay in *The Athenaeum* of November 1919 included his sharp perception of the poem as "the consummation of an experience", a perception which Walter de la Mare was feeling after when he wrote of Hardy's poems in the *Times Literary Supplement* of the same month that "We are as close to actual experience as words can bring us." Murry concluded (more fulsomely than we should care for today) with a tribute to the *Poems of 1912–13* which had grown out of Hardy's life:

It was fitting, then, and to some senses inevitable, that Mr Hardy should have crowned his work as a poet in his old age by a series of love poems that are unique for power and passion in even the English language. This late and wonderful flowering has no tinge of miracle; it has sprung straight from the main stem of Mr Hardy's poetic growth. Into *Veteris Vestigia Flammae* is distilled the quintessence of the power that created the Wessex novels and *The Dynasts*; all that Mr Hardy has to tell us of life, the whole of the truth that he has apprehended, is in these poems, and no poet since poetry began has apprehended or told us more. *Sunt lacrimae rerum.*[2]

Walter de la Mare also picked out the tears in the smallest things of life which by Hardy's alchemy were transformed into moments of universal experience. "Never," he wrote, "was the tinder of the mind more hospitable to the feeblest of actuality's sparks."[3] But it was Edmund Gosse who (helped by some notes supplied by Hardy) in the *Edinburgh Review* of April 1918 had perhaps come nearest to understanding, in those early years, how Hardy had learnt to build on a "buried emotion":

There is absolutely no observation too minute, no flutter of reminiscence too faint, for Mr Hardy to adopt as the subject of a metaphysical lyric, and his skill in this direction has grown upon him; it is nowhere so remarkable as in his latest volume, aptly termed *Moments of Vision*.

"No flutter of reminiscence too faint ... and his skill ... has grown upon him." It was in 1917, the year of this volume's publication, and the year in which, most significantly, he was beginning the labour of delving into the past of his own life in order to write his autobiography, that Hardy first made a note on his "buried emotion": by then it had become a most important principle in his art.

I was quick to bloom; late to ripen.
I believe it would be said by people who knew me well that I have a faculty (possibly not uncommon) for burying an emotion in my heart or brain for forty years, and exhuming it at the end of that time as fresh as when interred. For instance, the poem entitled "The Breaking of Nations" contains a feeling that moved me in 1870, during the Franco-Prussian war, when I chanced to be looking at such an agricultural incident in Cornwall. But I did not write the verses till during the war with Germany of 1914, and onwards. Query: where was that sentiment hiding itself during more than forty years?[4]

Some critics have assumed that this passage means that Hardy's poetry did not change: an old feeling could be resurrected many years later and regurgitated ready-made into a poem. Far from it. The steady "ripening" of those forty years, and the falling of the scales from his eyes at Emma's death, contributed their own distilled wisdom to each flutter of reminiscence.

How complex was the process can be seen in the poem which the poet himself cites in the above passage.

IN TIME OF "THE BREAKING OF NATIONS"

I
Only a man harrowing clods
In a slow silent walk
With an old horse that stumbles and nods
Half asleep as they stalk.

II
Only thin smoke without flame
From the heaps of couch-grass;
Yet these will go onward the same
Though Dynasties pass.

III
Yonder a maid and her wight
Come whispering by:
War's annals will cloud into night
Ere their story die.

1915

It was on August 18, 1870, that Hardy, during his magic week in Lyonnesse, scribbled a note of a simple pastoral scene which he observed from the rectory garden at St Juliot.

Sc. rusty harrow – behind that rooks – behind them, 2 men hoeing mangel, with bowed backs, behind that a heap of couch smoking, behind these horse and cart doing nothing in field – then the ground rising to plant[n.5]

The poem was not written until 45 years later. Hardy says it "contains a feeling that moved me in 1870". It is more than interesting to make a direct comparison of note with poem and see what has been added and what omitted – for example, there was no harrowing actually being done in the scene Hardy saw, nor was there any sign of "a maid and her wight".

But it is also instructive to look more closely at the poem, when we find it is considerably more than the description of a simple pastoral scene.[6] To begin with, there is the headnote in the first two manuscripts which locates the title's quotation "The Breaking of Nations" in the Biblical book of Jeremiah, chapter 51, verse 20. This verse reads (in the old Authorised Version of 1611 which Hardy knew so well):

> Thou art my battle-ax and weapons of war: for with thee will I break in pieces the nations, and with thee will I destroy kingdoms.

The next three verses complete the picture, throwing more light on the "mindsight" with which Hardy, when so much older, saw the scene. Note the characters who now enter:

> And with thee will I break in pieces the horse and his rider;
> and with thee will I break in pieces the chariot and his rider;
> With thee also will I break in pieces man and woman...
> old and young... the young man and the maid... the shepherd and his flock... the husbandman and his yoke of oxen... captains and rulers.

Readers of the whole chapter will find it full of the howling destruction of Babylon by the Old Testament Lord, who "maketh lightnings with rain, and bringeth forth the wind out of his treasures" – full of just that visionary, apocalyptic sense which, with another "horse and his rider", we have seen developing in Hardy as the 1914–18 war brought its horrors. Here too come the young man and the maid. The yoke of oxen, the shepherd and his flock build up the pastoral images; the captains and rulers broken in pieces match the destruction of the Great War and introduce the idea of "dynasties" to the watcher of this apparently idyllic and timeless scene.

But read further. Verse 31:

> One post shall run to meet another, to shew the king of Babylon that his city is taken at one end.

And that the passages are stopped, and the reeds they have burned with fire, and the men of war are affrighted.
For thus saith the Lord of hosts, the God of Israel; "The daughter of Babylon is like a threshing-floor, it is time to thresh her: yet a little while, and the time of her harvest shall come...." (Verse 37): "And Babylon shall become heaps... without an inhabitant...." (Verse 58): "Thus saith the Lord of hosts; the broad walls of Babylon shall be utterly broken, and her high gates shall be burnt with fire; and the people shall labour in vain, and the folk in the fire, and they shall be weary."

Gradually some of the deeper connotations and echoes felt by Hardy, and added to the original note of 1870, become apparent. The harrowing of the clods may reflect the harrowing of men and women's minds and the harrowing of Hell, the harrowing of souls as in the separation of tares from wheat, wheat from chaff on the threshing floor – images surely buried in the "heaps of couch-grass" of the second stanza, as in the description of Babylon put to judgement, "and her high gates shall be burnt with fire." Between seeing the scene and writing the poem, Hardy had also published the accurate and vivid description of the fire in *Desperate Remedies*, which began with the couch-grass smouldering on the ground ploughed and harrowed by Mr Springrove: he knew all about the sequence of cultivation and harvest and consummation.

But there are other layers, besides the Biblical and apocalyptic ones, which show how a single buried emotion can be transformed by the experience of the years and the images maturing in the mind. Some of the most revealing glimpses come through Hardy's further accounts of the genesis of this poem in his *Life*, which he had already begun to compile with Florence only a year or two after he wrote the poem. It is significant that he mentions the 1870 incident no less than three times in the book.

Towards the end of the *Life* (p 378) comes the passage we read a few pages back, specifically connecting this incident with the "buried emotion". The second reference (p 365) is in a group of diary notes Hardy made at the outbreak of the 'Great War' in 1914. To the note:

[1914] *August* onwards. War excitement. "Quicquid delirant reges, plectuntur Achivi!"[7]

Hardy added when compiling the *Life* (p 365):

It was the quotation Hardy had made at the outbreak of the Franco-Prussian war forty-four years earlier, when he was quite a young man.

This Latin quotation is part of the first reference to the poem in the *Life*, and it is the most revealing. It comes in an early chapter (V), which is headed "St Juliot". Paradoxically it is also the *last* reference: since having already written about the 1870 war in this chapter, he later went back and added nearly another 150 words.[8] (*Life*, pp 78–9). Carefully read, they show other layers that went into the making of the poem. Hardy is telling how he returned to St Juliot in August 1870, about three weeks after the onset of the war – and there found the "young lady in brown" of March changed into "a young lady in summer blue, which suited her fair complexion much better; and the visit was a most happy one." He continues (and I show the added passage in italics):

His hosts drove him to various picturesque points on the wild and rugged coast near the Rectory, among others to King Arthur's Castle, Tintagel, which he now saw for the first time; and where, owing to their lingering too long among the ruins, they found themselves locked in, only narrowly escaping being imprisoned there for the night by much signalling with their handkerchiefs to cottagers in the valley. The lingering might have been considered prophetic, seeing that, after it had been smouldering in his mind for between forty and fifty years, he constructed The Famous Tragedy of the Queen of Cornwall *from the legends connected with that romantic spot. Why he did not do it sooner, while she was still living who knew the scene so well, and had frequently painted it, it is impossible to say.*

H.M. Moule, who by this date knew of the vague understanding between the pair, sent them from time to time such of the daily and weekly papers as contained his leading articles on the war. Concerning such wars Hardy entered in his notebook: "Quicquid delirant reges, plectuntur Achivi!" On the day that the bloody battle of Gravelotte was fought they were reading Tennyson in the grounds of the rectory. It was at this time and spot that Hardy was struck by the incident of the old horse harrowing the arable field in the valley below, which, when in far later years it was recalled to him by a still bloodier war, he made into the little poem of three verses entitled "In Time of 'The Breaking of Nations'". Several of the pieces – as is obvious – grouped as *Poems of 1912–13* in the same volume with *Satires of Circumstance*, and three in *Moments of Vision*, namely, "The Figure in the Scene", "Why did I Sketch?", and "It never looks like Summer now", with doubtless many others, are known to be also memories of the present and later sojourns here in this vague and romantic land of "Lyonnesse".

Here (drafted in 1917 or 1918), is the first reference in the *Life* to this pastoral scene which Hardy had noted from the garden in 1870. It is already subtly changed in his mind, since he writes of "the incident of the old horse harrowing the arable field" – an incident which the original note specifically denies. (The poem he has now written is a more real experience than the scene itself.) The significance of the passage is the way in which he deliberately links this poem with Emma, Cornwall, and other poems about her, as well as with wars and tumults. During those 44 years the original scene, which held no young man or woman and a horse doing nothing at some distance from a stationary harrow, has moved into a far wider sphere, linked with Biblical apocalypse, dynasties, and long human history. Hardy has brought into the scene a young man and maid like the two who watched it themselves. He connects it too with Tintagel and Arthurian legend (was it *Idylls of the King* that they were reading in the rectory garden that afternoon?) and the romantic love of Tristan and Iseult long linked in his mind with that "Iseult of my own"; with the Greeks and battles of long ago and the unchanging tragedy of war; and with poems he wrote after 1912 about incidents that happened with Emma on August 22, 1870. This clear reference to the principle of the "buried emotion" is underlined in the first paragraph above, the later addition. The words he uses about the long gestation of *The Queen of Cornwall* are suggestive. Has not the

thin smoke without flame
From the heaps of couch-grass

a connection with the theme "smouldering in his mind for between forty and fifty years"?

In this added paragraph too he specifically alludes to Emma's death, and to his poetry, written late but enshrining the immortal.

> War's annals will cloud into night
> Ere their story die.

And there is another connection of great interest between the pastoral scene and the madness of wars.[8] Smith's Latin diction ıry defines the original, literal meaning of Horace's "delirant" as "to draw the furrow awry in ploughing". (It then proceeds through "deviating from a straight line" to committing follies, and raving.) It is not at all unlikely that Hardy, a very competent Latin reader, knew this even if it was a largely unconscious association.

There are many other associations or images that one could discuss in this poem.[9] The point is that in its development it is possible to see how a brief note, a simple "moment of vision" can be for Hardy the catalyst, not just for a poem written soon after when "recollected in tranquillity": but for the sifting of a lifetime of experiences and meditation, and the creation of something quite new.

Emma died when Hardy was 72; and in the next dozen years every flutter of reminiscence and buried emotion (many evoked not only by the shock of her death but also by his own autobiographical researches) could be brought to the surface and made new.

Satires of Circumstance, published in 1914, included the first fruits of this discovery, made in the *Poems of 1912–13*. *Moments of Vision* (1917) contains most of the finest mature crop. Let us look at just three poems which Hardy sets together in this volume, and which culminate in "During Wind and Rain", which some consider to be his greatest poem.

THE FIVE STUDENTS

> The sparrow dips in his wheel-rut bath,
>   The sun grows passionate-eyed,
> And boils the dew to smoke by the paddock-path;
>   As strenuously we stride, –

Five of us; dark He, fair He, dark She, fair She, I,
    All beating by.

The air is shaken, the high-road hot,
    Shadowless swoons the day,
The greens are sobered and cattle at rest; but not
    We on our urgent way, –
Four of us, fair She, dark She, fair He, I are there,
    But one – elsewhere.

Autumn moulds the hard fruit mellow,
    And forward still we press
Through moors, briar-meshed plantations, clay-pits
    yellow,
    As in the spring hours – yes,
Three of us; fair He, fair She, I, as heretofore,
    But – fallen one more.

The leaf drops: earthworms draw it in
    At night-time noiselessly,
The fingers of birch and beech are skeleton-thin,
    And yet on the beat are we, –
Two of us: fair She, I. But no more left to go
    The track we know.

Icicles tag the church-aisle leads,
    The flag-rope gibbers hoarse,
The home-bound foot-folk wrap their snow-flaked heads
    Yet I still stalk the course, –
One of us.... Dark and fair He, dark and fair She, gone:
    The rest – anon.

This journey through life as through the seasons, with individually observed details of natural life, could be by nobody but Hardy. (It is tempting, though unimportant, to try to identify the four others in this life, if indeed the poet himself is the speaker. He identified one – probably the "dark He" who disappears first – as his friend Horace Moule, who committed suicide in 1873. The phrase seems to come straight out of Emma's *Recollections* about her sister: "she dark, I fair", but Mrs Holder is not apparently one of the four. The dark "She" may be his sister Mary or Jane Nicholls, one of his early loves – for what it matters: curiosity about biographical detail may get in the way of the poem.) The reader is carried forward by its opening energy, and its graphic and characteristic imagery and vocabulary. "Strenuous" is a favourite Hardy word, and so is the negative form (as in "shadowless") which appears in more than 250 instances in the poems.[10] The urgency of the movement pulses through the intense first stanza and subsequent words like "press" and "on the beat", which gradually diminish as the cold and dark and silence take over. Hardy's typical body imagery is here – the sun "passionate-eyed", the trees' "fingers... skeleton-thin", the flag-rope gibbering hoarse – an inspired, idiosyncratic description. Compound words like "briar-meshed", "home-bound foot-folk" compress and yet widen the picture. The structure of the poem is satisfying, with its unifying refrain and the strange compelling sensation that we are all bounding involuntarily forward on a moving track as the seasons change, but with a helpless backward impulse as each friend in turn drops off. The seasons-as-life is not an original metaphor; but as so often Hardy makes it live by the details of his observation of nature – the sparrow's bathing place, the dew boiling to smoke, the earthworm's noiseless activity, the particular squeak of flapping rope. Yet there is as well an overview, a universalising of these seasons or stages of life in which we can recognise ourselves stylised against the backdrop of our natural setting, wondering whether in life we get anywhere however hard we run... while the world wheels inexorably, and the fate of each one – "elsewhere", "fallen", "anon", is typically understated.

The next poem, "The Wind's Prophecy", also tells of a journey: a journey through a day that is like the five students' journey through life. It too has a kind of refrain in each stanza as the wind pronounces in dialogue with the poem's speaker. Like "A Man was Drawing Near to Me" it pictures that drive from Launceston to St Juliot in March 1870 when Hardy was unwittingly about to meet Emma. At the time he was in fact recovering from the demise of his last love affair – a double one in which, if Millgate is right, he had moved on from Eliza Nicholls to her dark-haired sister Jane, who had finally herself rejected him and married an older man.

THE WIND'S PROPHECY

I travel on by barren farms,
And gulls glint out like silver flecks
Against a cloud that speaks of wrecks,
And bellies down with black alarms.
I say: "Thus from my lady's arms
I go; those arms I love the best!"
The wind replies from dip and rise,
"Nay; toward her arms thou journeyest."

A distant verge morosely gray
Appears, while clots of flying foam
Break from its muddy monochrome,
And a light blinks up far away.
I sigh: "My eyes now as all day
Behold her ebon loops of hair!"
Like bursting bonds the wind responds,
"Nay, wait for tresses flashing fair!"

From tides the lofty coastlines screen
Come smitings like the slam of doors,
Or hammerings on hollow floors,
As the swell cleaves through caves unseen.
Say I: "Though broad this wild terrene,
Her city home is matched of none!"
From the hoarse skies the wind replies:
"Thou shouldst have said her sea-bord one."

The all-prevailing clouds exclude
The one quick timorous transient star;
The waves outside where breakers are
Huzza like a mad multitude.
"Where the sun ups it, mist-imbued,"
I cry, "there reigns the star for me!"
The wind outshrieks from points and peaks:
"Here, westward, where it downs, mean ye!"

Yonder the headland, vulturine,
Snores like old Skrymer in his sleep,
And every chasm and every steep
Blackens as wakes each pharos-shine.
"I roam, but one is safely mine,"
I say. "God grant she stay my own!"

Low laughs the wind as if it grinned:
"Thy love is one thou'st not yet known."

Rewritten from an old copy

This is an unmistakably Hardyan world – the spectacular
pictures of land, sea, and sky, with their contrasts of flashing
light and darkness, their movement, and all the tumult of wind
and storm, enhanced by the short lines running over and the
internal rhymes ("The wind outshrieks from points and peaks.")
Many of us must often have heard the sea and wind in this mood,
and in a sky of racing clouds watched the rapid eclipse of "the
one quick timorous transient star." The lover on this journey is
certainly caught in a changing setting, where the wind rises in
ferocity as it breaks into, and at every point contradicts, his
thinking about the woman he is leaving behind; and where in the
last stanza the light changes dramatically. The threat in the
setting is evident from the first, with the "barren farms", the
wrecks and alarms; but it is not clear why. It may be that Hardy,
reworking the journey of 1870, is including with hindsight the
later trials of the unhappy marriage; but one doesn't know from
the poem why the journey should be so black. The detailed,
exhilarating pictures which dominate it and remain in the mind
seem not to be adequately supported or explained by the theme –
and the reader is not even sure that the traveller hears the wind's
message. It is for the next poem, "During Wind and Rain", to
achieve a near-perfect composition and balance, as the
understanding of the succeeding stages of a lifetime unfolds
within the lifetime of the poem.

DURING WIND AND RAIN

They sing their dearest songs –
He, she, all of them – yea,
Treble and tenor and bass,
    And one to play;
With the candles mooning each face. . . .
    Ah, no; the years O!
How the sick leaves reel down in throngs!

They clear the creeping moss –
Elders and juniors – aye,
Making the pathways neat

> And the garden gay;
> And they build a shady seat....
>   Ah, no; the years, the years;
> See, the white storm-birds wing across.
>
> They are blithely breakfasting all –
> Men and maidens – yea,
> Under the summer tree,
>   With a glimpse of the bay,
> While pet fowl come to the knee....
>   Ah, no; the years O!
> And the rotten rose is ript from the wall.
>
> They change to a high new house,
> He, she, all of them – aye,
> Clocks and carpets and chairs
>   On the lawn all day,
> And brightest things that are theirs....
>   Ah, no; the years, the years;
> Down their carved names the rain-drop ploughs.

Emma's *Recollections* read like a gloss on this poem: they reveal Hardy's indebtedness to her for some of his images, though of course the poem is much more than a reference to her memories. She writes of the first house she remembered in Plymouth – from which "in a deluging downpour of rain" she had watched the opening of the new railway line from London. In the garden was an unusual water-purifier – "a huge stone basin, a dripstone, and under which a bucket received the water drop by drop purified." Their next home had a fine garden, and

> a magnificent Elm tree of great age and girth showing itself high above the houses . . . But it has long since been cut down; all has been changed with the oncoming years.

> Ah, no; the years, the years.

Under the tree were

> long garden seats with long tables and a circular seat encircling it, nothing could have been better arranged by our elders.... At one end of our garden we had a poultry-

house... for there was a mania at that time for keeping handsome fowls... they were kept at the top of the large garden where rose trees had used to flourish.

The happy childhood included music round the piano.

They taught us to sing harmony and our four voices went well together... Sometimes my Mother and my Father sang their old songs together as in their youth.

Even yet another move did not disturb the child.

Bedford Terrace, North Road, was our next pleasant home. It was a fine Terrace... with the houses all standing high above... It stood so high that we could see right beyond the intervening houses to the Sound and harbour.

But change came with the years. At her grandmother's death they had to leave Plymouth, "and it was for ever lost to me." Their departure stood out in her memory.

The heavens poured down a steady torrent on our farewells, and never did so watery an omen portend such dullnesses, and sadnesses and sorrows as this did for us.[11]

It is during a quickening storm of wind and rain that Hardy looks back on the journey through life, the stages of the storm matching the more significant stages of life. At first only the rising wind makes itself known as, in contrast to the harmonious scene within, images of universal decay and finality swirl down in the sick leaves – "reeling" suggesting a variety of images from drunken or beaten helplessness to its opposite in a ghastly *danse macabre*. Then, like the emergent slug which warned Gabriel Oak of impending rain, other creatures take note of the portents, and the birds (explicitly white, not only because they are probably seabirds, but presumably also because white is often a sinister colour for Hardy) seeking shelter herald the hiss and lash of the destroying storm. The poem is tightly and carefully structured, the image in each stanza's last line connecting closely to that of the next stanza – as the storm birds lead to the fowls, the wall to the high new house. The reader is swung, in Hardy's most typical counterpoint, between contrasting themes: between memory and the intrusive present setting, the pictures deriving from the past and the single, final lines depicting the storm in the present; between candlelight and shadow, the harmony, happiness and brightness of the actors, and the heavy threat of the storm; between their busy occupations and the repeated interruptions and obstruction of "the years, the years," which, in token of this, alone of all lines do not rhyme with any other. This ballad-like refrain emphasises the theme of the lifetime passing. It checks us with "Ah, no;". It separates human life from the forces of Nature; and points to the storm which, in its destructiveness, its denial of all the past life images, becomes, particularly in the poem's final line, a concrete expression of Time – much as do the rain and darkness of "At Castle Boterel".

The final line indeed comes as something of a shock,[12] when the scene of the objects standing up on the lawn blends, as in a film, into the gravestone standing in the green of the churchyard. As the last lines of the other stanzas are often difficult to say, thick with consonants or alliteration, so is it particularly here: it enforces our attention with almost every word in the line heavily stressed, imitating the fundamental human labour of carving and ploughing.

The image of the plough is rich in underlying meanings. It can be linked with the earlier activity of clearing the creeping moss, which Thom Gunn likens to the burning of couch-grass, "a quiet clearing of space in nature so as to make room for human assertions."[13] But one can also think of clichés like "whole civilisations disappearing under the plough". It is a destructive and obliterating instrument which can reduce everything in its path to dust. Nature, with its rain that falls upon the just and the unjust, obliterates our own, personal, human patterns, as it has been doing in its interventions against our memories throughout the poem. (For the first time, in this line the image representing the Present now also includes the family, hitherto always kept safely in the Past.) It is another of Hardy's favourite contrasts and incongruities that he should make a gentle raindrop "plough". This idea appears elsewhere, particularly in "In Front of the Landscape",[14] where the faces from the past, which seem to obscure the view, are

> Some as with smiles,
> Some as with slow-born tears that brinily trundled
> Over the wrecked
> Cheeks that were fair in their flush-time, ash now with
> anguish,
> Harrowed by wiles.

Both tear and raindrop, Time and Nature, have an insidious activity,[15] and furrows can be drawn on faces as on the earth. Engraving of this kind is a favourite Hardy image: even as early as 1867 he had copied in his notebook a line from Corneille's *Le Cid* about the young hero and events which "Have graven his exploits upon his forehead."[16] His poems are full of it. In "Your Last Drive" he speaks of "read[ing] the writing on your face". "In a Former Resort after Many Years" tells how the old women he sees were once "fresh and furrowless", while his own

> former mind
> Was like an open plain where no foot falls,
> But now is as a gallery portrait-lined,
> And scored with necrologic scrawls."

In the final line of "During Wind and Rain" Hardy finds that what he has been drawing in the poem – a lifetime of memories, but described in the present as if they were still being lived – turns out to be drawn in dead names on a gravestone. The memories, the life, seem fresh and bright; but they end up superseded, merely a bare outline, a skeleton where once was flesh and blood; and an outline that is steadily eroded by the continuing rain. With his usual care for structure Hardy sees to it that the light downward reel of leaves at the beginning is matched by the stressed, implacable downward pitch of obliterating water at the end.

The power of this poem can be felt even though – or perhaps because – so much is left to the imagination. Hardy says nothing about who these people are – "he, she, all of them" – nor why he picks out certain of their activities, nor why, for example, their clocks and chairs should be out *all day*. He often deliberately writes his poem around a gap; and this invitation to participate, to make them work, gives readers part of their satisfaction in his poetry. It has much in common with the ballad tradition which is so important a background to his poems: here are the same mysteries, the same vivid depiction of only partially explained human actions. Like a ballad, this poem universalises and generalises human experience. We do not know who the speaker is, but he seems to speak for us as he reflects on the stages of human life and its setting within the world and time.

> I was quick to bloom; late to ripen.

It is arguable whether any other English poet has ripened so fruitfully, or so finely nourished his poetry with the wisdom and experience of great age.[17]

We stand on a high point in this exploratory journey. It is a moment to stop and draw breath, and from this vantage point to look down on how the particular configuration of this landscape came to be formed: what kind of mind and feeling it was which produced this poetry.

Notes

1   Eg poems already read here, like *Old Furniture, Logs on a Hearth, etc*

2   J.M. Murry, *op cit*, quoted in *Casebook*, 91. It is fitting that he should have ended with Virgil's famous (but untranslatable) line from *Aeneid* I about "the tears of things."

3   *Times Literary Supplement*, 27 November 1919, reprinted *Casebook*, 91–8.

4   *Life*, 378

5   The note was made on the endpapers of a German reader now in the possession of R.L. Purdy (*Millgate*, 129).

6   *Dennis Taylor* also examines this more fully than is possible here.

7   Horace, *Epistles*, I,ii,14, which may be translated: "Whatever

folly the kings commit, the Greeks will smart for it". (Smith's Latin-English Dictionary)

8   I am indebted to Dennis Taylor for these observations.

9   Eg the use of the words *stalk, wight*, and the symbolic value of the couch-grass in humanity's unending battle with Nature: (see later in this chapter.)

10 See also pp 152, 198.

11 *Some Recollections*, 2, 3, 8, 9, 19–21

12 Which Taylor compares with the shock of the eerie light change at the end of *The Wind's Prophecy*.

13 Thom Gunn, *op cit, Casebook* 223

14 See pages 289–90

15 Hardy made a point of this in an interview about Stonehenge reported in the *Daily Telegraph* of 24 August 1899. See the indispensable *Orel*.

16 Act I, sc. 1, 36

17 W.B. Yeats, whose greatest period was probably the last twenty years of his life, is the obvious comparison.

8

"OUT OF THY BRAIN AND HEART"

The Formation of the Landscape

"With Hardy's poetry, it is impossible to detach technique and imagination from character."
                                                    C. Day Lewis.

"The work of a great artist proceeds out of his inmost life."
                                                    W.R. Rutland.[1]

I have not yet referred to *The Dynasts*, the long verse and prose drama which, in seven Acts and "Fore" and "After Scene", surveys the Napoleonic Wars and their effects on human beings. Much more than even that, it is a philosophical reflection on the great web of humanity and on the Immanent Will – "this viewless, voiceless Turner of the Wheel" who, having set the world in motion, continues unconscious of it and its peoples:

> ... like a knitter drowsed,
> Whose fingers play in skilled unmindfulness,
> The Will has woven with an absent heed
> Since life first was; and ever will so weave.[2]

The Dynasts reflects both Hardy's strengths and his weaknesses. Written over many years, (its three-part publication completed in 1908) it also shows his originality: for it is neither novel nor stage play, but a work cast as for a film. The technique so often used in his novels (like the opening of *The Woodlanders*) where an initial panoramic view then settles and focuses on to one point is, with other cinematic skills, developed in *The Dynasts*. It shows Hardy not only as a thinker, but as an imaginative artist ahead of his time.

To study *The Dynasts* on this trip would be to keep walking until next year: other guidebooks exist and it is there for the reading – an original contribution to the discussion of

[180]

fundamental questions about the universe, God, humanity, and evil. But in this work, as in his other writings, it is the feeling human being, among all the potentates and vested interests of European politics and against all the workings of Fate or the Will, who is set firmly at the centre of the cosmos. As do his other writings, *The Dynasts* reflects its creator's mind and heart – not least in its emphasis on what he saw as the cardinal virtue: loving-kindness.[3] Whatever he actually achieved in his own life, loving-kindness – a compassionate respect for every individual being – was what he most admired. In some of the last lines of *The Dynasts*, the Chorus of the Pities hope for the amendment and reform of The Will:

"Nay; – shall not Its blindness break?
Yea, must not its heart awake,
      Promptly tending
      To Its mending
In a genial germing purpose, and for loving-kindness' sake?"

The theme runs through all his work. Another appeal is in a more personal poem which sprang from Hardy's own experience.

A BROKEN APPOINTMENT

You did not come,
And marching Time drew on, and wore me numb. –
Yet less for loss of your dear presence there
Than that I thus found lacking in your make
That high compassion that can overbear
Reluctance for pure lovingkindness' sake
Grieved I, when, as the hope-hour stroked its sum,
      You did not come.

You love not me,
And love alone can lend you loyalty;
– I know and knew it. But, unto the store
Of human deeds divine in all but name,
Was it not worth a little hour or more
To add yet this: Once you, a woman, came
To soothe a time-torn man; even though it be
      You love not me?

This beautiful lyric is like "I Look Into My Glass" and many others in its undercurrent of intense feeling and its scrupulous restraint under pain. It is finely structured, with its circling anguish and tolling repetition – "You did not come," – and the accumulation of tension in the first long sentence, pent up until "Grieved I".... It gives to "pure lovingkindness" and "high compassion" a quality "divine in all but name." Hardy not only felt it when a lack of compassion was shown to him: he cared about it for all creatures. This tenderness has been seen in many poems already – "The Inquiry", "Julie-Jane", "Drummer Hodge", "By the Barrows", "The Boy's Dream", "Tess's Lament", to name only a few. Two more are particularly good examples.

THE BLINDED BIRD

So zestfully canst thou sing?
And all this indignity,
With God's consent, on thee!
Blinded ere yet a-wing
By the red-hot needle thou,
I stand and wonder how
So zestfully thou canst sing!

Resenting not such wrong,
Thy grievous pain forgot,
Eternal dark thy lot,
Groping thy whole life long,
After that stab of fire;
Enjailed in pitiless wire;
Resenting no such wrong!

Who hath charity? This bird.
Who suffereth long and is kind,
Is not provoked, though blind
And alive ensepulchred?
Who hopeth, endureth all things?
Who thinketh no evil, but sings?
Who is divine? This bird.

This is one of six references I have counted in Hardy's poems (excluding *The Dynasts*) to the famous meditation on the nature of love which St Paul wrote to the early Christians at Corinth. (I

Corinthians, chapter XIII). He quotes no other Biblical passage so often. The poem's structure goes out of its way, again, to show that charity is divine. He often experiments with the triolet form, where the first line of each stanza must be repeated, but with a different meaning, at the end. As Patricia Clements writes, "The attraction of the form consists entirely in its rapid undoing and re-doing of meaning, and in its paradoxical use of repetition to convey change."[4] But Hardy makes far more of this than an exercise in prosody. There burns through the poem a passion which intensifies through the second stanza until it emerges, incandescent, in a controlled fury of unassailable assertions: and these break out of the expected triolet repetition in the last line.

Hardy wrote other sensitive poems about birds and animals (including one at the request of the RSPCA.) But into his poems about the sufferings of fellow-women and men went the heartache he knew life could bring, set against the joys he experienced, and his constant hope that one day things would mend. Few poets have meditated so deeply on a long life, mingling profound disillusion, grief, and hope; few have made such a compelling appeal for loving-kindness.

The original epigraph of "To An Unborn Pauper Child" was an echo of Hardy's thoughtful perusal of past local newspapers. It was from these that he had learnt of actual wife-selling incidents which sparked the opening of *The Mayor of Casterbridge*. From these some of the magistrates' edicts on women had remained in his mind – in sudden death, "And now she must be crowned";[5] in pregnancy, as in this poem, "She must go to the Union-house to have her baby". Contemporary fear of the Union or workhouse struck a deep knell in Hardy, partly from his perception of how his mother as a child had suffered from receiving "outdoor relief". Typically, however, a local and particular injunction led to a wide-ranging meditation on the kind of life such a child could expect to inherit.

TO AN UNBORN PAUPER CHILD

I

Breathe not, hid Heart: cease silently,
And though thy birth-hour beckons thee,
    Sleep the long sleep:
    The Doomsters heap

Travails and teens around us here,
And Time-wraiths turn our songsingings to fear.

II

Hark, how the peoples surge and sigh,
And laughters fail, and greetings die:
        Hopes dwindle; yea,
        Faiths waste away,
Affections and enthusiasms numb;
Thou canst not mend these things if thou dost come.

III

Had I the ear of wombèd souls
Ere their terrestrial chart unrolls,
        And thou were free
        To cease, or be,
Then would I tell thee all I know,
And put it to thee: Wilt thou take Life so?

IV

Vain vow! No hint of mine may hence
To theeward fly: to thy locked sense
        Explain none can
        Life's pending plan:
Thou wilt thy ignorant entry make
Though skies spout fire and blood and nations quake.

V

Fain would I, dear, find some shut plot
Of earth's wide wold for thee, where not
        One tear, one qualm,
        Should break the calm.
But I am weak as thou and bare;
No man can change the common lot to rare.

VI

Must come and bide. And such are we –
Unreasoning, sanguine, visionary –
        That I can hope
        Health, love, friends, scope
In full for thee; can dream thou wilt find
Joys seldom yet attained by humankind!

Comment on this poem may seem an impertinence. However

often it's read, the reader is drawn in each time as powerfully from "Breathe not, hid Heart", to all the gentleness and dignity of Hardy's approach.

Yet there is no sloppy sentimentality. The tenderness is given backbone by the painful tensions in the poem between what he knows about life with his mind, and hopes against hope with his heart. There is steel in the framework that only points up the gentleness: the tight metrical verse form, against which thrusts his affirmation of the supremacy of human feeling in life, its laughter, greetings, hopes, faiths, affections, and enthusiasms.

The contrasts and dissonances of life are always manifest. Though there are travails and teens (see a dictionary), there is also song-singing: honest acceptance of one does not deny the other. Long lines are balanced by expressive miniature lines:

> ... not
> One tear, one qualm,
> Should break the calm.

The language of poetry and philosophy is set against an intensely personal care for this tiny fellow human being, where the use of "thou" gives both intimacy and respect. Against the baby's helplessness and ignorance are arrayed all the forces of the Universe described in the Book of Revelation (or, The Apocalypse.) The "earth's wide wold" is scanned for "some shut plot", the weakness of the common lot is contrasted with the unattainable "rare", in a stanza where every word but one is in single syllables – which, as we say, a child could read. (Another profound statement about life, the opening of St John's Gospel, is similarly monosyllabic.) In the last stanza the diction makes particularly clear the rich and insoluble complexity of the human predicament. After all those Anglo-Saxon thumps and clots the elegant, lingering vowels and rhythms of three Latinate words – unreasoning, sanguine, visionary – give Hardy's game away. He knows the truth – the child "must come and bide". But despite what he knows, with a surge of that imaginative loving-kindness that he prized, he still hopes for the child, emphatically, the things that would make life what it was meant to be. Of these, love and friendship are paramount.

The Academy of 23 November 1901, in which this poem was first published, also carried an unsigned review of *Poems of the*

Past and Present. The writer returns repeatedly to Hardy's strength of feeling for his fellow humans.

> We remember no work that, between the lines, so urges kindness and tolerance between man and man. . . . Indeed, it has been left to Mr Hardy, among non-believers, to construct a new gospel of kindliness, a spiritualised 'service of man.' The ordinary agnostic who has serious thought for his fellows offers a hard materialism in the place of the religion in which he finds no solace. Mr Hardy, who is not ordinary, might be called an unbelieving mystic.[6]

Many poems support this assertion, among them two of his best-known because most frequently anthologised. "The Oxen" ends "Hoping it might be so." In "The Darkling Thrush", in a complex turnabout of the pathetic fallacy, Hardy credits the thrush with a supernatural happiness and "blessèd Hope" which he knows he cannot share. (The poem, with its fascinating echoes of Keats and Shelley – and the naturalist W.H. Hudson[7] – seems to be, as the nineteenth century ends, a rejection of the Romantic and pastoral lyric as well as a personal rejection of Victorian religious optimism.)

An earlier poem, "The Impercipient", had in the holograph a possible title variant: [The Agnostic]; and a headnote: "(Evensong; – Cathedral.)"

> Think some such mystery resides
> Within the ethic of my will."

This personification of The Will is particularly unpleasant; more often he is musingly vague or just downright ignorant. The poem remains an intellectual argument that might have been written in prose. It lacks the imagery and the compelling passion of Hardy's best poems. On the way to one such poem read "Doom and She", where sorrow rather than anger prevails. The Will is personified both as lord of Fate, or judgment, and as blind Mother Nature.

DOOM AND SHE

I

There dwells a mighty pair –
Slow, statuesque, intense –
Amid the vague Immense:
None can their chronicle declare,
Nor why they be, nor whence.

II

Mother of all things made,
Matchless in artistry,
Unlit with sight is she. –
And though her ever well-obeyed
Vacant of feeling he.

III

The Matron mildly asks –
A throb in every word –
"Our clay-made creatures, lord,
How fare they in their mortal tasks
Upon Earth's bounded bord?

IV

"The fate of those I bear,
Dear lord, pray turn and view,
And notify me true;
Shapings that eyelessly I dare
Maybe I would undo.

V

"Sometimes from lairs of life

Methinks I catch a groan,
Or multitudinous moan,
As though I had schemed a world of strife,
Working by touch alone."

VI

"World-weaver!" he replies,
"I scan all thy domain;
But since nor joy nor pain
It lies in me to recognize,
Thy questionings are vain.

VII

"World-weaver! what *is* Grief?
And what are Right, and Wrong,
And Feeling, that belong
To creatures all who owe thee fief?
Why is Weak worse than Strong?"...

VIII

– Unanswered, curious, meek,
She broods in sad surmise....
– Some say they have heard her sighs
On Alpine height or Polar peak
When the night tempests rise.

One may hardly have noticed the "vague Immense" in which
this poem begins, but one cannot fail to be moved by the chill
sterility, the lost beauty, of the Alpine heights where one is left.
Here is an early experiment with using the setting to unify the
poem and demonstrate the interaction between mind and world
– of the kind which culminated in poems like "Castle Boterel".
As usual Hardy does not attempt to "lift the 'burthen of the
mystery' of this unintelligible world".[17] As "A Dream
Question" ended with mystery, so do Doom's questions here:
and likewise the poet's own questions, in one of his most
vehement indictments of the ordering of the universe.

HAP

If but some vengeful god would call to me
From up the sky, and laugh: "Thou suffering thing,
Know that thy sorrow is my ecstasy,

That thy love's loss is my hate's profiting!"

Then would I bear it, clench myself, and die,
Steeled by the sense of ire unmerited;
Half-eased in that a Powerfuller than I
Had willed and meted me the tears I shed.

But not so. How arrives it joy lies slain,
And why unblooms the best hope ever sown?
– Crass Casualty obstructs the sun and rain,
And dicing Time for gladness casts a moan. . . .
These purblind Doomsters had as readily strown
Blisses about my pilgrimage as pain.

1866
16 Westbourne Park Villas

These tightly-knit lines of argument do not at first reading yield
their treasures. There seems nothing new in the theme of the
gods sporting with humankind – until it is turned, on the pivotal
"But not so", to Hardy's own individual angle: it is the chance,
random nature of life's buffetings that hurts, the offering of joy
and its pointless, unheeding withholding. Diction and rhythm
double the meaning.

How arrives it joy lies slain,
And why unblooms the best hope ever sown?

The hard, harsh teeth-clenched words of stanza two unfold at
once into a larger tone of long vowels and soft final consonants –
slain, sown, blooms; the human, personal voice and question
sounding not only against the fixed metrical frame of the sonnet,
but against the rigid voice of a mechanical universe.
("Mechanic" is a recurrent Hardyan term of abuse.) The answer
reflects that "mechanic speech" and "mechanic gear" and those
"mechanic repetitions" in its mouthful of stressed, crunching
consonants "Cráss Cásualty obstrúcts" – set in immediate
contrast to the simple basics of life, the sun and rain, which sing
themselves. Hardy's typical negative "unblooms" is particularly
poignant in the way it holds fruitful promise before our eyes
only to deny it. His "dicing Time" has a mincing cruelty quite
apart from its meaning; the "Doomsters" (Middle English, a
judge) are the last people who should be "purblind": the

discrepancies of life are everywhere in the poem. Here is one who is prepared to regard life as a pilgrimage, with all its overtones of purpose and stoicism; yet the slap in the face comes just as smartly. The life is strewn with the withered buds of a happiness that has never blossomed. The last word is pain.

"Hap", dated and placed in London in 1866, shows astonishing mastery of its medium, and Hardy's own idiom already clearly developed. Its pain and anger, so intensely felt, point to some of his suffering as a young man. By the turn of the century, when *Poems of the Past and Present* were published (November 1901), the dozen poems put together which all survey "God", "Nature", and humanity's lot are mostly less angry than exquisitely sad. In a fine poem, "The Bedridden Peasant to an Unknowing God", the suffering old man shames an uncaring God by his sublime humility and trust, which will not envisage a deity less principled than himself. Many later poems[18] show Hardy continually wrestling with these philosophical problems, in his own typical creative tension between opposites. On the one hand was the pull of his mind, which could accept abstractions about humanity and God, and the assertions in nineteenth-century scientific thought of man and woman's relative unimportance in the cosmic system. On the other hand was the pull of his heart, his instinctive certainty of the unique value of the sentient and moral human being, of the personal against the mechanical, the purposeful against the random; and a nostalgia for the old Christian certainties which he thought were superseded.

To these questions, Hardy was big enough to know that there was no final answer.

Thus things around. No answerer I....
    Meanwhile the winds, and rains,
    And Earth's old glooms and pains
Are still the same, and Life and Death are neighbours nigh.[19]

*   *   *   *   *   *

I have referred to Hardy's lively mind, concerned with contemporary thought until his death. In his portrayal of humanity up against an irrational and uncaring force, he was in many ways anticipating the theme of the absurdity of the human condition, a preoccupation of later writers like Camus,

Cocteau, Beckett, Ionesco, and Pinter – to which I shall return. He also wrote poems about social issues which are still ours. (I.A. Richards calls him "the poet who has most fully and courageously accepted the contemporary background.")[20] Three poems are about abortion, and one, beginning "O who'll get me a healthy child" touches on the grey areas of obstetric ethics which are under discussion in the 1980s. "A Jingle on the Times" (published 1917) satirizes the still-current preference for all that is controversial and violent, in art and news media as in life, and ends:

> Fighting, smiting,
>   Running through;
> That's now the civilised
>   Thing to do.

"The Lady in the Furs" ("I'm a lofty lovely woman", published in 1926) raises questions of poverty, ecology, and exploitation of workers and animals, that are still posed, and unsolved, today.

In his contemporary outlook, his questioning of religious dogma, his wide culture, classical and modern, and his deep interest in science and the arts, Hardy had something in common with Renaissance man, and it is there in the poetry. As a young man he had set out by methodical reading to compensate for his lack of formal higher education. For two years he read, apart from newspapers and reviews, nothing but poetry (and describes how nearly he might have been run down as he pursued his way among London traffic, his nose in Swinburne's new *Poems and Ballads*.) He not only quotes frequently from his favourite poets: he also writes poems about them.[21] The poem "Shelley's Skylark" was conceived as he looked out of a moving train.

SHELLEY'S SKYLARK

(The neighbourhood of Leghorn: March, 1887)

Somewhere afield here something lies
In Earth's oblivious eyeless trust
That moved a poet to prophecies –
A pinch of unseen, unguarded dust:

The dust of the lark that Shelley heard,
And made immortal through times to be; –

Though it only lived like another bird,
And knew not its immortality.

Lived its meek life; then, one day, fell –
A little ball of feather and bone;
And how it perished, when piped farewell,
And where it wastes, are alike unknown.

Maybe it rests in the loam I view,
Maybe it throbs in a myrtle's green,
Maybe it sleeps in the coming hue
Of a grape on the slopes of yon inland scene.

Go find it, faeries, go and find
That tiny pinch of priceless dust,
And bring a casket silver-lined,
And framed of gold that gems encrust;

And we will lay it safe therein,
And consecrate it to endless time;
For it inspired a bard to win
Ecstatic heights in thought and rhyme.

Though rarely anthologised, I find this one of Hardy's gems. Typically, he is moved by a little thing – like the memory of the frozen field-fare of his early childhood which was "light as a feather, all skin and bone... he had never forgotten how the body... felt in his hand: the memory had always haunted him."[22] But the little thing, the pinch of dust, is cradled in the great: "In Earth's oblivious eyeless trust" – (another idiosyncratic use of the negative.)[23] And passing through the incantatory repetition of "maybe... maybe..." the reader moves naturally, through magic casements, from the seen, limited, world to the unseen world of faery – where the valuable dust and the memory of the poet can be taken up and conserved for ever in a work of art that is imperishable, as the lark's song in its time was made imperishable. It is not the first time that we have seen Hardy meditating about poetic art.

The visual arts and music, however, meant almost as much to him. Having travelled through "the neighbourhood of Leghorn" in March 1887, he was by April writing sonnets in Rome; and in "The Vatican: Sala delle Muse", he was lamenting, to the apparition of a charmingly composite Muse ("an essence of all the Nine"), that he was an inconstant lover who cared for all the arts in turn – thus surely unacceptable? Form and Tune, Story and Dance and Hymn all held him:

– "Be not perturbed," said she. "Though apart in fame,
As I and my sisters are one, those, too, are the same.
　　　... These are but phases of one;
"And that one is I; and I am projected from thee,
One that out of thy brain and heart thou causest to be –
Extern to thee nothing. Grieve not, nor thyself becall,
Woo where thou wilt; and rejoice thou canst love at all!"

Love the arts he did – from his earliest years when music and dance moved him to tears, through his daily lunch-hour visits to the National Gallery as an apprentice, to his lifelong predilection for late Turner, and his meditations about Impressionism in poetry and art.[24] His poems are alive with colour: "the fair colour of the time", the "tinct of spring", "mornings beryl-bespread", the "colour and cast" of "earth's artistries", "hope-hues" and the unique "Earth is a cerule mystery".[25] From such a harvest of the seeing eye I choose just one poem which displays Hardy's sensitivity to visual beauty, and to the historic in pile and portrait.

A SPELLBOUND PALACE

(Hampton Court)

On this kindly yellow day of mild low-travelling winter sun
　　　The stirless depths of the yews
　　　Are vague with misty blues:
Across the spacious pathways stretching spires of shadows run,
And the wind-gnawed walls of ancient brick are fired vermilion.

　　　Two or three early sanguine finches tune
　　Some tentative strains, to be enlarged by May or June:
　　　From a thrush or blackbird
　　　Comes now and then a word,
While an enfeebled fountain somewhere within is heard.

　　　Our footsteps wait awhile,
　　　Then draw beneath the pile,
　　　When an inner court outspreads

As 'twere History's own asile,
Where the now-visioned fountain its attenuate crystal sheds
In passive lapse that seems to ignore the yon world's
    clamorous clutch.
And lays an insistent numbness on the place, like a cold hand's
    touch.
And there swaggers the Shade of a straddling King, plumed,
    sworded, with sensual face,
And lo, too, that of his Minister, at a bold self-centred pace:
    Sheer in the sun they pass; and thereupon all is still,
Save the mindless fountain tinkling on with thin enfeebled
    will.

No-one but Hardy would have chosen the word "stirless". Its
relaxed vowel and throw-away ending give space, depth and
silence to the scene.

The architecture naturally spoke too in a special way to him;
his poems are full of "storied towers", quoins, cornices and
vaults, "galleried naves and mighty quires".[26] "Copying
Architecture" was only one fruit among several of all the hours
he must have spent making drawings. In "The Abbey Mason" he
tells (in 109 couplets) an imaginary story of how the
Perpendicular style of Gothic architecture might have been
invented. In a letter to Sydney Cockerell in May 1912 Hardy
wrote about

what has struck me so often in relation to mediaeval art – the
anonymity of its creators. They seem in those days to have had
no personal ambition: and thinking of this last year I was led to
write a poem bearing on it.

He describes the master mason rebuilding Gloucester Cathedral
in the 1330s, perplexed, as the South transept rises, because the
old designs no longer fit:

"The upper archmould nohow serves
To meet the lower tracery curves:
"The ogees bend too far away
To give the flexures interplay."

He, and the work, come to a standstill. Then it is that chance and nature take a hand. His abortive diagrams, chalked on a board, have stood out all night through freezing rain; unable to sleep, in the "cadaverous dawn" he rises and stands before them in hopeless misery.

> He closelier looked; then looked again:
> The chalk-scratched draught-board faced the rain,
>
> Whose icicled drops deformed the lines
> Innumerous of his lame designs,
>
> So that they streamed in small white threads
> From the upper segments to the heads
>
> Of arcs below, uniting them
> Each by a stalactitic stem.
>
> – At once, with eyes that struck out sparks,
> He adds accessory cusping-marks,
>
> Then laughs aloud. The thing was done
> So long assayed from sun to sun. . . .

The laugh fades as the Abbot rebukes him for counting as a personal triumph what "the Almighty sent as guide"; and the mason's name is lost to history. The point that Hardy is making is only enunciated many years later in the poem by a succeeding Abbot, who says:

> ". . . Nay; art can but transmute;
> Invention is not absolute;
>
> "Things fail to spring from nought at call,
> And art-beginnings most of all.
>
> "He did but what all artists do,
> Wait upon Nature for his cue."

Ezra Pound called this Hardy's personal aesthetic. Hardy himself added his own ideas in several interesting notes about poetry being "a particular man's artistic interpretation of life" and the importance of the artist "going to Nature" with his own "idiosyncratic mode of regard."[27] This idiosyncrasy would also appear through that other vital principle, the buried emotion: the poet's own memories drawn out of himself as cue for the reflections of a lifetime.

These reflections were nurtured not only by Colour and

Form, but by Tune and Hymn, the music which profoundly
affected Hardy all his life.[28] We have already met the weird
"Jubilate", poems like "Leipzig" and "In the Nuptial Chamber"
and "The Ballad-Singer", which tell of the power of music;
poems remembering Julie-Jane – "Sing! How 'a would sing!" –
and the "softling song" of Emma's flitting, the airy quiver of the
old viol, the contralto voice "that lodges in me still with its
sweet singing... In the full-fugued song of the universe
unending". The list, too, is unending, for Hardy thought in
musical terms – about the "shore's sibilant tune", and "the wind
a lyre"; and how "soliloquies/Fell from him like an antiphonic
breeze."[29] He had only to see a piano, or hear a girl singing, to
write a poem about it; only to visit a museum of musical
instruments to imagine vividly the past experiences of each one.
Many of his poems are subtitled, like this:

A BYGONE OCCASION
(Song)
That night, that night,
That song, that song!
Will such again be evened quite
Through lifetimes long?

No mirth was shown
To outer seers,
But mood to match has not been known
In modern years.

O eyes that smiled,
O lips that lured;
That such would last was one beguiled
To think ensured!

That night, that night,
That song, that song;
O drink to its recalled delight,
Though tears may throng!

A little thing, you may say; but can anybody doubt the intensity
of his feeling for the joy of the moment and the power of song?
Out of so many poems about music let us read just one more.
Its background is linked with the Hardy family's never-

forgotten past in the "Mellstock" quire, about which he wrote a
dozen other poems.

TO MY FATHER'S VIOLIN

Does he want you down there
In the Nether Glooms where
The hours may be a dragging load upon him,
As he hears the axle grind
Round and round
Of the great world, in the blind
Still profound
Of the night-time? He might liven at the sound
Of your string, revealing you had not forgone him.

In the gallery west the nave,
But a few yards from his grave,
Did you, tucked beneath his chin, to his bowing
Guide the homely harmony
Of the quire
Who for long years strenuously –
Son and sire –
Caught the strains that at his fingering low or higher
From your four thin threads and eff-holes came outflowing.

And, too, what merry tunes
He would bow at nights or noons
That chanced to find him bent to lute a measure,
When he made you speak his heart
As in dream,
Without book or music-chart,
On some theme
Elusive as a jack-o'-lanthorn's gleam,
And the psalm of duty shelved for trill of pleasure.

Well, you can not, alas,
The barrier overpass
That screens him in those Mournful Meads hereunder
Where no fiddling can be heard
In the glades
Of silentness, no bird
Thrills the shades;
Where no viol is touched for songs or serenades,
No bowing wakes a congregation's wonder.

He must do without you now,
    Stir you no more anyhow
To yearning concords taught you in your glory;
    While, your strings a tangled wreck,
        Once smart drawn,
    Ten worm-wounds in your neck,
        Purflings wan
With dust-hoar, here alone I sadly con
Your present dumbness, shape your olden story.

Yes, Hardy is sad, but at 76, with so many dead whom he had loved, nostalgia is acceptable. I find this poem, and its sadness, more compelling at every reading. The intimacy of the address, as if the violin were a personal old friend, sharing reminiscences; the contrasting sweep of the enjambement into the rhythmic, unhurried circling of the great world, where one only stops for breath at "the night-time"; the vivid details of the man bowing – in church decorously, an associate: at the village jollities unpredictably, an individual; – these enchant one into his world. Then a hush comes as the eye slowly travels to the glades of the dead, where no bird sings, "No bowing wakes a congregation's wonder". This line seems to have unusual power. The tone and the stresses are different from the other last lines. Where the end of stanza II with its multiple alliterations and difficult diction reminds one of that strenuous fingering, this line uses the softer alliterative "w's" almost incidentally as part of the link between the two main words: "wakes" and "wonder" seem to bring readers out of those mournful glades into some broader plain, the Blessed Fields of simplicity and peace. Then – after a backward turn of the head for the "yearning concords taught you in your glory" – one sinks to an awareness that all is past. Time has performed its customary mutilation; but, again, the son and poet has "shaped" something that will last.

One could linger for many days on Hardy's musical poems – poems of a similar haunting sadness like "On the Tune Called The Old-Hundred-and-Fourth"; poems about the joys of the dance:

        Could I but will,
        Will to my bent,
    I'd have afar ones near me still

And music of rare ravishment
In strains that move the toes and heels!
And when the sweethearts sat for rest
The unbetrothed should foot with zest
Ecstatic reels.[30]

There is something hypnotic about the throb and zest of Hardy's

Rich-noted throats, and gossamered flingers
Of heels;

about the dust and glare, above all the human warmth and
passions inflamed by melody and dance which he knew so often
would end in tears. Yet despite this aspect of music, for him the
thought of it in his own life was usually healing.

So, to the one long-sweeping symphony
From times remote
Till now, of human tenderness, shall we
Supply one note,
Small and untraced, yet that will ever be
Somewhere afloat
Amid the spheres, as part of sick Life's antidote.[31]

* * * * * *

If for Hardy music was an essential part of sick Life's antidote, so
unquestionably was a sense of humour. What constitutes
humour is always slippery ground; and there are those who
think, because of his tragic view of life, that he had none. Their
impression does not fit the evidence. Harold Macmillan (Lord
Stockton) remembered Hardy as "a very merry old man full of
jokes";[32] presumably the man who provided the delicious pages
of Joseph Poorgrass, Clerk Crickett, Haymoss Fry, Granfer
Cantle singing "in the voice of a bee up a flue", The Distracted
Preacher, Old Mrs Chundle, and countless other comic
characters and situations. His earliest published poem, "The
Bride-Night Fire", first appeared (bowdlerized) in *The
Gentleman's Magazine* in November 1875; restored in dialect and
spice as now in *Wessex Poems*, it shows the same kind of light-
hearted, tongue-in-cheek humour as his other sketches of rural
life. A little earlier, while apprenticed to Arthur Blomfield in

London, he had actually published an amusing story called "How I Built Myself a House". It is to this period that "The Ruined Maid" belongs, a poem which we have seen is both superficially amusing and fundamentally witty in its play-off of hymn-tune metre against conventional moral. (He often enjoyed this rather esoteric – but meaningful – kind of joke, enshrining some of his poems of religious doubt, like "The Bedridden Peasant", in traditional hymn measures.) More than thirty years later he was still exploring the delights of expressive metre and comic rhymes in a poem about Liddell and Scott, the architects of the great Greek-English lexicon.

LIDDELL AND SCOTT
On the Completion of their Lexicon

(Written after the death of Liddell in 1898.
Scott had died some ten years earlier.)

"Well, though it seems
Beyond our dreams,"
Said Liddell to Scott,
"We've really got
To the very end,
All inked and penned
Blotless and fair
Without turning a hair,
This sultry summer day, A.D.
Eighteen hundred and forty-three.

"I've often, I own,
Belched many a moan
At undertaking it,
And dreamt forsaking it.
– Yes, on to Pi,
When the end loomed nigh,
And friends said: "You've as good as done,"
I almost wished we'd not begun.
Even now, if people only knew
My sinkings, as we slowly drew
Along through Kappa, Lambda, Mu,
They'd be concerned at my misgiving,
And how I mused on a College living
Right down to Sigma,

But feared a stigma
If I succumbed, and left old Donnegan
For weary freshmen's eyes to con again:
And how I often, often wondered
What could have led me to have blundered
So far away from sound theology
To dialects and etymology;
Words, accents not to be breathed by men
Of any country ever again!"

"My heart most failed,
Indeed, quite quailed,"
Said Scott to Liddell,
"Long ere the middle!...
'Twas one wet dawn
When, slippers on,
And a cold in the head anew,
Gazing at Delta
I turned and felt a
Wish for bed anew,
And to let supersedings
Of Passow's readings
In dialects go.
'That German has read
More than we!' I said;
Yea, several times did I feel so!...

"O that first morning, smiling bland,
With sheets of foolscap, quills in hand,
To write ἀάατος and ἀαγής,
Followed by fifteen hundred pages,
What nerve was ours
So to back our powers,
Assured that we should reach ὠώδης
While there was breath left in our bodies!"

Liddell replied: "Well, that's past now;
The job's done, thank God, anyhow."

"And yet it's not,"
Considered Scott,
"For we've to get
Subscribers yet
We must remember;

> Yes; by September."
>
> "O Lord; dismiss that. We'll succeed.
> Dinner is my immediate need.
> I feel as hollow as a fiddle,
> Working so many hours," said Liddell.

The whole poem is constructed to one end. As one hurtles through its short two- and three-foot lines, assigned to both speakers indistinguishably so that they resemble Tweedledum and Tweedledee, with ludicrous rhymes and situations like "Delta/felt a",

> And how I mused on a College living
> Right down to Sigma;

puns about dons, and rhyming of Greek words with English;[33] and as one passes from the picture of the slippered sages "smiling bland,/With... quills in hand" to the yawning, earthbound Liddell whose only thought now is food – one touches off, at the end, the final shower of sparks in this send-up of dictionary-making.

> "I feel as hollow as a fiddle,
> Working so many hours," said Liddell.

Hardy enjoyed words and metres so much that he often turned them to comic effect. "Is wary walking worth much pother?" booms "the Jersey boat with its funnel agroan". (This is in a poem called "The Contretemps", where a farcical situation of mistaken lovers' identities develops and is fully exploited – both as humour and, towards the end, as a part of life's web, which Hardy does not attempt to disentangle.) With his predominantly ironic cast of mind, he could not help seeing the funny side and the often ridiculous dissonances of serious or respectable happenings;[34] so that in "The Levelled Churchyard", when

> We late-lamented, resting here
> Are mixed to human jam,
> And each to each exclaims in fear,
> "I know not who I am!"

a wicked facility in rhyme prompts him to add:

> Here's not a modest maiden elf
> But dreads the final Trumpet,
> Lest half of her should rise herself,
> And half some sturdy strumpet!

Hardy's sense of the ludicrous was there in the little boy playing "This life so free" for the convict; it is often evident, as in the conversation between Henry VIII and Edward the Confessor ("The Coronation"), and the ironical skit on both "The Respectable Burgher" and the new Higher Criticism of the Bible which the man could not take. Seeing the limitations of both, Hardy could not resist a take-off of each.

Indeed his gift for caricature of some sacred cow is often verbally amusing. In "The Sick Battle-God" he genuinely hoped (in 1901) that the "zest for slaughter was dying out",[35] and ridiculed the "lurid Battle-God" and his heavies in a positively Jabberwockian skit on their fanatical and frenzied way of speech:

> On bruise and blood-hole, scar and seam,
> On blade and bolt, he flung his fulgid beam:
> His haloes rayed the very gore,
> And corpses wore his glory-gleam.

In gentler ways he mocks too – for example, the townee's unthinking assumptions about remote bucolic bliss.

THE MILKMAID

> Under a daisied bank
> There stands a rich red ruminating cow,
> And hard against her flank
> A cotton-hooded milkmaid bends her brow.
>
> The flowery river-ooze
> Upheaves and falls; the milk purrs in the pail;
> Few pilgrims but would choose
> The peace of such a life in such a vale.
>
> The maid breathes words – to vent,
> It seems, her sense of Nature's scenery,

> Of whose life, sentiment,
> And essence, very part itself is she.
>
> She bends a glance of pain,
> And, at a moment, lets escape a tear;
>   Is it that passing train,
> Whose alien whirr offends her country ear? –
>
> Nay! Phyllis does not dwell
> On visual and familiar things like these;
>   What moves her is the spell
> Of inner themes and inner poetries:
>
> Could but by Sunday morn
> Her gay new gown come, meads might dry to dun,
>   Trains shriek till ears were torn,
> If Fred would not prefer that Other One.

Here even the poet is mocked in his would-be pastoral idyll; the "inner poetries" of his Phyllis (of madrigal and eclogue fame) turn out to be not quite what he was expecting.

Hardy often laughed at himself and high poetic art if there was any danger of their becoming pompous. The same journey that produced "Shelley's Skylark" had also given him hs first view of Genoa the Proud, set on the "epic-famed, god-haunted Central Sea" of history and legend. One almost hears the violins; but suddenly they turn into a squawk.

GENOA AND THE MEDITERRANEAN

(March 1887)

> O epic-famed, god-haunted Central Sea,
>   Heave careless of the deep wrong done to thee
> When from Torino's track I saw thy face first flash on me.
>
> And multi-marbled Genova the Proud,
>   Gleam all unconscious how, wide-lipped, up-browed,
> I first beheld thee clad – not as the Beauty but the Dowd.
>
> Out from a deep-delved way my vision lit
>   On housebacks pink, green, ochreous – where a slit
> Shoreward 'twixt row and row revealed the classic blue through it.
>
> And thereacross waved fishwives' high-hung smocks,
>   Chrome kerchiefs, scarlet hose, darned underfrocks;

Often since when my dreams of thee, O queen, that frippery
    mocks:
    Whereat I grieve, Superba!.... Afterhours
    Within Palazzo Doria's orange bowers
Went far to mend these marrings of thy soul-subliming
    powers.

    But, Queen, such squalid undress none should see,
    Those dream-endangering eyewounds no more be
Where lovers first behold thy form in pilgrimage to thee.

After all those purple adjectives, when he is expecting the serene
marble front of classical grandeur, what he sees is rows of tatty
underwear on the line: and (rhyming "mocks" with smocks and
underfrocks) he ridicules himself and his stereotyped vision of
Genoa the Beauty, which can hardly take the knock of finding
her the Dowd.[36]

Perhaps the poem in which Hardy most thoroughly pokes fun
at himself is the delightful "Snow in The Suburbs" – though it's
only as one knows him well that this may become apparent. It is
on page 10. At first the picture of what is happening is quite
enough to keep the reader busy.

Those steps are still visible outside the house – no. 1, Arundel
Terrace, facing Wandsworth Common – where the Hardys
lived from 1878–81. After the minute description of the scene,
where the chief characters are the snow, the sparrow, and then
the cat, it is a surprise at the end to find human beings involved:
more than one has been watching it all the time. The watchers
are no more important than the other characters; rather less so in
fact, since only their single action is mentioned, taken
completely for granted in the sequence of natural events. This is
a pastoral poem, one of a small group in *Human Shows* (published
in 1925) in which Hardy seems able to detach from his usual
concerns and indulge himself with a less complex observation
and even enjoyment of nature – (though the poems are often
linked as metaphors of "the autumn of his life" and "the winter
of his days".)

This is not to say that the execution of this poem is simple.
Even the layout is expressive. As always, Hardy "was a man
who used to notice such things" as the strange behaviour of
snowflakes. As always, he is encouraging us to use our eyes and

see the extraordinary in the daily ordinary, or in the sight that has been taken for granted – and constantly to re-examine what we had thought was reality. Here's the reader at sparrow level, in the thick of the snow, muffled and silenced; and one almost feels the wet down one's neck as the sparrow, clown-like, is knocked off his perch, blinks and shakes himself under the avalanche. Characteristically, Hardy's grammar deliberately obscures whether it is snow or sparrow that "lights on a nether twig" – and that's the point, for individuality often becomes obscured as it melts into a generalising background.

Hardy made a dozen changes in this poem between his holograph for the printer and the version now in *Human Shows*. Though he may have made notes or an early draft while he was living at Upper Tooting, it is likely that this poem was effectively written during the 1920s – a mellower period when, recognised as the Grand Old Man of English letters, and thanks to Florence's self-sacrificing care of her octogenarian husband,[37] he seems to have been able to suspend the reiteration of his most tragic views. His changes all make for greater precision and more vivid imagery, like the palings "glued" where they had before been "joined", and "there is no waft of wind", where previously he had rather jauntily written "there's not a whiff of wind". He may also have (re-) read John Clare's "lodging snows" and preferred it to his earlier "waiting" lumps. (Hynes' three-volume edition of the poems makes many more such discoveries accessible.) But there is another way in which Hardy's years of experience and meditation contribute to this poem: for in it, with typical humour, he enjoys spoofing some of the tragic patterns that over the years have preoccupied him. Dennis Taylor, writing of the brief "Indian Summer" of Hardy's pastoral poetry, points to how in this poem "he burlesques many of his tragic images: the concatenations of accident, the webbed pattern of fate, the losing of one's way in a changing nature, the whiteness of death."[38] Seen like this, one cannot help enjoying with him the joke at his own expense.

Apart from the buffoonery in poems like "The Bride-Night Fire" and "Liddell and Scott", Hardy's humour is of the mind, a "thoughful laughter" – the awakening of which Meredith defines as the test of true comedy.[39] Indeed the long history of comedy in society has interesting affinities with Hardy. One thinks of its classical origins, with the ritual debate and struggle between the Alazon, or Impostor, and the Eiron – the mocker, or Socrates figure, who by irony draws out the comedy and the uncertainties of the character and scene. One thinks of comedy's complexity, its debt to surprise and chance and changes in fortune; and the links Kierkegaard made between the comedian and the religious person, who both see the contradictions at the heart of our deepest experiences. One recalls how comedy usually begins from the absurd or the inexplicable and is still usually left with the irreconcilable. One remembers the clear-eyed self-scrutiny which comedy requires, and its affirmation of the complexity of truth, seeing us, with all our absurdities, as we are – with a laughter that is both releasing and purging and, as others besides the great Molière have recognised, often close to tears. All these aspects of comedy are in some degree characteristic of Hardy's thinking and living, and may be found in his poetry.

Yet he is no Molière. He fits better the description by Landor which Meredith quotes in his lively essay: "Genuine humour and true wit require a sound and capacious mind, which is always a grave one." (John Weightman, reviewing a recent biography of Voltaire, wrote of him: "His superb wit, like all wit, depended on a keen sense of evil.")[40] Meredith's "great humourist ... has an embrace of contrasts beyond the scope of the comic poet"; his "stroke is worldwide, with lights of tragedy in his laughter." Meredith's observations have other interesting connections with Hardy. For him the humourist's "vast power ... built up of the feelings and the intellect in union, is often wanting in proportion and in discretion ... Humourist and satirist frequently hunt together as ironists in pursuit of the grotesque, to the exclusion of the comic."

Readers can explore their own ideas on these connections. As we now move away from Hardy's sense of humour to other aspects of his mind, it may appear that while his brow was often furrowed over life's tragedy, there were many times as well when on his face, as on ours when we read, lay what Meredith called "that slim feasting smile."

* * * * * *

The Comic Spirit's attributes, in Meredith's definition, included that of "unsolicitous observation." Hardy was too much a champion of humankind and too much wrung by his views of the inherent hostility of the universe to be unsolicitous (though his Immanent Will invariably is.) But his powers of observation are possibly unmatched. A description of him in 1894 picked out as

> his most noticeable feature, bright, deep-set eyes, keen as a hawk's, but, for all their watchfulness, full of a quiet *bonhomie*. Indeed, there is something not un-hawk-like about his whole physiognomy, with the predatory expression left out; in no other human face have I seen such a still intensity of observation.[41]

This power of observation is seen everywhere in his notes, novels, and poems. It is in "Snow in the Suburbs" and "A Spellbound Palace" and "Night-Time in Mid-Fall"; in the subtle intonations of the Ruined Maid and the country girl, in the curtain disturbed by the draught in "A Man Was Drawing Near To Me", and in countless other details. In the dramatic poem "At Wynyard's Gap" where two strangers meet on horseback in a desolate spot ripe for romance, the man in silence watches the woman, and observes:

> You stand so stock-still that your ear-ring shakes
> At each pulsation which the vein there makes.

These are lines which for David Wright illustrate Hardy's particular gift: "the imagination working and engaged, but the eye unwaveringly fixed upon the object."[42] In the poems already read here so evident is this faculty, and this use of every "minute observation" to create something greater, that there is hardly a need to linger – but let a last poem exemplify it all.

A COUNTENANCE

> Her laugh was not in the middle of her face quite,
>   As a gay laugh springs,
> It was plain she was anxious about some things
>   I could not trace quite.
> Her curls were like fir-cones – piled up, brown –
>   Or rather like tight-tied sheaves;
> It seemed they could never be taken down....
>
> And her lips were too full, some might say:

I did not think so. Anyway,
The shadow her bottom one would cast
Was green in hue whenever she passed
    Bright sun on midsummer leaves.
Alas, I knew not much of her,
And lost all sight and touch of her!

If otherwise, should I have minded
The shy laugh not in the middle of her mouth quite,
And would my kisses have died of drouth quite
    As love became unblinded?

1884[43]

*   *   *   *   *   *

"Bright sun on midsummer leaves". Some of Hardy's most typical images will be our care on almost the last lap of the journey; but one can not turn from this glimpse of the thinking and feeling person behind the poems without a hard look at what many people consider to be his most essential quality: his sincerity and concern for the truth.

Notes

1   Lewis, *The Poetic Image*, 152 (London 1947); Rutland, *Thomas Hardy: A Study of his Writings and their Background, ix* (Oxford 1938)

2   Fore Scene.

3   "A sentiment perhaps in the long run more to be prized than lover's love." (*Two on a Tower*, ch XLI). See also, for example, the poems *A Plaint to Man, God's Funeral, Often When Warring;* and the *Apology to Late Lyrics and Earlier.*

4   *PTH*, 148.

5   Hardy's original note for *The War-Wife of Catknoll* explained this phrase as "Old English for 'there must be a coroner's inquest over her.'"

6   Reprinted in *Casebook*, 47–8.

7   Hudson's description of the missel-thrush in his *Nature in*

Downland (1900) has been picked out by Carl J. Weber (*Hardy of Wessex*, London 1940/65) and subsequent writers.

8   The 1885 *Revised Version* has "peace". The Revd Islwyn Blythin of the University of Wales writes: "There is no question in my mind that the translation which [Hardy] pre-supposes in his poem is preferable to the traditional one, because the Hebrew 'shalom' really means 'wholeness'. If everything hangs together as it should, then all is well, but if not, all is woe! I doubt very much if there was such a translation available in Hardy's time, but would he, perhaps, have known an erudite clergyman?... My guess is that his own poetic, artistic *nous* would have led him directly to the heart of the matter." (Letter to the Revd Rupert Davies in response to my query.) The answer may well lie with Hardy's friendship with the Revd Henry Moule and his sons.

9   A note of April 1871, *Notebooks* 9. Also: "The sea... murmured, and he thought it was the pines; the pines murmured in precisely the same tones, and he thought they were the sea". *Tess of the d'Urbervilles*, ch LV

10 *Apology to Late Lyrics and Earlier; 1895 Preface to Jude the Obscure; Apology*, quoting from Wordsworth's *Intimations* Ode; Arnold, "Study of Poetry", *Essays in Criticism*, 2nd series; *Apology*.

11 *Lit. Notes II*, entries 2450, 2480; *Millgate*, 571

12 *Life*, 153

13 In *Thomas Hardy: A Writer and His Background*, ed Norman Page (London 1980), Roger Robinson on "Hardy and Darwin", and Lennart Björk on "Hardy's Reading", discuss this further. Glen Wickens' "Hardy's Inconsistent Spirits and the Philosophic Form of The Dynasts" in *PTH*, 101, is also helpful. After the 1914–18 War Hardy became much less hopeful about the progress of both The Will and humanity's "loving-kindness".

14 We must not forget how Hardy's imagination ran riot into the grotesque as he questioned mind and reality. Mary Jacobus links Hardy's mind and imagination with Ruskin's description of "'a diseased and ungoverned imaginativeness' in 'the contemplation of great powers in destructive operation, and generally for the perception of the presence of death.'" (The Stones of Venice, quoted in "Hardy's Magian Retrospect", *op cit*, 267)

15 Letter to L. Milman, 17 July 1893.

16 *Life*, 410, (see the note in *Collected Letters*, VI 48); *Life*, 403.

17 *The Dynasts*, Preface (1903)

18 Eg Aγυωστωι θεωι (*To the Unknown God*), *Before Life and After* (see page 279), *God's Funeral*, etc

19 *Nature's Questioning*

20 *Science and Poetry*, (London, 1926) 68, also quoted in *Casebook*, 110

21 *Life*, 49; letter to Swinburne, 1 April 1897. *A Pair of Blue Eyes* is full of allusions to *In Memoriam*, *Desperate Remedies* to Shelley; the poems about Keats are *Rome: At the Pyramid of Cestius near the Graves of Shelley and Keats*, *At a House in Hampstead*, *At Lulworth Cove a Century Back*; there are poems, for example, *To George Meredith* and *To Shakespeare*.

22 *Life*, 444

23 See pages 152, 171 and 198

24 Eg *Life*, 185, 216, 228–9, 329

25 *Four in the Morning*

26 *Barthélémon at Vauxhall*

27 Pound, *Confucius to Cummings*, 286, quoted in *Dennis Taylor*, 55; *Life* 383, 153, 225, 228

28 See for example my *Figures in a Wessex Landscape*, pp 21–3, 26–7, 241–7. Several of the hymn tunes Hardy mentions can still be found in *The English Hymnal*, *Congregational Praise*, etc

29 *Fetching Her, On The Way, I Met a Man*

30 *Could I But Will*. See eg *Great Things*, *In the Small Hours*, already quoted; and *At the Entering of the New Year*, *The Dance at the Phoenix*, *Reminiscences of a Dancing Man*; and *The Two Houses*, from which the next lines come.

31 *To Meet, or Otherwise*. Hardy's music, when young, included comparatively little from the classical repertoire. One has to remember that J.S. Bach was virtually introduced to the British public by Mendelssohn, Samuel Wesley and others only as the nineteenth century advanced. ("For many years Bach was known in England more by reputation than by experience" – see the New Grove Dictionary of Music, *Bach Family*, on the Bach Revival). But note Hardy's poem *Lines to a Movement in*

Mozart's E-Flat Symphony.

32 Presidential speech at the Hardy Festival, Dorchester 1968, as reported by Terry Coleman in *The Guardian* 10 July 1968, "Publishing Hardy under the Greenwood Tree"

33 Hardy probably enjoyed the irony of the meanings of these first and last words in the dictionary – the first two meaning "inviolable" and "hard, strong, etc", and the last meaning "egg-shaped" – the shape they must have felt their heads squeezed into after the great work, and its links with "egg-heads".

34 One could argue, from our sanitised Western viewpoint where the subject of death is only beginning to creep out from its social taboo, that Hardy's references to it are sometimes crude: there are the dead children "laid... like sprats in a tin" (page 61), and the dead lover in *The Fight on Durnover Moor*, "lamented where the worms waggle under the grass". They may reflect his (shall we say) down-to-earth countryman's background. He can hardly be blamed for speaking often of death – in Victorian times there was a good deal of it about.

35 *Life*, 365.

36 See Patricia Clements' fascinating essay in *PTH*.

37 See *Millgate*, 544–5

38 *Dennis Taylor*, 153

39 George Meredith, *The Idea of Comedy* (1877). See too his "Prelude" to *The Egoist*

40 *The Observer*, 21 September 1986

41 Rosamund Tomson, *The Independent*, N.Y., 22 November 1894, quoted *Millgate*, 322

42 "Notes on Hardy," *Agenda, op cit* 73

43 At his death Hardy left a holograph of *Winter Words* partly ready for publication. His wife Florence edited the manuscript for the printer and somehow in l. 10 here the word "bottom" was replaced by "lower" at the first printing. (See *Complete Poetical Works* vol III, 326.)

9

TRUTH

We have seen how Hardy's mind is like a powerful plough, continually turning over the soil in the search for the meaning of "existence in this universe." His own "attempts to explain or excuse the presence of evil and the incongruity of penalizing the irresponsible" he describes as "'questionings' in the exploration of reality." Accused, as he so often was, of pessimism, he roundly denied the charge, quoting a line from one of his early "In Tenebris" poems:

"If way to the Better there be, it exacts a full look at the Worst" – that is to say, by the exploration of reality, and its frank recognition stage by stage along the survey, with an eye to the best consummation possible: briefly, evolutionary meliorism.

Such an exploration of reality is "the first step towards the soul's betterment, and the body's also."[1]

TO SINCERITY

O sweet sincerity! –
Where modern methods be
What scope for thine and thee?

Life may be sad past saying,
Its greens for ever graying,
Its faiths to dust decaying;

And youth may have foreknown it,
And riper seasons shown it,
But custom cries: "Disown it:

"Say ye rejoice, though grieving,
Believe, while unbelieving,
Behold, without perceiving!"

– Yet, would men look at true things,

And unilluded view things,
And count to bear undue things,

The real might mend the seeming,
Facts better their foredeeming,
And Life its disesteeming.

February 1899

Whether he is considering a commonplace day, a bedridden old man or the imminent birth of a pauper child, often Hardy will look at the worst but still hope for the best; or look at the ugliness but see the intrinsic beauty. "Earth might be fair, and all her people one ..." But when the worst is inevitable, facing the truth with dignity is the mark of human integrity. "Mr Hardy, whatever else he disbelieves in," wrote *The Athenaeum's* anonymous reviewer of *Time's Laughingstocks,* "believes in the strength and permanence of truth ... [and he] will not ... have poetry at the expense of truth."[2] It was one of the qualities that had first attracted Hardy when, as an apprentice in London, he found that "a sense of the truth of poetry, of its supreme place in literature, had awakened itself in me."[3] It is the power of truth which, as the same reviewer continued, "curbs Mr Hardy's pessimism", and gives his poetry a strength and a nobility which lift rather er than oppress. "Mr Hardy offers no laurel to Despair."

"BETWEEN US NOW"

Between us now and here –
    Two thrown together
Who are not wont to wear
    Life's flushest feather –
Who see the scenes slide past,
The daytimes dimming fast,
Let there be truth at last,
    Even if despair.

So thoroughly and long
    Have you now known me,
So real in faith and strong
    Have I now shown me,

That nothing needs disguise
Further in any wise,
Or asks or justifies
    A guarded tongue.

Face unto face, then, say,
    Eyes my own meeting,
Is your heart far away,
    Or with mine beating?
When false things are brought low,
And swift things have grown slow,
Feigning like froth shall go,
    Faith be for aye.

Nothing could be more affirmative.

Although "Truth will be truth alway", Hardy was too wise
to think that it was simple or easily come by; or that it was the
same as certainty.

What of the world now?...
No more I know.[4]

Truth, Hardy knows, can be complex and ambiguous; and it
can appear different according to our standpoint. "A fool sees
not the same tree that a wise man sees." The nearest we seem
able to come to it is, as philosophers from Gorgias to Bertrand
Russell have said, that we believe it to be true.[5] In the face of
so much that is unknowable and unsayable, Hardy's way
forward is through honesty to his own experience, and
sincerity in thought and feeling. Even here there are questions
– for what does sincerity mean: and, sincerity to what or to
whom? Poets and critics admit that "clearly sincerity is a
value, even though one rather difficult to define – maybe it is
one of the ultimate values in literature" (Thom Gunn.)
"Whatever it is, it is the quality we most insistently require in
poetry. It is also the quality we most need as critics" (I.A.
Richards.)[6] That Hardy thought long and deeply on this is
shown not only by his poetry but by many notes he made and,
for example, a notable passage which he wrote for the last
chapter of *Tess of the d'Urbervilles,* but omitted from the final
text:

The humble delineator of human character and human contingencies, whether his narrative deal with the actual or with the typical only, must primarily and above all things be sincere, however terrible sincerity may be. Gladly sometimes would he lie, for dear civility's sake, if he dared, but for the haunting afterthought that: "this thing was not done honestly and may do harm." In typical history, with all its liberty, there are, as in real history, features that can never be distorted with impunity and issues which should never be falsified. And perhaps in glancing at the misfortunes of such people as have or could have, lived, he may acquire some art in shielding from like misfortunes those who have yet to be born. If truth required justification, surely this is an ample one.

Some years earlier he had made these notes:

(1883) *August.* Write a list of things wh. everybody thinks & nobody says; & a list of things that everybody says and nobody thinks.

July 19. In future I am not going to praise things because the accumulated remarks of ages say they are great and good, if those accumulated remarks are not based on observation. And I am not going to condemn things because a pile of accepted views raked together from tradition, and acquired by instillation, say antecedently that they they are bad.

(1901) *Dec 31st.* After reading various philosophic systems, & being struck with their contradictions and futilities, I have come to this: *Let every man make a philosophy for himself out of his own experience.* He will not be able to escape using terms and phraseology from earlier philosophers, but let him avoid adopting their theories if he values his own mental life.[7]

There are to be no secondhand opinions or accounts. If the experience of the moment is black, it must be accepted as present truth.

IN TENEBRIS I

"Percussus sum sicut foenum, et aruit cor meum" – Ps ci.[8]

Wintertime nighs;
But my bereavement-pain
It cannot bring again:
    Twice no one dies.

Flower-petals flee;
But, since it once hath been,
No more that severing scene
    Can harrow me.

Birds faint in dread:
I shall not lose old strength
In the lone frost's black length:
    Strength long since fled!

Leaves freeze to dun;
But friends can not turn cold
This season as of old
    For him with none.

Tempests may scath;
But love can not make smart
Again this year his heart
    Who no heart hath.

Black is night's cope;
But death will not appal
One who, past doubtings all,
    Waits in unhope.

If Hardy is "the poet who has most steadily refused to be comforted"[9] it is, as often seen in his poems, because he thinks life a travesty of what it should be and what in moments it can be; and because all its glory passes. But the joys are no less real because we must accept, and foresee, their transience.

HE FEARS HIS GOOD FORTUNE

There was a glorious time
At an epoch of my prime;
Mornings beryl-bespread,
And evenings golden-red;
    Nothing gray:
And in my heart I said,
"However this chanced to be
It is too full for me,
Too rare, too rapturous, rash,
Its spell must close with a crash
    Some day!"

The radiance went on
Anon and yet anon,
And sweetness fell around
Like manna on the ground
    "I've no claim",
Said I, to be thus crowned:
I am not worthy this: –
Must it not go amiss? –
Well... let the end foreseen
Come duly! – I am serene."
    – And it came.

Inevitably Hardy could see the many faces of truth:

Love is long-suffering, brave,
Sweet, prompt, precious as a jewel;
But jealousy is cruel,
    Cruel as the grave!

So as an old man looking back on life he described his "Private Man" as having come to terms with only modest expectations of life:

Tasting years of moderate gladness
Mellowed by sundry days of sadness[10]

and, more identifiably himself, in the poem published after his death:

HE NEVER EXPECTED MUCH
[or]
A CONSIDERATION

[A reflection] ON MY EIGHTY-SIXTH BIRTHDAY

Well, World, you have kept faith with me,
    Kept faith with me;
Upon the whole you have proved to be
    Much as you said you were.
Since as a child I used to lie
Upon the leaze and watch the sky,
Never, I own, expected I
    That life would all be fair.

'Twas then you said, and since have said,
    Times since have said,
In that mysterious voice you shed
    From clouds and hills around:
"Many have loved me desperately,
Many with smooth serenity,
While some have shown contempt of me
    Till they dropped underground.

"I do not promise overmuch,
    Child; overmuch;
Just neutral-tinted haps and such,"
    You said to minds like mine.
Wise warning for your credit's sake!
Which I for one failed not to take,
And hence could stem such strain and ache
    As each year might assign.

That childhood experience looking up at the sky, when
Thomas knew that he did not want to grow up, is recounted in
the *Life*, and inspired another late poem, "Childhood Among the
Ferns", as well as the similar incident in the life of the young
Jude. Even so young he was aware that life was not all green
gloss and sunshine; and it is reflected in the humdrum
understatement of "Just neutral-tinted haps and such". As
Hardy noted on New Year's Day, 1902: "Pessimism (or rather
what is called such) . . . is the only view of life in which you can
never be disappointed. Having reckoned what to do in the worst

possible circumstances, when better arise, as they may, life becomes child's play."[11]

So the sensitive and emotionally susceptible nature was kept in check by the scrupulous intellect and the historical awareness which cohabited in Hardy. Likewise the countryman-born refused a romantic idealisation of the natural world around him, seeing the blind-wrought havoc of the Drowsing Mother expressed in the cankers and poisons of wood and field.

IN A WOOD

From *The Woodlanders*

Pale beech and pine so blue,
        Set in one clay,
Bough to bough cannot you
        Live out your day?
When the rains skim and skip,
Why mar sweet comradeship,
Blighting with poison-drip
        Neighbourly spray?

Heart-halt and spirit-lame,
        City-opprest,
Unto this wood I came
        As to a nest;
Dreaming that sylvan peace
Offered the harrowed ease –
Nature a soft release
        From men's unrest.

But, having entered in,
        Great growths and small
Show them to men akin –
        Combatants all!
Sycamore shoulders oak,
Bines the slim sapling yoke,
Ivy-spun halters choke
        Elms stout and tall.

Touches from ash, O wych,
        Sting you like scorn!
You, too, brave hollies, twitch
        Sidelong from thorn.

Even the rank poplars bear
Lothly a rival's air,
Cankering in blank despair
If overborne.

Since, then, no grace I find
Taught me of trees,
Turn I back to my kind,
Worthy as these.
There at least smiles abound,
There discourse trills around,
There, now and then, are found
Life-loyalties.

1887: 1896

1896 may have been one of the worst years in Hardy's life – the bitter attacks on *Jude*, the book's final contribution to his marriage breakdown, the waning of his hoped-for relationship with Mrs Henniker; the year of "Wessex Heights" and "In Tenebris" I and II. But he could still see clearly that all was not lost, and with characteristic realism qualify the human condition as part glorious, part fallen:

There, now and then, are found
Life-loyalties.

This recognition of things as they are and could be is everywhere in his poetry: it is shown in his frequent choice of the everyday incident, the commonplace in life, to provoke a philosophical reflection. "There is enough poetry in what is left [in life], after all the false romance has been abstracted, to make a sweet pattern."[12] It is shown in his steadfast rejection of the merely sentimental.

HER INITIALS

Upon a poet's page I wrote
Of old two letters of her name;
Part seemed she of the effulgent thought
Whence that high singer's rapture came.
– When now I turn the leaf the same
Immortal light illumes the lay,
But from the letters of her name
The radiance has waned away!

1869

No rose-coloured romantic light clings to this dead passion. This is seen all the more clearly for the structure of the poem. The repetition of "the letters of her name" and of the image of light in both halves of the poem conditions us to expect sameness; and as if to stress the sameness the poem pivots on the word "same" in a position of maximum exposure. But the surprise of the last line shows us, in particular contrast to the immortal light which still floods the page, the faded, denatured letters which are *not* the same, which have become nothing. Hardy has his dreams, and values them as part of the life of the imagination: but in honesty to himself he must ask and answer:

what do we know best?
That a fresh love-leaf crumpled soon will dry.[13]

The imagination is always submitted to the cold light of day, and to the everyday surroundings of life. Hardy's realism is holistic. He does not lift situations out of the wider context of the experience but includes it in his scrutiny. So his settings symbolise this wider context. Some are set in glorious sunshine, some in drab, fly-blown waiting-rooms or in a bleak cold house, at a sodden sheep-fair, or where nettles mask a grave. He has no sentimentality either about human failings. He sees how we cloak reality from ourselves. In the poem "My Cicely" we saw how the lover deliberately closed his eyes to the fact of his former lover's degeneration and chose to cling to the illusion of her death; and Hardy implicitly criticizes him, showing his rejection and separation from the landscape itself. The lover speaks:

So, lest I disturb my choice vision,
   I shun the West highway,
Even now, when the knaps ring with rhythms
   From blackbird and bee;

And feel that with slumber half-conscious
   She rests in the church-hay
Her spirit unsoiled as in youth-time
   When lovers were we.

In another poem, "In Front of the Landscape", the speaker's vision of the landscape around him is "blotted to feeble mist" by "the intenser/Stare of the mind" – the ghosts of past people and scenes he sees surging in a tide of images across his view. It ends in an intricate irony characteristic of Hardy. His speaker is blinded by his self-absorption and cannot see the real landscape; whereas "passing people" look at him and, similarly self-absorbed, cannot see his equally "real" inner thoughts.[14]

   Hardy's ironic detachment is a powerful aid to his "hawk's vision" of life; and as usual there is a strong counter-pull from his feelings of compassion. The two in harness make for an experience that we know to be real and true.

"AH, ARE YOU DIGGING ON MY GRAVE?"

"Ah, are you digging on my grave
   My loved one? – planting rue?"
– "No: yesterday he went to wed
One of the brightest wealth has bred.
'It cannot hurt her now', he said,
   'That I should not be true.'"

"Then who is digging on my grave?
   My nearest dearest kin?"
– "Ah, no; they sit and think, 'What use!
What good will planting flowers produce?
No tendance of her mound can loose
   Her spirit from Death's gin.'"

"But some one digs upon my grave?
   My enemy? – prodding sly?"
– "Nay: when she heard you had passed the Gate
That shuts on all flesh soon or late,

> She thought you no more worth her hate,
>   And cares not where you lie."
>
> "Then, who is digging on my grave?
>   Say – since I have not guessed!"
> – "O it is I, my mistress dear,
> Your little dog, who still lives near,
> And much I hope my movements here
>   Have not disturbed your rest?"
>
> "Ah, yes! *You* dig upon my grave ...
>   Why flashed it not on me
> That one true heart was left behind!
> What feeling do we ever find
> To equal among human kind
>   A dog's fidelity!"
>
> "Mistress, I dug upon your grave
>   To bury a bone, in case
> I should be hungry near this spot
> When passing on my daily trot.
> I am sorry, but I quite forgot
>   It was your resting-place."

After the sugary language of the dead woman there is liberation in the gentle, but total, honesty which, by the end, makes the reader come to rest on the hard bedrock of the truth.

This poem was first published in 1913. Hardy (by now a Georgian poet) was able to reject, as he always had done, Victorian sentimentality. It is interesting to look at what Ezra Pound in 1917 was hoping for in the poetry of the twentieth-century:

> It will, I think, move against poppy-cock, it will be harder and saner, it will be what Mr Hewlett calls "nearer the bone". It will be as much like granite as it can be, its force will be in its Truth ... I mean it will not try to seem forcible by rhetorical din, and luxurious riot. We will have fewer painted adjectives impeding the shock and stroke of it. At least for myself, I want it so, austere, direct, free from emotional slither.[15]

One knows just what Pound means by "emotional slither"; and one rarely meets it in Hardy. Nor does one often meet "rhetorical din" (unless deliberately, on the part of some "dramatic impersonator"); for Hardy's restraint, his very lack of rhetoric, is among the ways by which his sincerity is expressed. He drew strength from "the force of reserve, and the emphasis of understatement."[16] If we look back to "The Whitewashed Wall" (p 11) we see something of this strength through deep simplicity and understatement, through

> Its whitewashed bareness more than the sight
> Of a rose in richest green.

The homely conversational tone, with that pivoting "Well," which we have come to understand in Hardy, lowers our defences and lulls our expectations. But there is an inexorable accumulation of power as one reads, until almost the last moment: and here it flows out unchecked in those strangely magical last four lines. As a perceptive unnamed reviewer wrote of this poem on publication:[17]

> It seems to be prosaically told. At least there is no line, until you reach the last four, that stops you with its beauty; and you run through the beauty of the last four to reach the end; and then the beauty of the whole takes you and flows back through the whole poem.

In those bare, mainly monosyllabic lines, where a word like "labouring" glows with unexpected depth, Hardy enables us mainly by suggestion to share in the vivid experience of a dreaming woman, and to catch the finality in her son's "sheet of white".

In place of rhetoric Hardy concentrates and distils essential emotion; and he can do it with the plainest of words and the most ordinary of metres. In the following poem the tone varies between lyric warmth and heroic austerity.

THE END OF THE EPISODE

> Indulge no more may we
> In this sweet-bitter pastime:
> The love-light shines the last time
> Between you, Dear, and me.

There shall remain no trace
Of what so closely tied us,
And blank as ere love eyed us
Will be our meeting-place.

The flowers and thymy air,
Will they now miss our coming?
The dumbles thin their humming
To find we haunt not there?

Though fervent was our vow,
Though ruddily ran our pleasure,
Bliss has fulfilled its measure,
And sees its sentence now.

Ache deep; but make no moans:
Smile out; but stilly suffer:
The paths of love are rougher
Than thoroughfares of stones.

The gentle and almost childlike musings about "the flowers and thymy air" shine out between the sterner lines; and how effective is the unusual choice of "ruddily" (and its extra syllable in the line) – a word which, though often associated with health, also carries overtones of its exact opposite, the overflow into apoplexy, and the glare of sinister fires. The alliteratively linked phrase "Though ruddily ran our pleasure" may suggest in the dimmest recesses of the mind something like a blood-tinged stream in flux; the evocation of bliss is sharply cut off as soon as it appears. The warmth and fluency of this stanza turn into the flinty suppressions of the last.

In this restraint and detachment there is always a self-effacement. However strong the emotion, however thoughtful a meditation, Hardy contrives to stand back, showing first what caused his emotion rather than the emotion itself – so that the reader both shares individually in the experience and also finds it to be a universal one, a cause for common reflection. He tells a story or paints a picture, but he himself is often absent.

A LIGHT SNOW-FALL AFTER FROST

On the flat road a man at last appears:
How much his whitening hairs

Owe to the settling snow's mute anchorage,
And how much to a life's rough pilgrimage,
    One cannot certify.

The frost is on the wane,
And cobwebs hanging close outside the pane
Pose as festoons of thick white worsted there,
Of their pale presence no eye being aware
    Till the rime made them plain.

A second man comes by;
His ruddy beard brings fire to the pallid scene:
    His coat is faded green;
    Hence seems it that his mien
    Wears something of the dye
Of the berried holm-trees that he passes nigh.

The snow-feathers so gently swoop that though
    But half an hour ago
The road was brown, and now is starkly white,
A watcher would have failed defining quite
    When it transformed it so.

Near Surbiton

This poem is one of the most fascinating examples of Hardy's art. What is it about? Apparently, unexciting suburbia. Why is it worth turning into a poem? From its opening, on a "flat" road, to its end, it is all about muteness and uncertainty and realisation: the cloaking of snow, the cloaking of identities, the cloaking of change, the uncloaking of awareness. The reader is led through one uncertainty after another: "no eye being aware"; "hence seems it...", "something of the dye"; "A watcher would have failed defining quite/When it transformed it so."

The tentativeness shifts. Momentarily it clarifies and then it dulls again, heightening one's impression of instability and unknowing. It is, one senses, after a long stillness that a man "at last" appears. The reader knows nothing about him and cannot even tell his age by his hair. Then time and temperature-change reveal something else. In the true Hardyan situation, the world moving onward shows us something mutely present all the time which we have been too blind to see – the cobwebs now outlined in frost. And then there is a surge of colour, green and red and

fire as the second man comes by; until he too blends into the
green and red of hollies and loses such identity as he had. We are
adrift in the silent eddy of snowflakes; and it is "starkly" that the
surprise comes, that the world has changed – yet how, or when,
it happened, we hardly know. The watcher we faintly inferred
from the first stanza's "one" has receded into a conditional tense
as if he or she were only hypothetically there. Are we the
watcher or is there another? Do we as readers have any link with
either watcher or watched, who have mingled with their
surroundings? All these blurred identities are dramatised in the
obscure double "it" of the last line, when subject and object are
the same word, and one hardly fathoms what the first "it"
means.

It isn't known exactly when Hardy wrote this poem – or
wrote it first (he and Emma lived in Surbiton for the winter of
1874–5). But it is clear from the holograph prepared for
publication in 1925 that he originally wrote it without the
second stanza. This is added, at the bottom of the holograph
page, to the originally complete poem. The interesting thing is
that he had used a very similar image in *Tess of the d'Urbervilles*
(published in 1891, but re-read by Hardy for the Wessex Edition
of 1912–14 and the Mellstock Edition of 1919–20). The
difference between the two images in novel and poem is a subtle
one. In *Tess* (chapter 43):

> Cobwebs revealed their presence on sheds and walls where
> none had ever been observed till brought out into visibility by
> the crystallizing atmosphere, hanging like loops of white
> worsted from salient points of the outhouses, posts, and gates.

While this is part of an outdoor description of an unusually
severe winter, in the poem one realises that the cobweb is seen
from the *inside*. We look outwards, through the pane and
through the cobwebs: but we do not know at what point we have
become aware of them, aware of the changes taking place in the
road outside and the road of life, the changes symbolised in the
ambiguous, or twofold, whitening of the hair. During this half-
hour, one of the most certain facts in the poem, our watching of
a scene (through that favourite Hardy metaphor, the window of
the mind) becomes a realisation that the scene-changes mirror,

and clarify, our life's changes: the poem has been a new experiencing of life.

* * * * * *

We began to read "A Light Snow-Fall after Frost" as an example of Hardy's self-effacement and his power to draw us in, without pressure, to find the truth in an experience ourselves. He does not want to come between the reader and the picture, either by his own rhetoric or as an intrusive narrator. The identity of the speaker in many of his poems is a puzzle – even in an intensely personal poem like "The Phantom Horsewoman". In several poems he surprises us by revealing at the end that the person we thought was the narrator was in fact listening to somebody else.[18] It is one of many questions readers have to consider. If the puzzle of the narrator's identity is partly to reflect both the ambiguities of life and the universality of human experience, it also keeps Hardy almost anonymous. He is free to draw a picture, and a conclusion, with as little emphasis as he likes: a picture, perhaps, of almost nothing, the most ordinary incidents of life, which he turns into a moment of understanding.

LIFE AND DEATH AT SUNRISE

(Near Dogbury Gate, 1867)

The hills uncap their tops
Of woodland, pasture, copse,
And look on the layers of mist
At their foot that still persist:
They are like awakened sleepers on one elbow lifted,
Who gaze around to learn if things during night have shifted.

A waggon creaks up from the fog
With a laboured leisurely jog;
Then a horseman from off the hill-tip
Comes clapping down into the dip;
While woodlarks, finches, sparrows, try to entune at one time,
And cocks and hens and cows and bulls take up the chime.

With a shouldered basket and flagon
A man meets the one with the waggon,
And both the men halt of long use.

> "Well," the waggoner says, "What's the news?"
> "– 'Tis a boy this time. You've just met the doctor trotting
>   back.
> She's doing very well. And we think we shall call him 'Jack'."

> "And what have you got covered there?'
> He nods to the waggon and mare.
> "Oh, a coffin for old John Thinn:
>   We are just going to put him in."
> "– So he's gone at last. He always had a good constitution."
> "– He was ninety-odd. He could call up the French Revolution."

So unprententious is this poem, and so prosaic its dialogue, that
at first one may wonder at the point of it. But as so often with
Hardy there is enough to keep the reader unfolding many layers
of meaning and allusion.[19] There is in fact a relaxed lightness of
tone that his critics often miss, as he raises the absurd babel of
sound from the tuning orchestra of bird and cock and bull and
matches their activities with the beginning of the human day –
just as the encounter of dawn and night in the mists up the
hillside is matched by the meeting of the messengers of life and
death, of Jack and John, of human kind eternally renewing itself.
Simon Gatrell recalls Hardy's echo of *The Winter's Tale*, "Thou
mettest with things dying, I with new-born". The same
Olympian view of first and last things in the human story (as
observed by the waking hills) is strengthened by the evocation of
the French Revolution.

This apparently throw-away line at the end is paralleled by
others in Hardy's poems – like the last line, for example, of
"Julie-Jane", or a poem about the tragedy of love, betrayal, and
suicide, "The Rash Bride", which ends at the graveside with the
simple note:

> We sang the Ninetieth Psalm to her – set to Saint Stephen's
>   tune.

These endings tie us to reality, do not let us escape into
sentimentality, remind us that it is in everyday things that we
have to find meaning, and answer "the eternal question of what
Life was".

Hardy continues to ask this question; but he will not answer it
for others. He puts before us a situation and we can take it or
leave it. Often there is a moral problem posed, or a riddle of life

which his particular cast of mind appreciated, which both he and we have to solve for ourselves – if we can. He will neither push himself beyond what he sees as truth – only "now and then, are found/Life-loyalties" – nor will he push readers. In fact, he will not even help them to understand, but keeps them at arms' length, to make their own discoveries by puzzling over his obscurities. We saw this in the blank walls and ellipses of "All's closed now" and "No answerer I . . ." Look at these two poems.

JUST THE SAME

I sat. It all was past;
Hope never would hail again;
Fair days had ceased at a blast,
The world was a darkened den.

The beauty and dream were gone,
And the halo in which I had hied
So gaily gallantly on
Had suffered blot and died!

I went forth, heedless whither,
In a cloud too black for name:
– People frisked hither and thither;
The world was just the same.

From the extraordinary, transfixed, "I sat" at the opening, to the simple end, the poem vibrates with tremendous emotion. But when one comes to examine the words (like "hail") and the specific nature of this experience, the meaning is obscure. Has the world changed to a darkened den, or is it just the same? Is it a criticism, or just a fact, that people are frisking so incongruously while the dark cloud envelops and the blast withers, and is the "hail" an effect of the blast, or of amiable good manners?

This is Hardy giving the essence of an experience; if the reader does not understood, well, life is incomprehensible anyway, and each must find the truth in his or her own way. Similarly in this poem:

THE MISSED TRAIN

How I was caught
Hieing home, after days of allure,

And forced to an inn – small, obscure –
At the junction, gloom-fraught.

How civil my face
To get them to chamber me there –
A roof I had scorned, scarce aware
That it stood at the place.

And how all the night
I had dreams of the unwitting cause
Of my lodgment. How lonely I was;
How consoled by her sprite!

Thus, onetime to me ...
Dim wastes of dead years bar away
Then from now. But such happenings to-day
Fall to lovers, may be!

Years, years as shoaled seas,
Truly, stretch now between! Less and less
Shrink the visions then vast in me. – Yes,
Then in me: Now in these.

In the first three stanzas one thinks one knows what he is talking about. Then begin the ellipses and the broken lines, until in the last stanza, apart from the wonderful image "Years as shoaled seas", nothing is really clear; and Hardy just isn't telling any more.

He pushes us away, partly for privacy, partly so that we work for ourselves, and partly because often for him there is no answer to the problem of suffering, no means of understanding the riddles of the universe. He faces this not only with stoicism[20] but with humility.

THE YEAR'S AWAKENING

How do you know that the pilgrim track
Along the belting zodiac
Swept by the sun in his seeming rounds
Is traced by now to the Fishes' bounds
And into the Ram, when weeks of cloud
Have wrapt the sky in a clammy shroud,
And never as yet a tint of spring

Has shown in the Earth's apparelling;
   O vespering bird, how do you know,
     How do you know?

How do you know, deep underground,
Hid in your bed from sight and sound,
Without a turn in temperature,
With weather life can scarce endure,
That light has won a fraction's strength,
And day put on some moments' length,
Whereof in merest rote will come,
Weeks hence, mild airs that do not numb;
   O crocus root, how do you know,
     How do you know?

February 1910

AN AUGUST MIDNIGHT

I

A shaded lamp and a waving blind,
And the beat of a clock from a distant floor:
On this scene enter – winged, horned, and spined –
A longlegs, a moth, and a dumbledore;
While mid my page there idly stands
A sleepy fly, that rubs its hands...

II

Thus meet we five, in this still place,
At this point of time, at this point in space.
– My guests besmear my new-penned line,
Or bang at the lamp and fall supine.
"God's humblest, they!" I muse. Yet why?
They know Earth-secrets that know not I.

Max Gate, 1899.

Hardy may feel the limitations of his understanding, but he always pursues what he believes to be the truth, just as he pursues the search for "a way to the Better", no matter what he finds.

HE PREFERS HER EARTHLY

This after-sunset is a sight for seeing,
Cliff-heads of craggy cloud surrounding it.
    – And dwell you in this glory-show?
You may; for there are strange strange things in being,
    Stranger than I know.

Yet if that chasm of splendour claim your presence
Which glows between the ash cloud and the dun,
    How changed must be your mortal mould!
Changed to a firmament-riding earthless essence
    From what you were of old:

All too unlike the fond and fragile creature
Then known to me.... Well, shall I say it plain?
    I would not have you thus and there,
But still would grieve on, missing you, still feature
    You as the one you were.

This fine evocation of Emma as a "firmament-riding earthless
essence" recalls both "The Phantom Horsewoman" and "A
Woman Driving" (whose last stanza was quoted on p 113).
However ethereal the vision, he prefers her visible presence,
warts and all, and his honesty usually extends to recognition of
his own warts. Here, however, is the one area in which Hardy
appears to delude himself, or to stray from the truth: Emma's
death. The shock and guilt he experienced may have been so
personally unbearable that he deceived himself and others; and
as years passed he came to believe the account of her death and
its unexpectedness which he had everywhere given.

"Best Times" shows something of his difficulty. This poem
reviews the happiest times of their life together, from
Sturminster Newton backwards to Hardy's first arrival at St
Juliot.

BEST TIMES

We went a day's excursion to the stream,
Basked by the bank, and bent to the ripple-gleam,
    And I did not know
    That life would show,
However it might flower, no finer glow.

I walked in the Sunday sunshine by the road
That wound towards the wicket of your abode,
    And I did not think
    That life would shrink
To nothing ere it shed a rosier pink.

Unlooked for I arrived on a rainy night,
And you hailed me at the door by the swaying light,
    And I full forgot
    That life might not
Again be touching that ecstatic height.

And that calm eve when you walked up the stair,
After a gaiety prolonged and rare,
    No thought soever
    That you might never
Walk down again, struck me as I stood there.

Rewritten from an old draft

The "old draft" is thought to be one of the earliest poems Hardy wrote after that catastrophic November day when he "saw morning harden upon the wall". Only the previous day he must have been aware of Emma's painful drag up the stairs to her attics in Max Gate. At some point, he changed the poem significantly to fit the story he had always maintained. In the earliest version, which got as far as the holograph, the last stanza had begun:

And that calm evening when you climbed the stair,
After a languid rising from your chair....

* * * * * *

Hardy said that his *Poems of 1912–13* were "an expiation". It was not until 1922 that he published "Best Times" and, at the end of the same volume, a poem called "Surview", whose epigraph was a line from Psalm 119, "I thought on my ways". This may have been a healing farewell to guilt. Certainly the tone of many poems in the succeeding volume, *Human Shows*, is mellow and genial, as befits what Dennis Taylor calls the "Indian summer" in which Hardy wrote more pastoral poems, and probably more light-hearted ones, than at any other time. In "Surview", courageously placed as the prominent last poem of

Late Lyrics and Earlier, he appraises his own failure to attain to St Paul's model of love.

SURVIEW

"Cogitavi vias meas"

A cry from the green-grained sticks of the fire
  Made me gaze where it seemed to be:
'Twas my own voice talking therefrom to me
On how I had walked when my sun was higher –
  My heart in its arrogancy.

"You held not to whatsoever was true,"
  Said my own voice talking to me:
*"Whatsoever was just you were slack to see;
Kept not things lovely and pure in view,"*
  Said my own voice talking to me.

"You slighted her that endureth all,"
  Said my own voice talking to me;
*"Vaunteth not, trusteth hopefully;
That suffereth long and is kind withal,"*
  Said my own voice talking to me.

"You taught not that which you set about,"
  Said my own voice talking to me;
"That the greatest of things is Charity...."
– And the sticks burnt low, and the fire went out,
  And my voice ceased talking to me.

This honest poem reflects something of Hardy's high principles. Few poets have set their sights on "lovingkindness", and measured themselves so sternly against the truth. But Hardy cared about truth, and knew that one of its faculties is that it "shall make you free" – a statement attributed to Jesus only a few verses beyond his refusal to condemn a woman caught in adultery. In "The Revisitation", for example, it was recognising the truth which set the soldier free – "Soon I got the Route elsewhither". It is no accident that at the end of his long life Hardy's final farewell, in the posthumous *Winter Words*, ended with this:

And if my vision range beyond

The blinkered sight of souls in bond,
  – By truth made free –
I'll let all be,
And show to no man what I see.

[*He Resolves to Say No More*]

Notes

1 *Apology to Late Lyrics and Earlier.* The "questionings" come from Wordsworth's *Ode: Intimations of Immortality,* l.142.

2 8 January 1910. *Casebook,* 58.

3 *Life,* 385.

4 *To a Lady; A Night of Questionings.* "Art has the curious faculty of seeking truth without at the same time pretending to certainty." – G.D. Martin, *Language, Truth and Poetry* (Edinburgh 1975), 1.

5 Blake, *Proverbs of Hell;* Russell, quoted by G.D. Martin, *op cit,* 72; for a relevant Gorgias quotation see, for example, the entry under *Truth* in Brewer's *Dictionary of Phrase and Fable.*

6 Gunn, *op cit, Agenda,* 44–5; I.A. Richards, *Practical Criticism* (London 1929), Pt III, ch 7.

7 *Life,* 162, 161, 310.

8 Psalm 101, 5 in the Vulgate is 102, 4 in the Authorised Version, where it reads: "My heart is smitten, and withered like grass."

9 I.A. Richards, *Science and Poetry,* 68, quoted *Casebook,* 111.

10 *The Face at the Casement:* some published versions had "But O, too, Love is cruel"; *A Private Man on Public Men.*

11 *Life,* 15–16; *Jude the Obscure,* ch II; *Life,* 311.

12 *Life,* 114.

13 See *On a Fine Morning. A Young Man's Exhortation.*

14 Ronald Marken develops this in his excellent essay, *PTH,* 92. This poem is discussed again in Chapter XI.

15 Pound, "A Retrospect", Credo, in *The Literary Essays of Ezra Pound*, ed T.S. Eliot (London 1954).

16 *Life*, 363.

17 *Times Literary Supplement*, 1 June 1922.

18 Eg *The Paphian Ball, The Choirmaster's Burial*.

19 Jean Brooks in her excellent *Thomas Hardy: The Poetic Structure* (London 1971), Dennis Taylor and Simon Gatrell in *PTH* discuss this poem.

20 Cf *The Impercipient, Nature's Questioning*, etc.

10

MOON IN THE BRANCHES

Patterns of Life

Beside the path on this journey have been rue and bane, roses and thorns, iris and peony and thymy air. The reader has been lit by moon and stars, sunshine and paradisal skies, or choked in fogs and dashed with wind and rain, meshed in webs, imprisoned in tombs, confined with the whirr of manic clocks, or warmed by the lilt of song and dance. This is the natural domain of Hardy's imagination and memory, the deep well from which his images spring.

If we were to discuss imagery as it deserves, we should be on a lifetime's pilgrimage and this would be a different book. Many poets and critics have illuminated (and befogged) this complex subject and divergence of opinion is wide. Let us try to agree on a few signposts.

All human life is an exploration of meaning, a search for an order and a pattern which makes sense and gives delight – "the abiding impulse in every human being to seek order and harmony behind the manifold and the changing in the existing world". Those are a physicist's words, quoted by a poet.[1] Though in different ways, poet and scientist both search for reality. We have to use words as part of the search: but words are limited and limiting. We can never adequately describe in words, for example, the power of love; and we can also subtly (but severely) maim our understanding by the names we give to things or people, our tendency to pigeon-hole and categorize, and our resistance to the necessary continual change of those categories.

In the "real world", in "reality", nothing stands on its own. Reality is a tissue of relationship; and when we search for reality it can never be isolated, either from the world we live in or from ourselves. Hardy noted, as the idea for *The Dynasts* germinated in him, "The human race to be shown as one great network or tissue which quivers in every point when one point is shaken, like a spider's web if touched".

> Man is all symmetry,
>   Full of proportions, one limb to another,
>   And all to all the world beside:
>   Each part may call the furthest, brother:
> For head with foot hath private amity,
>   And both with moons and tides.[2]

So the search for reality cannot be mere dry dissection. If it involves humanity it involves mind, spirit and senses, a passion in the search, and the great pool of consciousness and sub-consciousness where feeling, imagination and intuition are guide, prophet, and queen.

Out of this pool comes, in our exploration of the relationships of this world – between things and feelings and thoughts – the deep need for metaphor. A seed lying in darkness, it germs and swells and buds into the light, where following it one finds revealed something of the pattern of the world. Imagery helps us to make connections. By its revelations and its beauty it answers our search and, like a draught of cool spring water, satisfies the thirst for understanding.

An image is not just a word-picture. It has to create for us a new understanding, a new experience, not just of the two (or more) things related, but of our conception of them. When Hardy ends a story of the death of love with:

> And the west dims, and yellow lamplights shine:
> And soon above, like lamps more opaline,
>   White stars ghost forth, that care not for men's wives,
>   Or any other lives.[3]

– our perception of the difference between the "yellow lamplights" of the town and the cool, distant "opaline" stars includes not only something about each, but about their place in our human situation. We look at them with new eyes. And when "white stars ghost forth" that perception grows again, not only with the absoluteness of whiteness and neutrality, but with the overtones of unhappy death, the pale uncertainties and alienations of the universe. The known of our senses has carried us across into the unknown, transcendent world beyond.

An image must persuade us of its truth. Not all do. We all know about mixed and muddled metaphors (like the Deputy Head's actual advice to the new prefects, "If the First Years shoot their horns, well, pull them up, and sit on them.") But, more seriously, even good poets can, and do, produce images that are imperfectly or unconvincingly conceived or carried through, either in themselves, or because they fail to fit and illuminate the general theme of a poem. One of Hardy's most curious is in an early poem (1866) in which he blames himself for an unworthy desire to escape from a friend's pain:

A CONFESSION TO A FRIEND IN TROUBLE

Your troubles shrink not, though I feel them less
Here, far away, than when I tarried near;
I even smile old smiles – with listlessness –
Yet smiles they are, not ghastly mockeries mere.

A thought too strange to house within my brain
Haunting its outer precincts I discern:
– *That I will not show zeal again to learn*
Your griefs, and, sharing them, renew my pain. . . .

It goes, like murky bird or buccaneer
That shapes its lawless figure on the main,
And staunchness tends to banish utterly
The unseemly instinct that had lodgment here;
Yet, comrade old, can bitterer knowledge be
Than that, though banned, such instinct was in me!

1866
16 Westbourne Park Villas

What does a reader visualise? What is a murky bird? And what is a pirate doing here, and the vastness of the seas, when the only other image is one of lodging and precincts? One can argue that Hardy wished to show how foreign was this intrusive thought to true friendship, wished to outlaw it from his mind; but for many people the image is probably hard to accommodate, and unproductive of that bound of delight and revelation which an apt connection gives. Yet it is often by the very strangeness of his images that Hardy makes one think about ordinary and extraordinary human experience. It is possible to be arrogant or superficial in the quick dismissal of an image which does not immediately speak to one, or which seems to have lost its freshness. For others it may speak; or the poet's purpose may have escaped us. When some Hardy character, for example, conventionally describes his lost love as "pure as cloistered nun", Hardy may be deliberately showing an unimaginative man who thinks in clichés and is rigid of mind. He often uses a conventional image like this; or he may transform it by his own particular alchemy to give a new freshness an idea one had thought exhausted:

> I hid him deep in nodding rye and oat –
> His shroud green stalks and loam;
> His requiem the corn-blade's husky note –
> And then I hurried home....[4]

Many of his brief undeveloped metaphors are vivid, springing from the observant artist's eye, or his penetrating mind and awareness of words and sounds. In the same (anti-) war poem the reader sees at once the picture, and the significance, when

>   dykes of dead
> Lay between vale and ridge;

one hears only too clearly

>   that ever upspread from the dank deathbed
> A miles-wide pant of pain;

and, more cheerfully, in "At Tea", how

> The kettle descants in a cosy drone.

Hardy's most interesting imagery, however, is, predictably, developed at some length and more subtly, as part of his continuing search into reality. Certain images are explored repeatedly in series after series of poems. Among these one can pick out groups of poems about light (including sun and moon), about fire, about music, about leaves and trees, birds, fairs, imprisonment, railways and things mechanical, stairs, windows and clocks, one who returns, and webs, patterns and silhouettes of all kinds. So rich and complex is this imagery pattern that here

I can only lift a corner of the covering and point to what lies underneath.

Let us, for example, pick out a poem (written on his 73rd birthday) in which the whole poem – a picture of the dismantling of a fair – is an image of something else.

EXEUNT OMNES

I

Everybody else, then, going,
And I still left where the fair was?...
Much have I seen of neighbour loungers
Making a lusty showing,
Each now past all knowing.

II

There is an air of blankness
In the street and the littered spaces;
Thoroughfare, steeple, bridge and highway
Wizen themselves to lankness;
Kennels dribble dankness.

III

Folk all fade. And whither,
As I wait alone where the fair was?
Into the clammy and numbing night-fog
Whence they entered hither.
Soon one more goes thither!

2 June 1913

He stands, like the ghosts who were once "neighbour loungers", watching the end of the fair, but so lost in his reverie that when he suddenly rouses, he finds it is all over. The first stanza has pulled us from the hearty present into the past; and in the second, the "littered spaces" may remind us of the years-cluttered mind; the strange "wizening" of hard surface and stone may call up more vividly the emaciation of old age; and then the people fade away, back into the "numbing night-fog" from which they came. It is not until the last line that this image of life as a fair, and its ending as death, becomes clear – but it is a clarity within obscurity, within the mist of the question-marks, for what do we really understand about life or death? The puzzle is underlined by the rhyme scheme: all are feminine endings, except, paradoxically, the stressed masculine endings used just where the uncertainties are emphasised, either in a question-mark or the confusion of darkness and fog.

Dark is a word, and an idea, which Hardy uses frequently:

The thing is dark, Dear. I do not know.

[*In the Vaulted Way*]

And hence our deep division, and our dark undying pain.

[*Had You Wept*]

Like so many other recurrent words in his poems, it is a part, like a jigsaw piece, of his understanding of life's pattern and puzzle. We cannot study here all the single words which he develops as images or symbols; but we can notice a few as examples before picking out two or three for a harder look.[5] One finds, for instance, that *shine* tends (though not invariably) to be associated with unhappiness or transience, while *glow* is more often the tone of happiness. We have noticed too how often he uses a negative form like *unbe, unblooms, moveless, stirless* – sometimes to suggest most poignantly its positive. Music too is a natural image – he calls a poet *that high singer,* speaks of *the human tune,* or the dying father whose wheezy breathing was echoed by a robin *in antiphon.* (Excluding reference to bees' hum and birdsong, or dance alone, over 250 poems refer to music.[6] We have read several poems where *birds* – tiny powerless creatures – are images of triumph over time and death and cruelty, of aspiration and hope, and of zest in living and the constant renewal of life. *The landscape* is another vital image: in poems like "The Wind's Prophecy" and "A New Year's Eve in War Time" the landscape or weather around a person images the tumult within. So at the frozen death of a marriage one Christmas "the trees went on with their spitting amid the icicled haze".[7]

If frost is always a symbol of misery, *fire* is an even more important image in Hardy's series of explorations through over a hundred poems. We have already seen the slow, timeless burning of couch grass and the consuming of the old traces of love's flame, the embers of memory, with "spent flames limning ghosts", the dying fire as shadow to the dying day, the essential domestic security of the hearth, where to be "friendless, fireless",[8] is most to be pitied. Fire is the comparison used for the revealing sun in "The Revisitation", for the "liquor-fired" face of "My Cicely"; for "love's burn" and "the one who kindled gaily/Love's fitful ecstasies!"[9] Fire has overweening power. "Some have fire in the eyes"; some are "fire-filled prophets"; some suffer "words that burned/ My fond frail happiness out of me". Savagely, when fed an old photograph, the fire, as Time's destroyer, "gnawed at the delicate bosom's defenceless round... Till the flame had eaten her breasts, and mouth, and hair".[10]

Above all, fire brings a sharp moment of crisis – the blinded bird's "stab of fire" – or of illumination, when something is "flashed home", when Barnes' coffin was revealed as it "flashed the fire of the sun", when a solution "bursts in a flame... upon me!" The moment of understanding is often painful, its premonition ominous – like the partnership of "phantasmal fears,/And the flap of the flame", and the desperate misery of a loveless marriage prefigured, as

> Above the level horizon spread
> The sunrise, firing them from foot to head
> From its smouldering lair,
> And painting their pillows with dyes of red.[11]

Just as *shine* is often sinister, so is *red* – the colour of blood and war and too-seductive peony lips. Colours and light form other important clusters of poems. There is a "secret light of greens" which is not merely conventional as an image of youth, spring, and immortality, but can turn ominously "yellow-green" in "green-rheumed clouds", like the "witch-flame's weirdsome sheen" which distorts our view of reality.[12] Colours are used as metaphysical counters – in the purple light of paradise and love, in "hope-hues", and when "primal rightness took the tinct of wrong". White is often the colour of death: that hatred of frost, which he links with fear and Time's destruction, may be behind this reiterated theme:

> Care whitely watching, Sorrows manifold

and

And my dream was scared, and expired on a moan,
And I whitely hastened away.[13]

Close to white are the neutral tones, the ashen pallor of misery
and suffocating time which we have already met. These tones
are lifeless and faded, utterly denuded of light.

Light is perhaps most important of all: the light in human eyes,
the light of sun and star-shine and lighthouse, and above all the
light, the gaze, the probing of the moon. (It is no surprise to learn
that the hymn "Lead, kindly light", sung at his obsequies, was
one of Hardy's favourites.) Readers of the *Life* will recall his love
of Turner's painting, particularly "in his maddest and greatest
days", when, Hardy writes, recognising "the impossibility of
really reproducing on canvas all that is in a landscape, [Turner]
gives for that which cannot be reproduced a something else
which shall have upon the spectator an approximate effect to
that of the real. . . . Hence, one may say, Art is the secret of how
to produce by a false thing the effect of a true. . . ." How does
Turner produce this effect? Chiefly by bringing to bear his own
inner vision, his total self, upon what he sees; and by his use of
light. Hardy had been at the Royal Academy when he wrote
those words. "Turner's watercolours: each is a landscape *plus* a
man's soul. . . What he paints chiefly is light as modified by
objects. . . ."[14] For Hardy light had something of the same
importance as for Turner, an atmosphere which he breathed like
air. If one looks back at many of the poems in this book, they
show light linked with music and laughter, beauty, love, joy,
truth, life and immortality, vision, and the imagination. The
second stanza of "Thoughts of Phena" is an extended metaphor
of life as a light which can dim and go out. Even the programme-
seller in the shadowy theatre of "The Two Rosalinds" was,
significantly and typically, "Hovering mid the shine and shade as
'twixt the live world and the tomb". The "discovered curl of
hair" was once of "brightest brown" and still "beams with live
brown as in its prime". The faithless lover in "The Shiver"
turned to "one of far brighter brow"; and as an old man, Hardy's
mindsight lingers through the mists of time on the remembered
glory of an early love:

Mid this heat, in gauzy muslin
See I Louie's life-lit brow.[15]

Light is to do with "illumination" and the poet's vision – the "effulgent thought" of the high singer in "Her Initials", the floods of light in the poet's bower. It is to do with joy – the dance, lit first by candles and then by the early tints of dawn; the glorious time, "beryl-bespread", when "the radiance went on".[16] The unique bursting of the suffocating cell of Time is achieved into a realm of magic lights.

"SHE OPENED THE DOOR"

> She opened the door of the West to me,
> > With its loud sea-lashings,
> > And cliff-side clashings
> Of waters rife with revelry.
>
> She opened the door of Romance to me,
> > The door from a cell
> > I had known too well,
> Too long, till then, and was fain to flee.
>
> She opened the door of a Love to me,
> > That passed the wry
> > World-welters by
> As far as the arching blue the lea.
>
> > She opens the door of the Past to me,
> > > Its magic lights,
> > > Its heavenly heights,
> > When forward little is to see!

1913

Those magic lights of the past – "when you were all aglow" – were only heightened by the darkness of soul of poems like "In Tenebris". It may have been to acknowledge the power of both darkness and light in life that he placed immediately before the "In Tenebris" group one of the most characteristic and revealing of his shorter poems.

THE SELF-UNSEEING

> Here is the ancient floor,
> Footworn and hollowed and thin,
> Here was the former door
> Where the dead feet walked in.

> She sat here in her chair,
> Smiling into the fire;
> He who played stood there,
> Bowing it higher and higher.
>
> Childlike, I danced in a dream;
> Blessings emblazoned that day;
> Everything glowed with a gleam;
> Yet we were looking away![17]

Though this poem begins somewhat bleakly with its concrete, precise evocation of a place haunted, visibly and tangibly, by the past, the moment the past is remembered as alive the warmth and light begin. The picture of childhood is of glow and gleam, and a deliberate fusion of the heraldic word "emblazon" (again an inscription or engraving, a favourite image), and the later word "emblaze" with its glow/fire meanings. The innocence and simplicity of childhood are quite without visible shadow; the only hint of a figurative one is in the last line.

Most of Hardy's light poems, and his view of life, include the inevitable complement of darkness and shadows – the shadows of our confusion or unheed, shifted by the gradual revelations of the moving moon or the dawn of light, or its photographic opposite, the brightness of transient happiness clouded by the oncoming shadows of slow awareness.

IN HER PRECINCTS

> Her house looked cold from the foggy lea,
> And the square of each window a dull black blur
>   Where showed no stir:
> Yes, her gloom within at the lack of me
> Seemed matching mine at the lack of her.
>
> The black squares grew to be squares of light
> As the eveshade swathed the house and lawn,
>   And viols gave tone;
> There was glee within. And I found that night
> The gloom of severance mine alone.

Kingston-Maurward Park

As "the black squares grew to be squares of light" so did the speaker's realisation grow and change. (Something similar happens near the end of "The Wind's Prophecy".) Hardy's awareness of light, dark and shadow was natural for one whose youth was spent by candle and lamplight; but it must also have been absorbed from his early favourite reading of nineteenth-century Gothic novels such as Harrison Ainsworth's and the elder Dumas' – from the dark streets around Old St Paul's and the shadowy apartments of Windsor Castle and the Louvre. As an architect he was trained, and saturated, in Gothic art at the heyday of the Gothic Revival. His understanding of light and shadow is carried over into his poetry – and into the delicate, significant drawings he made for *Wessex Poems*, particularly those reproduced here. He would have affirmed many of Ruskin's observations about the power of shadow and the realisation of how it moves with the changing light of passing time. "Light deprived of all shadow ceases to be enjoyed as light". Architecture "should express a kind of human sympathy by a measure of darkness as great as there is in human life.... All ... must be done by spaces of light and darkness."[18] We have seen this in many poems – in the shifting shadows of the tree on the white Druid stone, the "stretching spires of shadow" at Hampton Court, where only the unreal "Shades" of history pass "sheer in the sun"; the funeral shades in "The House of Silence" contrasted with "floods of light"; and, in that only half-countenanced laugh, the shadow cast by the girl's bottom lip which "was green in hue whenever she passed/Bright sun on midsummer leaves".

The shadows often bring a message. In "The Later Autumn", when "gone are the lovers", and all is moving towards decay,

> Couch-fires abound
> On fallows around,
> And shades far extend
> Like lives soon to end.

Often in the repeated experience of Hardy's poetry, the shadows grow alongside the light-pattern, hardly perceived; when they finally become apparent, their message is that we are blind until it is too late.

BEFORE AND AFTER SUMMER

I

Looking forward to the spring
One puts up with anything.
On this February day
Though the winds leap down the street,
Wintry scourgings seem but play,
And these later shafts of sleet
– Sharper pointed than the first –
And these later snows – the worst –
Are as a half-transparent blind
Riddled by rays from sun behind.

II

Shadows of the October pine
Reach into this room of mine:
On the pine there swings a bird;
He is shadowed with the tree.
Mutely perched he bills no word;
Blank as I am even is he.
For those happy suns are past,
Fore-discerned in winter last.
When went by their pleasure, then?
I, alas, perceived not when.

In a similar pattern, "Noonshine riddles the ribs of the sunshade"; one recalls the lines and tangles of "The Pedigree" and his father's violin, the "red-veined rocks far West", the "gated ways" and the revealed network of the frosted cobweb, the leafy patterns of "Under the Waterfall" and the tracery of bare branches recurrent through Hardy's poetry. Patterns of all kinds are probably his most searching images. Again it is clear how Gothic principles influenced him, their designs being rooted in nature's intricate curls of leaf and branch and bud. In his autobiography he wrote explicitly about the parallels between poetry and architecture, the unexpected straying of "curved leafage" as of apparently freak metres, and how he "carried on into his verse . . . the Gothic art-principle in which he had been trained – the principle of spontaneity, found in mouldings, tracery, and such like". (Like most of the *Life*, the passage is worth reading.)[19]

But apart from Gothic design's debt to nature, Hardy finds another link. In his *Memories of Church Restoration,* a paper delivered in 1906 to the Society for the Protection of Ancient Buildings, he draws specific attention to where the "essence and soul of an architectural monument" lies. It is not in the material in which it is built, but in the

> forms to which those materials have been shaped. We discern in a moment that it is in the boundary of a solid – its insubstantial superfices or mould – and not in the solid itself, that its right lies to exist as art.

He goes on to say that some of the most perfect examples of Gothic art (like Salisbury Cathedral's north-east aspect, or Merton College chapel's east window) would be just as beautiful if done in some other similar materials "and the old substance be made to vanish for ever". Then comes the perception of the vital link with nature.

> This is, indeed, the actual process of organic nature herself, which is one continuous substitution. She is always discarding the matter, while retaining the form.[20]

So these patterns are linked in his mind with the processes of nature, the inevitability of change, decay and renewal: all the themes of Time's march and product, and the dissynchronisation of mind and surrounding world, which exercised him most.

Almost the first sight of Hardy's world in this book was a quick look at a poem called "The Prospect". There the pattern of branches and veins imaged the experience of his love, first seen under the green trees of summer, then as it developed, until its skeletoned winter. The pattern changes, covering both the evolving stages of the love and life, and the changing world. Often the change in the pattern brings one of those moments of revelation, when the speaker finds he is out of step.

> The summerhouse is gone,
> Leaving a weedy space;
> The bushes that veiled it once have grown

> Gaunt trees that interlace,
> Through whose lank limbs I see too clearly
> The nakedness of the place.[21]

One can trace in many other poems this pattern of Emma under the boughs, as in "The Going" and "At the Word 'Farewell'" (where it clearly represents fate), and in "Epeisodia" where

> Under boughs of brushwood
> Linking tree and tree
> In a shade of lushwood
> There caressed we!

But when the lushness ends, what is left is the skeleton of "The Prospect" and other poems where Hardy identifies himself, once his love is over, as a dead tree – "leaves around me falling". In "The Tree and the Lady":

> I'm a skeleton now,
> And she's gone, craving warmth. The rime sticks like
> a skin to me:
> Through me Arcturus peers; Nor' lights shoot into me;
> Gone is she, scorning my bough!

As his early love waxes:

> the pattern grows
> Of moonshades on the way:

and

> Where three roads joined it was green and fair,
> And over a gate was the sun-glazed sea.

But as it wanes, all is changed:

> Yes, I see those roads – now rutted and bare.

Where once green branches waved,

> What now I see before me is a long lane overhung

With lovelessness, and stretching from the present to the grave . . .[22]

There is far more to be seen in Hardy's patterns – patterns of light, lines of all kinds, dapple and fleck, silhouettes and binding gossamer webs. We have glanced at the Gothic influence at their source, but not at the many other strands of historic and contemporary thought which he absorbed and interpreted: nor have we contrasted his use of pattern with that of other poets; nor how we are caught inside a pattern, symbolising our inflexible minds, unable to adapt to a changing world. These fascinating glens lie too far from the highway you and I must tread to reach home before nightfall. But we must in any case travel by the light of the moon; for so many of Hardy's patterns involve the moon, and, apart from them, it is also one of his most important images.

Hardy's significant moon has already been encountered in several of the seventy-odd poems he wrote about it. In "Jubilate" the moon reveals how things are: it may be "hazy mazy" if we are caught in a romantic vision; it may be altering our idea of reality as it "greened our gaze" in "Once at Swanage"; it may reveal reality to come or reality past, as in the silhouetted figure of "Wessex Heights". The moon may seem, as it did in "Julie-Jane", to preside over human activities, indeed over "all that haps beneath the moon". In "The Pedigree" it was cold and ominously watery and framed by the window, imaged as the inquisitive eye of the poet. All these attributes and more belong to the moon in his poems.

If there were time to launch into about a dozen of these very beautiful moon poems, one might get some idea of the complexity of its role. One could trace, as Jon Stallworthy absorbingly does,[23] how in his novel, Hardy sees the moon which accompanies each incarnation of Jocelyn Pierston's *Well-Beloved*, not only as *her* symbol, but as his own – as if the moon/Beloved were really "his wraith, in a changed sex", his double, a mirror-image whom he loves in a narcissistic way. (In *The Well-Beloved* it becomes clear that this self-love is closely linked with the creative artist's love for his creations. Something of this link appears in "The Pedigree"; and other poems like "I Looked Up From My Writing" and "The Convergence of the Twain" (p 293) connect the moon, or "moon-eyed fishes", with the poet.) In the following poem, much of the complex relation between poet and moon is the background for a typical Hardy premonition that love is doomed to die.

HONEYMOON-TIME AT AN INN

At the shiver of morning, a little before the false dawn,
  The moon was at the window-square,
Deedily brooding in deformed decay –
  The curve hewn off her cheek as by an adze;
At the shiver of morning a little before the false dawn
  So the moon looked in there.

Her speechless eyeing reached across the chamber,
  Where lay two souls opprest,
  One a white lady sighing, "Why am I sad!"
  To him who sighed back, "Sad, my Love, am I!"
And speechlessly the old moon conned the chamber,
  And these two reft of rest.

While their large-pupilled vision swept the scene there,
  Nought seeming imminent,
  Something fell sheer, and crashed, and from the floor
  Lay glittering at the pair with a shattered gaze,
While their large-pupilled vision swept the scene there,
  And the many-eyed thing outleant.

With a start they saw that it was an old-time pier-glass
  Which had stood on the mantel near,
  Its silvering blemished – yes, as if worn away
  By the eyes of the countless dead who had smirked at it
Ere these two ever knew that old-time pier-glass
  And its vague and vacant leer.

As he looked, his bride like a moth skimmed forth, and
      kneeling
  Quick, with quivering sighs,
  Gathered the pieces under the moon's sly ray,
  Unwitting as an automaton what she did;
Till he entreated, hasting to where she was kneeling,
  "Let it stay where it lies!"

"Long years of sorrow this means!" breathed the lady

As they retired. "Alas!"
And she lifted one pale hand across her eyes.
"Don't trouble, Love; it's nothing," the bridegroom said.
"Long years of sorrow for us!" murmured the lady.
  "Or ever this evil pass!"

And the Spirits Ironic laughed behind the wainscot,
  And the Spirits of Pity sighed.
  "It's good", said the Spirits Ironic, "to tickle their minds
With a portent of their wedlock's after-grinds."
And the Spirits of Pity sighed behind the wainscot,
  "It's a portent we cannot abide!

"More, what shall happen to prove the truth of the
    portent?"
  – "Oh; in brief, they will fade till old,
And their loves grow numbed ere death, by the cark
  of care."
  – "But nought see we that asks for portents there? –
'Tis the lot of all." – "Well, no less true is a portent
  That it fits all mortal mould."

Hardy's moon is so often "corpse-cold", "chilly", and
"frozen", and it is often associated with things that are
"frigid".[24] Here the opening, and repeated, "shiver of morning"
and its succeeding "false dawn" are ominous images for a
honeymoon. Equally sinister is the unspeaking gaze of the moon,
that prying concentration "at the window square" of a Selene so
violently maimed that, reaching the savage word "adze", one is
shaken. It presages the shattering of the glass, which, against the
innocence of the couple (who do not know at first what has
broken), itself becomes a sinister object, leering, besmirched by
generations of smirking eyes which contrast with the united,
single eye of the bride and groom. I like Stallworthy's suggestion
that the pier glass's "Cyclopean eye... is... shivered,
seemingly by the basilisk gaze of the moon". He goes on to
develop the idea first mooted by Pierston's cherishing of Selene
as a "sisterly divinity", while he feared Aphrodite – preferring
the sterility of the moon to the demands of Venus, which (like
Sue Bridehead) Pierston cannot really face. The similarities in
age, vocation, temperament, and amatory history between
Pierston and Hardy are inescapable. Was it the fundamental

frustration, and irony, of his life that the childless poet, whose heart leapt so frequently to the throbbings of new love, (often love that was safely unattainable,) instinctively cherished the moon goddess because he feared Aphrodite too much to be able to reach consummation? This would help to explain that voyeuristic eye (also present in poems like "The Burghers"), the dwindling of the line's reflections in "The Pedigree", and the same implication of sterility in the fragmentation of the pier glass – where no more successions of eyes will replace each other in future.

At the end of "The Pedigree" the moon was "stained"; and at her most tragic moment the Trampwoman, in a familiar pattern,

> lay weak,
> The leaves a-falling on my cheek
> The red moon low declined.[25]

The moon often presides over human suffering.

> Sinking down by the gate I discern the thin moon,
> And a blackbird tries over old airs in the pine,
> But the moon is a sorry one, sad the bird's tune,
> For this spot is unknown to that Heartmate of mine.
> [*The Difference*]

> Now I am dead you come to me
> In the moonlight, comfortless;
> Ah, what would I have given alive
> To win such tenderness!
> [*An Upbraiding*]

The moon often symbolises the indifference of Nature; and often it is a part of those potent patterns which tell of the human mind locked with the earth over an ever-widening chasm of disharmony and disjunction. As a stifled presentiment germs:

> I looked back as I left the house,
> And, past the chimneys and neighbour tree,
> The moon upsidled through the boughs.
> [*I Looked Back*]

When ghosts from the past seem to fill the house, and the visitor's sight,

> A bough outside is waving,
>   And that's its shade by the moon.
>
> [*The Strange House*]

The rejected husband of "The Burghers"

>   stood as in a drowse,
> And the slow moon edged from the upland nigh,
> My sad thoughts moving thuswise.

In another fine poem, "On the Esplanade", which begins:

> The broad bald moon edged up where the sea was wide,
>   Mild, mellow-faced;

the watcher describes the seaside scene and various elements in it, some revealed by the moon, which he did not then understand. It ends:

> Yea, such did I mark. That, behind,
> My Fate's masked face crept near me I did not know!

The mild and mellow moon has led him on to view and try to understand the meaning of the scene; but by the end, the moving of the moon has become the creeping of Fate, which will limit him and curb his vision. So the moon is a double symbol, part of the terrible disjunction of life: as it swells and grows, it takes us with it, our imagination growing and spreading with hope and joy. As it wanes we realise, shrinking, that we are bounded by the cruel laws of the universe, of Time, and of Fate.

In "The Telegram", an increasingly resentful bridegroom tells how his bride longs to go to the death-bed of her former lover.

> – The yachts ride mute at anchor and the fulling moon is fair,
> And the giddy folk are strutting up and down the smooth
>   parade,

And in her wild distraction she seems not to be aware
That she lives no more a maid.

So rapt her mind's far-off regard she droops as in a swoon,
And a movement of aversion mars her recent spousal grace,
And in silence we two sit here in our waning honeymoon
At this idle watering-place. . . .

What now I see before me is a long lane overhung
With lovelessness, and stretching from the present to the
grave . . .

In her "wild distraction" she goes with the fulling moon; but
already the honeymoon is waning, the two patterns – individual
and universal – are out of phase, and the future will be dark and
leafless.

(Hardy's own drawing at the end of 'Her Death and After'.)

*   *   *   *   *   *

If the moon and patterns of light and shade, tree and leaf and
web[26] are some of Hardy's most complex images, another
pattern of life is also fundamental to his thinking. It is that of
return.

In "Amabel" (1865) he returns to his love and finds with
horror what Time has wreaked. In "Seeing the Moon Rise",
(August 1927, only months before his death), he laments that
where:

We used to go to Froom-hill Barrow
To see the round moon rise
Into the heath-rimmed skies,

now, though "hoping to go again, high yonder,/As we used", they cannot:

> Feet once quick are slow.

"My Cicely" and "The Revisitation" both tell of lovers returning to past scenes; in the *Poems of 1912-13* the poet returns to Cornwall and then, in finality, to "Where the Picnic Was". "Welcome Home" is about an émigré who tries a return to his uncaring native village; "The Country Wedding" is the fiddler's tale of how he played at a couple's marriage, and returned to play for their burial. "The Seven Times" describes Hardy's own seven journeys to St Juliot, and "A Daughter Returns" presents a very different reception by a father from that given to the Ruined Maid.

Many of these poems of return highlight the difference between the Returner's dream and the reality. Time and Circumstance (or Fate) have pursued their inexorable march, but he or she has stood still: the mind is again out of step with the world it lives in. The human response to time passing is too often to become inflexible, to shut itself into a pattern that it knows, and to refuse to face – or become disconcerted by – the facts. From this inflexibility we awake too late, as the Returner too late discovers. In Hardy's case his own backward gaze too often imprisons him in the past. The following poem shows his mental return to his wife's death on its tenth anniversary, links her again with the pattern of trees and dappled sunlight, and shows him caught like a ram in the thicket of the pattern that has grown up round him.

TEN YEARS SINCE

> 'Tis ten years since
> I saw her on the stairs,
> Heard her in house affairs,
> And listened to her cares;
> And the trees are ten feet taller,
> And the sunny spaces smaller
> Whose bloomage would enthrall her;
> And the piano wires are rustier,
> The spell of bindings mustier,
> And lofts and lumber dustier

Than when, with casual look
And ear, light note I took
Of what shut like a book
Those ten years since!

November 1922

Why is Hardy so preoccupied with the theme of return? The answer lies in his perpetual probing into reality, and in the patterns of life that people make for themselves. The return is to give the mind a chance to take a second look at the incomprehensible, only part-seen, experiences of life; and to correct the rigid pattern in which we have insensibly allowed ourselves to be caught. When we take a second look we have only two options: to entrench ourselves in our first opinion (or prejudice), or to accept a change. The lover of "My Cicely" cannot accept the truth of the new situation; the lover of "The Revisitation" can and does, and is released for a new journey. To both (and to many Hardy characters) the revelation comes in a critical moment of illumination, like fire, for which he subtly prepares the reader. Looking at these poems of return, one finds that careful repetition, on the way to the climax, makes readers feel they have been here before and know what is going to happen; when something unexpected breaks the pattern, their shock is the greater, the moment of vision all the more acute. Children love repetition in a story, and familiar landmarks on a journey – they feel secure. Hardy is concerned to lead on readers' expectations in the same way. In "The Revisitation" the early stanzas remind us that the lover is retracing a familiar route: "up the lane I knew so well"; "round about me bulged the barrows/As before"; "... rose the peewits, just as all those years back"; and there is the Sarsen stone, on which so many times they had sat. (Ironically Agnette asserts: "It is *just* as when we parted!" – it seems the same, and indeed it *is* the same, because the same pride that separated them before will separate them again.) Then the sun burns its fiery illumination deep into their hearts.

We have also seen how in "Her Initials" Hardy plays on the word "same" to break the stanza into two different halves. Though in each half he repeats "the letters of her name", in the second they are quite changed; and though the first effulgent light still "illumes the lay", it has faded now from her name.

When "She Revisits Alone the Church of Her Marriage" the constant refrain is "Where all's the same". But though the church may be the same, the woman has changed. She has to come into line with reality: to revisit in order to revise.

Only Hardy could have written the following poem of return.

THE VOICE OF THINGS

Forty Augusts – aye, and several more – ago,
   When I paced the headlands loosed from dull employ,
The waves huzza'd like a multitude below,
   In the sway of an all-including joy
      Without cloy.

Blankly I walked there a double decade after,
   When thwarts had flung their toils in front of me,
And I heard the waters wagging in a long ironic laughter
   At the lot of men, and all the vapoury
      Things that be.

Wheeling change has set me again standing where
   Once I heard the waves huzza at Lammas-tide;
But they supplicate now – like a congregation there
   Who murmur the Confession – I outside,
      Prayer denied.

Instantly recognizable are all those favourite images and words – thwarts, toils, the huzza'ing waves, and "all the vapoury things/That be".[27] Three times the speaker visits and revisits the Cornish coast. Each time, it seems, the waves are in sympathy with his mood. The first time they roar his joy; the second, their hiss and bubble shift tantalisingly with his own uncertainties and disillusionment. A third time he returns and stands on the same spot. But this time all is changed: the waves have left him beached, alienated, isolated, rejected as he was by the congregation of "The Impercipient". His expectations have been cruelly dashed, and his experience must be adjusted accordingly.[28]

We keep seeing how Hardy's fundamental concern is to make sense of reality, to bring a degree of order into his understanding of experience. The goal of imagery includes just this; and imagery, connections and patterns are a natural part of his search. He pursues it too through metre, rhyme, choice of words, and other devices of his craft. Nearly the last stage of this journey of understanding will be an "eye-sweep" (his word) over this craftsmanship and its integral importance in the poems. But as we stop looking primarily at imagery, let us leave it reading a beautiful lyric which embodies many of Hardy's recurrent images for understanding life.

SHUT OUT THAT MOON

Close up the casement, draw the blind,
    Shut out that stealing moon,
She bears too much the guise she wore
    Before our lutes were strewn
With years-deep dust, and names we read
    On a white stone were hewn.

Step not forth on the dew-dashed lawn
    To view the Lady's Chair,
Immense Orion's glittering form,
    The Less and Greater Bear:
Stay in; to such sights we were drawn
    When faded ones were fair.

Brush not the bough for midnight scents
    That come forth lingeringly,
And wake the same sweet sentiments
    They breathed to you and me
When living seemed a laugh, and love
    All it was said to be.

Within the common lamp-lit room
    Prison my eyes and thought;
Let dingy details crudely loom,
    Mechanic speech be wrought;
Too fragrant was Life's early bloom,
    Too tart the fruit it brought!

1904

Hardy won't have the moon this time at the casement – she has done enough damage and could do more. There is chilling evidence in the silenced lutes and the entombed listeners. We are isolated too from the everlasting stars. Love, so often symbolised by that stepping through the casement into the night,

> When, having drawn across the lawn
> In darkness silently
> A figure flits like one a-wing
> Out from the nearest tree ...

– love is past, sterile and scentless, withered from the bloom and flower of Hardy's world into sour acidity, and the understanding

> That sweets to the mouth in the belly are bitter, and tart,
> and untoward.[29]

So when the death of love stills the creative impulse, what is there left? Only some of his most pejorative words: *common, prison, dingy,* and *mechanic speech* – that "matrimonial commonplace and household life's mechanic gear" which the returning lovers see as they reach her home in "The Dawn After the Dance":

> And there stands your father's dwelling with its blind bleak
> windows telling
> That the vows of man and maid are frail as filmy gossamere.

Notes

1 Niels Bohr, quoted in C. Day Lewis, *The Poetic Image* (London 1947), 36

2 *Life,* 177; George Herbert, *Man*

3 *The Harbour Bridge*

4 *The Peasant's Confession*

5 Other interestingly recurrent words to pursue might be, for example, *gear, labouring, mechanic, shine.* . . .

6 Already looked at in Chapter VIII.

7 *One Who Married Above Him*

8   *The Singing Woman*

9   *Two Serenades; In a Eweleaze near Weatherbury*

10 *A Winsome Woman; Quid Hic Agis? In the Vaulted Way; The Photograph*

11 *In the Old Theatre, Fiesole; The Last Signal; Aristodemus the Messenian; A New Year's Eve in War Time; A Conversation at Dawn*

12 *Middle-Age Enthusiasms; Once at Swanage*

13 *The Seven Times; Before Life and After; And There Was A Great Calm; The Dream-Follower*

14 *Life*, 216

15 *Louie*

16 *The House of Silence; He Fears His Good Fortune*

17 The place of the "former door" is still visible at his birthplace. (National Trust, Higher Bockhampton.)

18 Ruskin, *Modern Painters*, vol III, Pt IV, ch III, §14; Seven Lamps of Architecture, Ch III, §24

19 *Life*, 300–1

20 *Orel*, 213–14

21 *Where They Lived*

22 *First Sight of Her and After; Where Three Roads Joined; The Telegram*

23 Eg *At Moonrise and Onwards, In Sherborne Abbey, A Cathedral Façade at Midnight, At Rushy Pond, A Hurried Meeting*, etc; Jon Stallworthy, *Read by Moonlight, PTH*; see also J. Hillis Miller's introduction to *The Well-Beloved* (London, New Wessex edition 1975)

24 *In the Moonlight; At a Pause in a Country Dance; At Rushy Pond; In Sherborne Abbey*

25 *The Trampwoman's Tragedy*

26 We have not looked in detail at Hardy's webs: see for example *A Hurried Meeting; Bereft, She Thinks She Dreams; A Wasted Illness; Last Week in October; An Experience*, and many others

27 Hardy's development of the concept of "things" is a fascinating

pursuit – see Patricia Clements' essay in *PTH*

28   We have seen the same to be true, though comically, of his expectations of "Genova the Proud"

29   *Great Things; In Tenebris III*

11

CRAFT – FOR A PURPOSE

In "Shut Out That Moon" it is interesting to notice how the rhymes develop. In the first stanza, only the short lines rhyme. In the second, "lawn" and "drawn" are only obliquely removed, almost echoing "moon/strewn/hewn"; and moreover they rhyme together where one doesn't expect it – as if, with their long nostalgic vowels and soft final consonants, they were the lingering memory of those days when all was fair. In the third stanza the rhyme explicitly links scent and sentiment, in the way Proust later made famous;[1] but the fact that these two long lines now unexpectedly rhyme, as well as the short ones, only makes the unrhyming "love" (and its ironical "all it was said to be") more pointed. In the last stanza, all the predominant rhyme vowels of the poem are gathered: the "oo" of the first stanza, the "or/aw" of the second, which, in the third, were completely lost (save in "forth") as the sharper "ee" sounds accompanied the falseness of our expectations. The stresses too are part of the message. They were the elegant, melodious dactyls of "Clóse ŭp the cásemĕnt", "Brúsh nŏt the bóugh" and "fórth ŏn the déw-dashed láwn"; the alliteration is not obtrusive, but lends order and strengthens the framework. In the last stanza the words change from "glittering", "lingeringly", "sentiments", to shorter staccato onomatopoeic words with hard consonants; and for the first time every line rhymes. If our eyes and thought are prisoned, so shall our ears be in the mesh of this tight rhyme; the direct linking of all those opening restrictive images with Life's blighted early bloom reinforces the meaning. The imprisonment of the soul, the loss of beauty, the silencing of the poet's lute into mere mechanic speech are all part of that soured fruit.

Hardy is a giant of metrical, rhyming, and verbal variation. Dennis Taylor reckons that in 1089 poems, he uses 799 metrical forms, of which he has invented 629. (He compares this with Swinburne's 420 different forms, Tennyson's 240, and Robert Browning's 200.[2] This fact is impressive; but this is not the place to burrow into the lengthy tables furnished by research students who have valiantly examined the stresses and rhymes of every two-line, three-line, four-line, and up to 26-line stanza which Hardy wrote. The important thing about his craftmanship is not so much what he did (though this can be fascinating), as why and how he did it – in his pursuit of reality, to use every possible way of shaping and extending meaning. Every gift and layer of experience – like his musical ear and his intelligent study of the classics – added to his awareness of the power of metre, or measure, to "carry a rational content", to contribute essentially to what he was trying to say.

We have seen how Hardy, tongue in cheek, used hymnal Long Measure to raise the ghost of morality in "The Ruined Maid". More seriously, many of his most agnostic poems are ironically cast in the (even more) Common Measure of hymns of faith – his recognition that tension and paradox are at the heart of life. This recognition is one of the most important elements in his poetry; and he used metre, the language of stresses and speech rhythms, to express it. His rhythms image all the rhythms of life: the rhythms of our inner life of thought and spirit, and the conflicting rhythms of the universe, which at times synchronise but usually end in a clash of dissonance and mistiming. So the metrical framework can represent the straitjacket of fate, time and circumstance against which the human heart bursts in its own rhythms of longing and suffering. "Hap" is a good illustration because it is cast in the tight mould of the sonnet and the iambic pentameter. The rhythm we know so well in a line like: "Whĕn Í | cŏnsí | dĕr hów | mў líght | ĭs spént | " is broken, in "Hap", by the harsh stresses of lines like:

Thăt thy lóve's lóss ĭs mý háte's prófitĭñg

– the stresses of our normal speech which are required to express the conflicting demands of "my" and "thy". "Hap" shows the human voice responding in all its individuality to the inhuman, "mechanic" rigidity of the universe.

As we have seen along the way, Hardy scrutinizes many of the other tensions of life; and almost any poem shows a skilful use of metre to convey the meaning. In "Julie-Jane", the sprightly openings of the first three stanzas – with the caesurae stressing the speaker's lingering reflections on her particular qualities – are slowed into a sadder tone in the fourth stanza by the change of rhythm which heralds the new facts the reader is about to learn. Something similar happened in "The Ballad Singer" and "Former Beauties". In "A Wife Waits", the errant husband has his own rhythm of anapaests throughout the poem, while his wife's patient spondees match her steadying arm:

> Wíll's | ăt t̄he dánce | iñ t̄he Clúb- | rŏom belów,
> Whére | thĕ tăll líqu- | ŏr-cŭps fóam;
> I on the pavement up here by the Bow,
> Wáit, wáit, tŏ stéadў hĭm hóme.

And as she recalls, while he now dances with a "loving companion", how he once promised to be true to her –

> Sáid hĕ lŏved nó óne but me

– his stressed assertion breaks his own usual rhythm: and so we know it to be false.

We have met other interruptions to the rhythm which tell of the difficulties of understanding or execution – like the fingering lines in "To My Father's Violin", or the stammering breaks and the fall from the triple metres of "The Voice". In that poem it was clear how much the rhythm revealed about the weakening voice and the predominating wind – when the words' meaning alone could not. Often Hardy's reticence – his "Thus I . . . ; but lo, Me!" – is expanded and contradicted by his expressive metre. It often tells something which he would not, in other words, make explicit, something "too sunk in to say".[3]

Sometimes the metre is used as part of a visual expression of meaning. "Thoughts of Phena", for example, is the only "line of writing" about her that he possesses: the metrical offering is the only relic. The shape on the page of "Snow in the Suburbs" carries in the rather uneven arrangement of the middle stanza just what happens in the haphazard cascade of snow. The poem "Regret not Me" is even more interesting in this respect. It begins:

> Regret not me;
> Beneath the sunny tree
> I lie uncaring, slumbering peacefully.

In the next four stanzas, all similarly shaped, the speaker looks

back on the joys of his life that one assumes is now over, filling
out the details implied by the form of the poem, the shape of a
burial mound. Then:

> Now soon will come
> The apple, pear and plum,
> And hinds will sing, and autumn insects hum.

> Again you will fare
> To cider-making rare,
> And junketings; but I shall not be there.

For the first time, the caesura of the last line is marked by a semi-
colon instead of a comma; and for the first time there comes this
ominously explicit and rather severe "but I shall not be there". It
contrasts with the apparent bonhomie that follows.

> Yet gaily sing
> Until the pewter ring
> Those songs we sang when we went gipsying.

> And lightly dance
> Some triple-timed romance
> In coupled figures, and forget mischance;

> And mourn not me
> Beneath the yellowing tree;
> For I shall mind not, slumbering peacefully.

The reader at first may take this poem at its face value; though
he or she may feel a twinge of something sour in the inversion of
"regret not me" and "mourn not me", and the insistence of the
dead man that his friends (or friend?) should sing and dance just
as usual – there is something here of the "Don't mind me!" of
colloquial sarcasm. But the metre also speaks. In the penultimate
stanza Hardy makes a pun on his rather self-conscious
arrangement of lines (a two-foot, then three-foot, then a four-
foot line which breaks by its caesura into two two feet lines like
the first.) His "triple-timed romance" occurs in his triple-timed
line; and he goes on to increase the pun in the "coupled figures"
which come in that two-foot half of the next line. The puns
check us, and focus our attention. One does not know who the

(human) coupling figures are; nor whether by his unexpected urging of them to forget "mischance" the speaker is really suggesting they will forget *him* as they couple again: but there is an unhappy undercurrent here which suggests that the speaker's nonchalance may be only affected. Shirley Neuman circles the puns: "By drawing attention to the artifice of the form, the poet has also drawn attention to the artifice of the emotion its surface expresses and has pointed the reader to the poem's underlying emotion: an ironic bitterness that the dead are so quickly forgotten."[4]

Hardy inevitably uses puns – not for cheap laughs, but because he was quick-witted and saw connections, and how double meanings reflect life's complexities. The "burnt circle" – image and fact – of "Where the Picnic Was" is expanded as the "circle of friends" by the use of "band", with its etymological connection with "bond" and wedding ring, "anything by which a person is bound."[5] When Hardy writes of the old woman who is

> Here by the baring bough
> Raking up leaves[6]

the ear alone would not tell the difference from "bearing" – and the reminder of it speaks of deprivation and passing time. In "At Castle Boterel" one may well read a double meaning into the simple (but momentous) "Saw us alight". In the poem "Before Life and After"[7] when the poet writes:

> But the disease of feeling *germed*

the meaning ranges from seedtime to decline and morbidity.

Hardy's choice of words is admirably rich, like a many-veined seam of gold running through all his poems. When, in an apparently humdrum metre, he writes a phrase like

> And shaken words bitter to madness,[8]

one knows, in a kind of awe, that this is what human feelings are like. He can differentiate between many states of emotion, like the "heartsome zest" of "Joys of Memory", the "throbbings of noontide" in "I Look into My Glass", the "ruddily ran our

pleasure" of "The End of the Episode", the crushed pain of "a
time-torn man" in "A Broken Appointment". He can be
markedly precise and accurate: in the surgical image "Eyes
couched of the mis-vision that blurred me"; in the "opalised"
state of the drinking-glass under the watefall; in the loving
catalogue (relic of the small boy riveted to his Napoleonic
magazine?) of the soldiers' gear in "The Alarm";

> "Now, to turn to marching matters: –
>   I've my knapsack, firelock, spatters,
> Crossbelts, priming-horn, stock, bay'net, blackball,
>   clay,
> Pouch, magazine, and flint-box that at every quick-step
>   clatters; –
>   My heart, Dear; that must stay!"

(Magnificent, you may say, but not necessarily poetry – but
then the following stanza begins:

> – With breathings broken
> Farewell was kissed unspoken,
> And they parted there as morning stroked the panes:

and one may think Hardy has restored something of the balance
of life.)
   He was never afraid of unusual or rare words, like "stillicide"
or "embowment", or "nonage"; or the unusual use of them that
we saw in "Just the Same", or

> What will you do when Charley's seen
> Dewbeating down this way?[9]

(in a poem of monosyllables where even the half-dozen
disyllables stand out.) He used dialectal words if they enriched
the meaning, unearthed archaic words (like the Middle English
verb "to small"), and had no hesitation in inventing words like
mindsight, subtrude, wonderwork, "a look of love so
thoroughsped". "At a Pause in a Country Dance" vividly
pictures the young mother dancing with her lover, looking out
"where the frozen moon lit frozen snow", while

the fiddlers six-eighted
With even more passionate vigour.

He had an extraordinary ability to mix "poetic" with racy or slang words without any loss of credibility. "Nobody Comes" was written when he was 84.[10]

NOBODY COMES

Tree-leaves labour up and down,
    And through them the fainting light
    Succumbs to the crawl of night.
Outside in the road the telegraph wire
    To the town from the darkening land
Intones to travellers like a spectral lyre
    Swept by a spectral hand.

A car comes up, with lamps full-glare,
    That flash upon a tree:
    It has nothing to do with me,
And whangs along in a world of its own,
    Leaving a blacker air;
And mute by the gate I stand again alone,
    And nobody pulls up there.

9 October 1924

One moment the spectral lyre intones; the next, a car "whangs along in a world of its own". Of course: the car, in its own world, which "has nothing to do with me", its lamps at full glare only isolating the poet the more in his blacker air – of course it whangs along, and that word, too, emphasises his isolation. Could there be any better description of how

the fainting light
Succumbs to the crawl of night,

or how those "Tree-leaves labour up and down"? (Hardy's use of the word "labour" is fairly frequent and often inspired, like the dreaming woman "deep in the labouring night".)[11]

And then he uses negatives in a special way. We noted how effective are the "stirless depths of the yews" at Hampton Court, and the speaker's "moveless hands" in "The Phantom

Horsewoman". Another example:

> Then did the Quick pursue the Dead
> By crystal Froom that crinkles there;
> And still the viewless quire ahead
> Voiced the old holy air.
>
> [*The Dead Quire*]

We saw how final is the phrase "Waits in unhope" ("In Tenebris"), how anguished the evocation of its opposite in "And why unblooms the best hope ever sown?" in "Hap", and in many other poems. But much more than this, Hardy grasps the tension between negation and affirmation which is fundamental to human life; and to declare this he can twist and turn his meaning between these two poles with great artistry. In the following poem, one of his finest, he looks back, not to Wordsworth's trailing clouds of glory, but to a time he postulates when human beings were unaware of suffering.[12]

BEFORE LIFE AND AFTER

> A time there was – as one may guess
> And as, indeed, earth's testimonies tell –
> Before the birth of consciousness,
> When all went well.
>
> None suffered sickness, love, or loss,
> None knew regret, starved hope, or heartburnings;
> None cared whatever crash or cross
> Brought wrack to things.
>
> If something ceased, no tongue bewailed,
> If something winced and waned, no heart was wrung;
> If brightness dimmed, and dark prevailed,
> No sense was stung.
>
> But the disease of feeling germed,
> And primal rightness took the tinct of wrong;
> Ere nescience shall be reaffirmed
> How long, how long?

This poem needs the space and sensitive study which Jean

Brooks gives it in her admirable book.[13] Here Hardy, as always, involves us as readers in his creative process as we move between his two kinds of positive and negative ("None ... none ... none ...", "if something ... no ...") and his ambiguous rhythms – finding that life and its paradoxes in the universe are no more easily scanned than some of his lines. The dignified restraint of his tone still allows (and the more potently) his deep feeling for human suffering to come through, even before the climax of the last line; for the words he has chosen – "If something winced and waned, no heart was wrung ... No sense was stung" – highlight human bodily pain as well as its mental equivalent. Jean Brooks points out the precision of "winced", a word meaning "*involuntary* shrinking", and therefore apt for a condition of unconsiousness. After this poem, it is no wonder that she writes: "Hardy's emotional manipulation of negation is masterly".

He is also a master of implication and understatement. He named "the force of reserve, and the emphasis of understatement" as of "the principles that make for permanence".[14] In his most anthologised poem, "The Oxen", he contrives never once to use the word "stable", nor in "The Whitewashed Wall" the word "death". His poems bristle with "thwart things" he only hints at, things he will not divulge, people described only as "he" or "she", people whose ignorance of what is going on only matches our own:

> Of the churchgoers through the still meadows
>   No single one knew
> What a play was played under their eyes there
>   As thence we withdrew.
>
>   [*At the Wicket Gate*]

> O were it but the weather, Dear,
>   O were it but the miles
> That summed up all our severance,
>   There might be room for smiles.
>
> But that thwart thing betwixt us twain,
>   Which nothing cleaves or clears,
> Is more than distance, Dear, or rain,
>   And longer than the years!
>
>   [*The Division*]

One of his poems about "their happiest time" at Sturminster Newton shows not only this power of implication, but also how much is implied through the prosody.

OVERLOOKING THE RIVER STOUR

The swallows flew in the curves of an eight
  Above the river-gleam
  In the wet June's last beam:
Like little crossbows animate
The swallows flew in the curves of an eight
  Above the river-gleam.

Planing up shavings of crystal spray
  A moor-hen darted out
  From the bank thereabout,
And through the stream-shine ripped his way;
Planing up shavings of crystal spray
  A moor-hen darted out.

Closed were the kingcups; and the mead
  Dripped in monotonous green,
  Though the day's morning sheen
Had shown it golden and honeybee'd;
Closed were the kingcups; and the mead
  Dripped in monotonous green.

And never I turned my head, alack,
  While these things met my gaze
  Through the pane's drop-drenched glaze,
To see the more behind my back....
O never I turned, but let, alack,
  These less things hold my gaze!

As the poet watches from his window, the reader is caught up with him in the darting swallows' flight, by the recurring anapaests and iambs that describe them. Yet a brake seems to work against them, a brake applied by the extra stresses in the shorter lines like

Iň thĕ wét Júne's lást béam.

By the third stanza, the smooth flight is blocked too by the hard impeding consonants – "Closed were the kingcups"; and the fragile balance between the gleam of light and the gleam of wetness has been lost to the drip of rain. So our misgivings, prompted by the contradictions of the metre, and the altered day, are confirmed as we reach the last stanza. The poet stops describing his idyllic moment: it has become for him a moment of revelation, when he realises that what he *didn't* see was far more important. We are now significantly slowed by the second and third lines, "thése thíngs" being heavily stressed; and the stress moves to "the more behind my back" – a subtle use of "more" as a noun, which gives no clue at all as to what kind of thing(s) it refers to. Then there is an impassioned echo of the swallows in the anapaests of

Ŏ névĕr Ĭ túrned

braked again sharply by the caesurae and the "but" which follow; till the rhythm of the last line is turned upside down with the agonised stress on "thĕse léss thìngs". By this characteristically skilful use of rhythm Hardy has told more than in his ambiguous words. The shift in the stress has made "these things", whose description forms most of the poem, only at the very last moment of realisation into "these *less* things". It is masterly writing.

Hardy's understatement is often that of irony – an irony made plain very often by this skilled use of prosody, as in "Regret Not Me", and the very effective stresses of "How She Went to Ireland".

HOW SHE WENT TO IRELAND

Dora's gone to Ireland
    Through the sleet and snow;
Promptly she has gone there
    In a ship, although
Why she's gone to Ireland
    Dora does not know.

That was where, yea, Ireland,
    Dora wished to be:
When she felt, in lone times,
    Shoots of misery,

> Often there, in Ireland,
>   Dora wished to be.

> Hence she's gone to Ireland,
>   Since she meant to go,
> Through the drift and darkness
>   Onward labouring, though
> That she's gone to Ireland
>   Dora does not know.[15]

These two poems are like many other "layered" ones where a repeated line leads through the poem, gradually telling more, until revelation only comes at the end – like the children of "Unrealized", who describe all the naughty things they are doing, about which, as refrain,

> Mother won't know.

For five stanzas of mishaps, Mother doesn't know; then comes the last:

> How we cried the day she died!
>   Neighbours whispering low...
> But we now do what we will
>   Mother won't know.

Sometimes Hardy's inclination to understatement is reinforced by the need for brevity and compression – when, for example, he has to illustrate in a few words the passage of time.[16] Sometimes his compression seems a part of his awkwardness.

FOUR IN THE MORNING

> At four this day of June I rise:
> The dawn-light strengthens steadily;
> Earth is a cerule mystery,
> As if not far from Paradise
>   At four o'clock,

> Or else near the Great Nebula,
> Or where the Pleiads blink and smile:
> (For though we see with eyes of guile

The grisly grin of things by day,
    At four o'clock

They show their best.) . . . In this vale's space
I am up the first, I think. Yet, no,
A whistling? and the to-and-fro
Wheezed whettings of a scythe apace
    At four o'clock? . . .

– Though pleasure spurred, I rose with irk:
Here is one at compulsion's whip
Taking his life's stern stewardship
With blithe uncare, and hard at work
    At four o'clock!

Bockhampton

The cheerfulness one catches from this poem may burst into laughter at

    – Though pleasure spurred, I rose with irk.

Some may think it Hardy at his most cussedly angular. And yet, isn't the compression valid, making space for the more important lines; is it not in fact vivid, exact, onomatopoeic, masterly? And does it not help to extend the range of the poem, with its breathtaking "Earth is a cerule mystery", into just that unique magisterial sweep of Hardy's eye which, expressed with stimulating variety, takes in the whole beauty and contrariety of the universe as well as its most important element, an individual human being? I see in this poem, too, another of Hardy's self-mockeries – that of the pedantic rhapsodist outdone by the "simple", wholesome, resilient rural labourer.

The triolet-like refrain "At four o'clock" chimes the hour through the poem, each time with a slightly different emphasis. In some poems Hardy repeats a word for a much more important purpose. In many poems, by stripping off one layer after another to the climactic end, he reminds the reader how, in life, understanding only gradually dawns. In other poems he will take one word and develop it, coming back to it again and again, but each time with a subtly different meaning: showing how significance changes for us as understanding grows. (Something similar is in the change of stress by which "these things" become "these less things". There is a hint of it too in some of Shakespeare's sonnets and the conceits of the "Metaphysical" Poets – or even, almost in parody, in D.L. Sayers' *Gaudy Night* (chapter XVIII) where Peter Wimsey completes Harriet's unfinished sonnet by using "sleep" four times in as many lines, each time with a different emphasis.) But Hardy goes further: in his study of how meaning and reality are constantly changing for people, he is drawn to "a kind of progressive redefinition", as Patricia Clements puts it, "of the words he uses."[17] In his earliest poem, "Domicilium", one sees how the word "wild", which appears three times, seems to change its meaning.

DOMICILIUM

It faces west, and round the back and sides
High beeches, bending, hang a veil of boughs,
And sweep against the roof. Wild honeysucks
Climb on the walls, and seem to sprout a wish
(If we may fancy wish of trees and plants)
To overtop the apple-trees hard by.

Red roses, lilacs, variegated box
Are there in plenty, and such hardy flowers
As flourish best untrained. Adjoining these
Are herbs and esculents; and farther still
A field; then cottages with trees, and last
The distant hills and sky.

Behind, the scene is wilder. Heath and furze
Are everything that seems to grow and thrive
Upon the uneven ground. A stunted thorn
Stands here and there, indeed; and from a pit
An oak uprises, springing from a seed
Dropped by some bird a hundred years ago.

                      In days bygone –
Long gone – my father's mother, who is now
Blest with the blest, would take me out to walk.
At such a time I once inquired of her
How looked the spot when first she settled here.
The answer I remember. "Fifty years

Have passed since then, my child, and change has marked
The face of all things. Yonder garden-plots
And orchards were uncultivated slopes
O'ergrown with bramble bushes, furze and thorn:
That road a narrow path shut in by ferns,
Which, almost trees, obscured the passer-by.

"Our house stood quite alone, and those tall firs
And beeches were not planted. Snakes and efts
Swarmed in the summer days, and nightly bats
Would fly about our bedrooms. Heathcroppers
Lived on the hills, and were our only friends;
So wild it was when first we settled here."

Clements traces the sequence. "Wild" is first used for the
honeysuckle climbing the cottage walls. Then: "Behind, the
scene is wilder", as he pans out to the surrounding heath. But
fifty years before, his grandparents were the lone inhabitants of
this place, surrounded by bramble and furze, bats and snakes, the
present trees unplanted.

> "Heathcroppers
> Lived on the hills, and were our only friends;
> So wild it was when first we settled here."

By the end of the poem, we have revised our opinion of what
wildness really is; we have had to adjust our focus from those
first "wild honeysucks", which now seem mere tame garden
flowers.
   "Domicilium" is written mainly in Wordsworthian blank
verse, though it begins with three six-line stanzas. The last lines
of the first two stanzas rhyme together. The only other rhyme is
an interesting example of that repetition which makes for
familiarity: one hears how the child who asked his grandmother
what her home used to be like unconsciously echoes her in his
poem.

> At such a time I once inquired of her
> How looked the spot when first she settled here.

There's no hint, however, of the extraordinary skill in rhyme and its use which Hardy was to display even a few years later. The early poem, "Amabel", is like "Tess's Lament" in its repeated falling resonances of regret, the "knell" which seems to echo round and round with never an end: even in 1865 or 66 he was obviously aware of how a rhyme scheme could contribute to the total meaning of a poem. This is the most important thing about his use of rhyme; but perhaps before looking at it more closely, one should in passing note some of the other ways in which Hardy shows himself a virtuoso of rhyme.

He is a master of the deceptively simple, the apparently inevitable rhyme – as, for example, in "I Look Into My Glass" or "On a Discovered Curl of Hair", "Silences" or "Drummer Hodge". Poems like "Night-Time in Mid-Fall" or "Once at Swanage" show how he can rhyme every line in two stanzas without any seeming forced. He frequently rhymes two or even three syllables at a time – like the "constellations/reverberations/ improvisations" of "A Singer Asleep", the "flooring/ignoring" of "Song to an Old Burden", and 35 stanzas of double rhymes in "The Revisitation". He makes triple rhymes like "slenderly/ tenderly" and "history/mystery" and the receding voice of the wind/woman in "listlessness/wistlessness". When he wants to, he can find rhymes unlimited: sometimes for a joke,[18] as in "Liddell and Scott", to send up dictionary-making; sometimes for some other special effect. In "The Flirt's Tragedy", for example, every single one of its 29 stanzas ends in the vowel-sound "oo", leading up to the climax of the last word: "slew". (The rhymes here are sometimes too ingenious; but apart from the crescendo effect, they also unify a setting which spans many years and countries.) We have seen how he repeated one rhyme throughout "The Haunter"; sometimes he will choose to stress a theme word by rhyming every stanza to it – as in "Under High-Stoy Hill", where all four stanzas end in the characteristic, past-laden word "behind".[19] He can use internal rhymes with apparently no difficulty – like those in "The Wind's Prophecy", or "The Going of the Battery", where the soldiers' wives lament their husbands' departure for the Boer War in seven stanzas of double internal rhymes:

> – Yet, voices haunting us, daunting us, taunting us,
> Hint in the night-time when life beats are low
> Other and graver things.... Hold we to braver things,

Wait we, in trust, what Time's fulness shall show.

Hardy delights in every kind of unusual rhyme scheme. Look, for example, at the verse from "The Sick Battle-God" quoted on p 209: the internal rhymes at "wore/gore" in the last two lines are maintained through eleven stanzas. He can also successfully rhyme most unlikely words: like the "bird/ ensepulchred" of "The Blinded Bird" or, in "A Wet Night" the two words "mire-bestarred" and "calendared". We saw in "To Sincerity" and "Regret not Me" how easily he singly rhymes a three-line stanza; sometimes he deliberately links pairs of stanzas by one of the rhymes, even throughout a poem of 49 stanzas like "A Conversation at Dawn".[20]

One of the most interesting examples of stanza-linking clearly shows how much Hardy rhymed for meaning rather than just for the chime. Let us thankfully leave the list of virtuoso skills, and concentrate, in a short time and space, on a few poems in which one can see him exploring, and answering, much deeper purposes through rhyme. This has already been seen in poems such as "The Ballad-Singer" and "The Inquiry", "During Wind and Rain", "Copying Architecture in an Old Minster", "Under The Waterfall", and countless others where the rhyme leads to new meaning. Sometimes the word "rhyme" is given special importance – indeed this occurs significantly often. One of his most characteristic poems is:

THE RIFT

(Song: Minor Mode)

'Twas just at gnat and cobweb-time,
When yellow begins to show in the leaf,
That your old gamut changed its chime
From those true tones – of span so brief! –
That met my beats of joy, of grief,
    As rhyme meets rhyme.

So sank I from my high sublime!
We faced but chancewise after that,
And never I knew or guessed my crime...
Yes; 'twas the date – or nigh thereat –
Of the yellowing leaf; at moth and gnat
    And cobweb-time.

Once again, inner and outer landscape chime together; and the fundamental importance of rhyme is imaged as the life harmony of two people. Of these twelve lines, five are rhymed with "rhyme"; and inescapably, as the autumn comes round again the change of chime in the "true tones" is echoed in "yellowing leaf" and "cobweb-time" – "Yes; 'twas the date". So much does Hardy feel the power of association[21] that he often short-circuits an explanation by using a phrase like "my November" or "our Maytime" as straight images for youth and old age.

Another poem which stresses rhyme and uses it to bring new meaning is "In Front of the Landscape" – whose general purport was summarised on p 177. The speaker's inner visions obscure the real view.

IN FRONT OF THE LANDSCAPE

[I]

Plunging and labouring on in a tide of visions,
    Dolorous and dear,
Forward I pushed my way as amid waste waters
    Stretching around,
Through whose eddies there glimmered the customed
        landscape
    Yonder and near

[II]

Blotted to feeble mist. And the coomb and the upland
    Coppice-crowned,
Ancient chalk-pit, milestone, rills in the grass-flat
    Stroked by the light,
Seemed but a ghost-like gauze, and no substantial
    Meadow or mound.

The "speechful faces, gazing insistent" included those he had dearly loved.

[VI]

Then there would breast me shining sights, sweet seasons
    Further in date;
Instruments of strings with the tenderest passion

      Vibrant, beside
Lamps long extinguished, robes, cheeks, eyes with the
      earth's crust
      Now corporate.

[VII]

Also there rose a headland of hoary aspect
      Gnawed by the tide,
Frilled by the nimb of the morning as two friends stood
      there
      Guilelessly glad –
Wherefore they knew not – touched by the fringe of an
      ecstasy
      Scantly descried.

[VIII]

Later images too did the day unfurl me,
      Shadowed and sad,
Clay cadavers of those who had shared in the dramas,
      Laid now at ease,
Passions all spent, chiefest the one of the broad brow
      Sepulture-clad.

[IX]

So did beset me scenes miscalled of the bygone,
      Over the leaze,
Past the clump, and down to where lay the beheld ones;
      – Yea, as the rhyme
Sung by the sea-swell, so in their pleading dumbness
      Captured me these.

With this stanza Hardy pauses in his description, and readers
must pause to notice how the rhymes have led them steadily
from stanza to stanza. One finds that the long lines do not rhyme
– this is rare enough in his poetry to make one take notice. But
the short lines do: lines two and six with each other, line four
taking us forward to the next stanza's lines two and six, whose
rhyme it gives. As the rhymes continue thus, plaiting the poem
together like the ribbons of a Maypole dance, one sees how the
speaker's mind is "captured"

> – Yea, as the rhyme
> Sung by the sea-swell.

It's an intrusive simile, even if one remembers the two preceding "tides", which were visually rather than aurally evoked; but, in its prominent place, Hardy is determined to make us notice the rhyme, and the connections, once more, between inner and outer perception.

There are three more stanzas, during which he regrets that it is only now they are dead that he truly sees all these people. The moment of understanding has come, and has done its work. As he (mentally and physically) looks up, and notices the muttering passers-by, there is a change:

[XII]

> Hence wag the tongues of the passing people, saying
>   In their surmise,
> "Ah – whose is this dull form that perambulates, seeing
>   nought
>   Round him that looms
> Whithersoever his footsteps turn in his farings,
>   Save a few tombs?"

This is the last stanza. As Ronald Marken points out,[22] according to precedent one would expect the last line to rhyme with the second, "surmise": but it does not. The truth has been made plain, and there is no more need to move forward. The introduction of "tombs" not only surprises, and underlines the irony of the passers' limited vision; but its finality resounds. It links his inner vision, all that has "loomed" for him, with the reality of the outer world, the tombs that are all that is left there of the lives that are past.

Hardy's capacity to surprise (which Philip Larkin so much appreciated) appears in his metre and rhyme schemes, where nothing is totally predictable. Sometimes it is not so much surprising us, as keeping us wondering, or actually breathless – like the long-awaited verb "Grieved I," of "A Broken Appointment", or an occasion when the first rhyme is withheld for several lines. This happens in "Proud Songsters", the apparently simple little poem at which, earlier on p 40, I promised another look. Reading this poem aloud, we are probably struck by the everyday language of the first three lines, by the way we fall over ourselves around the short line "In bushes/Pipe", and, now familiar with Hardy's poetry, by an uneasy, conscious waiting for a rhyme. We know that he often uses an awkward rhythm to underline the counterpoint of life, and that his sense of irony is rarely in abeyance, so that there's some incongruence between our idea of mellifluous nightingales and, here, their almost comic piping ("In bushes"), especially when one sobers at once with the foreboding note of "as if all Time were theirs". Our watchfulness for a rhyme is not satisfied until the end of the fifth line, when we breathe again. And then comes, immediately, another rhyme, which turns all the suspense upside down by suddenly completing three rhyming lines out of six – heady stuff. But then we cannot linger. The second stanza's "growing", "nightingales", and "thrushes" lace it up with the first; and after its first statement, that might come from the stock market, the second stanza opens out, and broadens – not only in its meaning and time-scale, but also aurally, with the word "twain". Its soft open vowel continues the "pairs/wears/theirs" sounds of the first stanza; but the final "n" lengthens it musically, and by the time we reach those significantly spaced words

> But only particles of grain,
> And earth, and air, and rain

– we are caught up in the repeating cycle of life and death in a kind of pure ethereal essence... (Ronald Marken suggests a similar view when he writes: "The implications grow vaster as the images become, literally, more particular, more elemental, more harmonious".) He also points out, in his excellent essay, that the rhyme scheme of "Proud Songsters" is unique in Hardy's round thousand of poems. It shows him yet again fashioning his rhymes so that they are no mere aural adornment, but so that the sound expresses and expands the meaning.

These proud songsters and their many companions in his poems – the blinded bird, the swallows and moorhens, sea-mews, peewits, larks and gamebirds, thrushes and nestlings, cuckoos and linnets, and Dorset blackbirds with their "Pretty de-urr!": all the "hopping casement-comers" and "winged pipers overhead" which flock through his writings – these, it could be said, like Shelley's skylark

> inspired a bard to win
> Ecstatic heights in thought and rhyme.[23]

* * * * * *

On Hardy's 81st birthday a presentation was made to him on behalf of over a hundred younger writers. Part of the encomium ran: "The craftsman in you calls for our admiration as surely as the artist". It was one of many tributes he received during his long life, which included the Order of Merit, a (refused) knighthood, honorary doctorates and fellowships, the proposed creation of a university chair in his name, poems about him by fellow poets, and on his 83rd third birthday an appreciation in the *Sunday Times* by his old friend Edmund Gosse. (Referring to Brahminical religious laws, by which a man reaching his 84th year becomes a Saint, Gosse jocularly dubbed him St Thomas of Max Gate.) Yet he never became Poet Laureate. Judging by some of his poems of occasion he would have made a good one. One of these was the poem he wrote for the charity matinée in aid of the *Titanic* disaster fund. It is a brilliant poem, a *tour de force* in many ways typical of its creator, so densely packed that it needs to be read and re-read and pondered. Its tone, icily impersonal, is not Hardy's most usual or attractive; until we see what he is writing about, it may not engage our sympathy. But as an example of his greatness as artist and craftsman and viewer of life it has a proper place as we near the end of this exploration.

THE CONVERGENCE OF THE TWAIN

(Lines on the loss of the *Titanic*)

I

> In a solitude of the sea
> Deep from human vanity,
> And the Pride of Life that planned her, stilly couches
>   she.

II

> Steel chambers, late the pyres
> Of her salamandrine fires,

Cold currents thrid, and turn to rhythmic tidal lyres.

III

Over the mirrors meant
To glass the opulent
The sea-worm crawls – grotesque, slimed, dumb, in-
different.

IV

Jewels in joy designed
To ravish the sensuous mind
Lie lightless, all their sparkles bleared and black and
blind.

V

Dim moon-eyed fishes near
Gaze at the gilded gear
And query: "What does this vaingloriousness down
here?" ...

VI

Well: while was fashioning
This creature of cleaving wing,
The Immanent Will that stirs and urges everything

VII

Prepared a sinister mate
For her – so gaily great –
A Shape of Ice, for the time far and dissociate.

VIII

And as the smart ship grew
In stature, grace, and hue,
In shadowy silent distance grew the Iceberg too.

IX

Alien they seemed to be:

No mortal eye could see
The intimate welding of their later history,

X

Or sign that they were bent
By paths coincident
On being anon twin halves of one august event,

XI

Till the Spinner of the Years
Said "Now!" And each one hears,
And consummation comes, and jars two hemispheres.

Almost anyone else, called to write upon the *Titanic* disaster, would probably have evoked the suffering of the last scenes and the bereaved, perhaps the faults of the ship's design, possibly something about the massive forces of Nature ranged against human endeavour. Hardy's approach is uniquely his. From the first moment he sounds the note of human vanity, and by his quotation from the First Letter of John (Chapter II, verse 16), sets an agenda which he proceeds to fill out imaginatively with a brilliant brush of sensuous imagery.

> For all that is in the world, the lust of the flesh, and the lust of the eyes, and the pride of life, is not of the Father, but is of the world.
>
> (1611 translation, "Authorised Version")

The eye travels slowly over the motionless wreck, as the ear catches the sea's gush and whine through the empty chambers, and one first senses the poles of cold and heat which vibrate throughout the poem. Here is the lust of the eyes unsatisfied – the seeing mirror slimed, the jewels blackened and dead, both recalling all those human expectations unfulfilled, blind and dumb and indifferent. The "moon-eyed fishes", suggests Jon Stallworthy, "in the necessary absence of the moon, embody the narrator's detached imagination, and into [their] mouths is put the question he must answer:

'What does this vaingloriousness down here?'"[24]

Well: almost exactly half-way through the poem, it turns (as often) on this one compendious word. The scene has been graphically set, in passive stillness disturbed only by the languid movements of sea-worm and fish, the ship "couched" in solitude as if awaiting her fate. Now, at the word "Well:" comes a sense of movement, of urgency, of purpose and fulfilment, which accelerates to the end of the poem. (I think of Donald Davie's description of Hardy as "the poet of technology, the laureate of engineering" – and this poem "like an engine, a sleek and powerful machine" whose rhymes "slide home like pistons in cylinders".)[25] But it is not just the rhymes that slide home. No longer described as a mere passive object, infiltrated by the sea, the ship is now seen as part of a purpose, "fashioned", in her feminine way, as the mate for that Shape of Ice which the urgent Immanent Will is preparing as her twin half ("a grim parody of the platonic symbol of perfection".)[26] The Shape is given "sinister" personality; the smart ship grows, like a woman, "in stature, grace and hue", and is a "creature of cleaving wing". The choice of "cleaving" was a late inspiration for Hardy, a flash of genius. Its overtones amplify the poem's meaning – overtones of "parting or dividing" (the water) and of "piercing or penetrating" as in the sexual metaphor and Biblical injunction to a man to "leave father and mother and . . . cleave to his wife: and they twain shall be one flesh". It keeps too its simpler meaning of "to stick fast or adhere" which perfectly fits its relation to the iceberg.[27] The sexual metaphor implied from the beginning is continued in the word 'welding' as this wedding of Shape and gaily fashioned creature is prepared, a union of sinister Ice and created Fire in which it is the Ice which overcomes and turns her marriage into death. And as, below the surface, the Iceberg penetrates the unconscious ship, the moment of consummation comes and meaning is made violently clear.

Hardy's change of tone and language in the second half – from passivity to urgency, from sensuous description to metaphorical and symbolic diction – is deliberately made to enhance the meaning. The first half conveys the picture of the aimless object on the seabed. The second half gathers up that object into the wider and deeper significance of the whole universe's pattern. Patricia Clements writes: "Reaching backwards in time, he finds the pattern of which the *Titanic*'s wreck is an item. She becomes now a part of the blind figure in the mind of the Immanent Will."[28] Yet again Hardy is seeking to order the material of life to make meaning, to find reality.

But this poem is different in stance from his others in its total impersonality, its apparent negation of human consciousness and significance, so that the reader may feel excluded or uncomfortable. Stallworthy links its icy sterility with the "frigid circuit" of the moon poems. Patricia Clements calls it a poem "less about convergence than about the division of matter from mind." William Pritchard says that Hardy "spin[s] out an explanation that doesn't explain anything".[29] The poem is a living thing: like most of Hardy's poems, expressive of life's ambiguities, ironies, and inscrutabilities, and requiring an active and creative response from the reader, who must make of it what he or she will.

Notes

1   Eg "Tous ces souvenirs... nés d'un parfum..." (*Du Côté de Chez Swann*, Pléiade edition, I 186.) Proust greatly admired Hardy's work and discussed Hardy's novels in his own.

2   This counts the complete poems in *The Dynasts*. The figures in brackets are based on the work of John Fletcher.

3   *The Master and the Leaves*

4   *PTH*, 42

5   *Shorter Oxford English Dictionary*

6   *Autumn in King's Hintock Park*

7   See below, page 279

8   *The Church and the Wedding*

9   *To Carry Clavel*

10   That evening he was expecting his wife Florence to return to Max Gate after an operation in London.

11   *The Whitewashed Wall*

12   See also, for example, the end of his note in *Life*, 149, and the note of April 7 in *Life* 218

13   Jean Brooks, *op cit,* 44ff

14   *Life,* 363

15   Dora Sigerson Shorter, who died in July 1918, had asked to be buried in Ireland.

16   Eg as in *A Church Romance*

17   *PTH,* 147

18   As in *Lorna the Second* and *A Refusal*

19   In *Long Plighted,* a poem in which we gradually revise our understanding of the meaning of "long", he rhymes each stanza with "years".

20   One stanza was quoted on page 251; the next stanza's third line rhymes with "lair".

21   As discussed in Chapter IV with *Under the Waterfall*

22   *PTH,* 22

23   Marken, *op cit, PTH,* 19; *Shelley's Skylark*

24   *PTH,* 177

25   Donald Davie, *Thomas Hardy and British Poetry,* 17

26   Stallworthy, *PTH,* 177

27   Genesis II, 24; Matthew XIX, 5; Mark X, 7, etc. We must also note Jesus' emphasis on the word "twain" (A.V. translation). Definitions from the OED.

28   *PTH,* 153

29   "Hardy's Anonymous Sincerity", *Agenda* 106

12

AFTER SCENE

It is impossible to read Hardy's poetry without being aware of his own individual voice. I believe that, although he ceased writing in 1927, this voice has particular resonances with what he might have called the soundings of men and women and society several generations later. Is this because Hardy's thinking was ahead of its time, or is it because he was plucking at chords which are universal to human experience? Poetry has been called "felt thought":[1] Hardy not only records emotions, but analyses and re-examines their cause in the light of the whole human condition, as part of his continuing enquiry into reality.

That reality, in the twentieth century, has included the uprooting of more people probably than ever before. With an exponentially increasing world population, incessant wars over much of the globe, famines, political upheavals causing millions of refugees, the regaining of independent status by former colonies, migration in search of work – these and other factors have combined to create vast numbers of people who have no easy physical or spiritual base. In addition, in the Western industrialised countries, a post-1945-war period of full employment, wider educational and entrepreneurial opportunities and greater economic parity did much, for a time, to level out class distinctions, so that many who were socially mobile were also déracinés, moving between different cultures.

On several levels, Hardy was one of these. He achieved the miracle, in Victorian England, of climbing out of a peasant background into the middle class – but not without pain and bitterness, reflected in his work all his life. Even when his reputation was established, he reports the difficulty of getting *The Mayor of Casterbridge* published in volume form, "the publisher's reader having reported to Smith, Elder, and Co that the lack of gentry among the characters made it uninteresting". (One can compare, for example, Stan Barstow's similar initial difficulties almost a century later.) It is no wonder that Hardy's political comments sometimes touch on the big issues of the later twentieth century, like privilege – an issue evident as much in Maoist and post-Mao China and in the USSR as in tribally-divided African states and capitalist Western ones. "I am against privilege derived from accident of any kind," noted Hardy in 1888, "and am therefore equally opposed to aristocratic and democratic privilege. (By the latter I mean the arrogant assumption that the only labour is hand-labour)..."[2]

But it was not only in social class that he moved between two cultures. In his chosen field of literature he spanned the gap between centuries of oral tradition and the written tradition of the educated élite. In his poetry the dominant voice is that of the ballad, with its solidarity of "ordinary people" and its universalising of human experience; the natural rhythms of our speech are for Hardy poetic. While today's culture in mass-media societies may be increasingly oral–visual rather than written, Hardy with all his debt to writers and thinkers of the past and yet his "passion for the human voice"[3] may be more helpfully bridging our contemporary divisions than we realise.

The same is true of the priority which tends to be given by modern society to technology and scientific methods, over against the fruit of the imagination, human experience, and the interpretation of life through art. Though Hardy was interested in new technology[4] and kept up his scientific reading until his death, we have seen how he characterised the "dead" world where art and imagination were excluded as "mechanic". This leads us directly into the dilemma of late twentieth-century thought, which is beginning to question the values and practices which have been increasingly dominant since the Enlightenment, or Age of Reason. I believe that in this dilemma Hardy is particularly involved and has important things to say to us. Let me expand this.

In his book *Foolishness to the Greeks* Lesslie Newbigin gives an excellent "profile" of our post-Enlightenment culture. I hope to evade dangerous over-simplification if I pick out simply as markers some salient points, which readers must fill out for themselves. Since Newton, our culture has increasingly affirmed that *cause and effect* are the laws governing the real world (or nature, i.e., all that exists.) Any idea of a *purpose* behind the universe has been largely abandoned in the West (though in the late twentieth century some scientists are beginning to think differently.[5] This analytical and mathematical way of thinking has been applied to all forms of human knowledge; and we have thought that the application of reason, liberated from dogma and superstition, and embodied in the triumphs of science, is sure to bring progress and understanding.

The subjection of all human life to this analysis was, with the Industrial Revolution, a factor in the break-up of the craftsman's work. Hitherto seen through from start to finish by its creator, human work was now broken down into separate processes and shared out, much of it characterised by the repetitive action of machinery and certainly by an absence of any sense of purpose (except the need for a wage-packet.) The new science of economics teaches that production is only for consumption; and the market becomes the link between the divided work processes and the consumers. "Gross National Product", points out Dr Newbigin,

> refers only to what enters the market. It excludes the work of the housewife, of the gardener growing his own food. It includes the operations of the gambling syndicate, the arms salesman, and the drug pusher.[6]

The consequences are important for society. First, with work removed from the home, two worlds evolve: that of the work area (the public), where economic and impersonal values rule; and that of the home and family (the private), "that remains under another vision of how things are."[7] Second, the growth of huge cities becomes a world without landmarks, where individual identities are easily blurred. Third, the bureaucracy needed to organise all this treats individuals impartially, therefore anonymously and as replaceable, reducing the elements of human life to what can (now) be computerised; and finally, it largely destroys personal responsibility.

It is, however, difficult to describe human behaviour in terms solely of cause and effect, without the category of purpose.

> A strange fissure thus runs right through the consciousness of modern Western man ... With dedicated zeal he purposes to explain the world as something that is without purpose.

In his constant attempt to enthrone *objective facts* as the only test of reality, with *values* relegated to a world of private options which is quite separate, and irrelevant to the analysis of reality, Western man (rather more than Western woman) has come to the paradox of asserting that to reach 'the truth' "the only really valuable things are value-free facts".[8]

Now Hardy himself exhibits these "fissures" of the post-Enlightenment man and woman.

> (1881) *May 9.* After infinite trying to reconcile a scientific view of life with the emotional and spiritual, so that they may not be inter-destructive I come to the following....[9]

He leapt to learn new "facts", to study and apply scientific thinking, to embrace Darwin's theories. Yet he knew also that human consciousness is a fact that cannot be explained by mechanistic determinism alone; that "Feeling... [is] the great motor force of human life", and that in addition to the dichotomy between head and heart, there is, for further complication, the enslavement of soul to body, the "'Fatal Dependence' – that of the cerebral functions on the nutritive economy."[10] In him the world of "private values" was highly developed, with its emphasis on the individual and on relationships between people, and his own particular emphasis on loving-kindness – which meant not only sympathy, but the kind of honouring of a person's need which we met in "A Broken Appointment". All this runs counter to the law of the market and value-free facts.

Then, on the one hand, he rejected what he regarded as the English Church's belief in the supernatural, and hoped for its "rationalization"; but on the other, many of his statements and poems (like "The Shadow on the Stone", the *Poems of 1912–13*, and "Night-Time in Mid-Fall") show his own willing "suspension of disbelief" in the supernatural; and he continued to value the Church's ethical standpoint and its cohesive vision of purpose in human life.[11] Hardy indeed condemns the First Cause (sometimes significantly called the Immanent Will) for creating a world apparently without purpose – certainly not with the purpose of individual happiness. Much of his poetry is informed by a vision of what human happiness and fulfilment could be, were it not thus sabotaged.

It is sabotaged too by "'man's inhumanity to man' – to woman – and to the lower animals"[12] – a value-judgment. We have seen how with the 1914–18 war Hardy gave up all belief in "the gradual ennoblement of man", and saw everywhere the deterioration of human values and relationships.[13] Seeing beyond the terrible death-roll and manifold destruction of that war, his vision of limitless horror, as humanity becomes increasingly enslaved by its own inventions and its own moral lawlessness, is only too relevant to today's nuclear dilemma and profit-controlled society.[14]

Hardy points to other dilemmas we know. With characteristic irony he called himself "a harmless agnostic" who hardly held "any views about anything whatever".[15] Though a typical understatement, this sounds like wisdom today, in a society where the slick televised answer, a Prime Minister's invariable infallibility, the instant assessment of "truth" or "fact" in black and white, and the standardization of thought by the majority, are in fashion. Hardy had begun to see the power of the press even in 1912, when, in a plea for "an appreciation of what is real literature", he partly attributed to bad newspaper reporting the fact that, "while millions have lately been learning to read, few of them have been learning to discriminate."[16] This is still a central question in British society today. Hardy closely identified with Matthew Arnold's judgment that "Poetry is at bottom a criticism of life ... the greatness of a poet lies in his powerful and beautiful application of ideas to life – to the question: How to live."[17] (It must be understood that Hardy was concerned more with the emotional, intellectual, and spiritual problems of living, rather than with political or economic systems.[18]) He esteems art as an expression of living truth about human life, as the opposite of "mechanic speech", as a kind of pointing to landmarks in the landscape, a vision of truth and beauty and the ultimate nature of things in human experience.

This vision is not that of received analytical Enlightenment thinking. It's a vision that keeps before us the unknowability of facts and the inexplicabilities of life, the desire for a sense of purpose in existence, and the importance of personal, human, values. Yet Hardy held it in a proper tension with his championing of reasoned thinking, hoping to see "harmful conventions shaken – in this country at least – by lucid argument and, what is more, human emotions."[19]

He would, I think, have been quite at home with much scientific thought of the late twentieth century, which is beginning to see that its methods do not explain everything. (You and I can touch on so little here. Graham Dunstan Martin, in his admirable *Language, Truth and Poetry*, devotes some time to discussing the common ground (though the different language) of art and science, both of which "appertain to a single frame of mind, one that admits complexity and uncertainty... and is healthily suspicious of claims to absolute truth.")[20] In fact Hardy sometimes assimilates his scientific knowledge to his value/ purpose attitude: Darwin's teaching that all creation is one becomes with Hardy part of the reason for good relations between humans and animals. (Read the poem "The Wind Blew Words".)

In a sense such a doctrine of creation fell easily into place with Hardy, whose formative years spent in deep country had given him a relation to nature as close, and as unconscious, as breathing. A town boy will pick a flower while a country boy won't: "It grows in his soul – he does not want it in his buttonhole."[21] But even as a schoolboy he spanned two worlds in his own life, walking daily between the bustling market town and the unchanged ways of centuries in his own isolated hamlet. Later, living in London, he was always conscious of the tension between rural and urban cultures. In his article *The Dorsetshire Labourer* (and others) he lamented the demise of certain rural values, but fully recognised the poverty which drove men into the towns – to a general loss of individual identity and personal responsibility, and a most damaging obliteration of their roots.

This loss of a sense of continuity and history (seen, for example, in *The Woodlanders* and *Jude the Obscure*)[22] – with all its oral and cultural tradition, its sense of every individual secure in a recognised, contributing, place in the human network – was one of Hardy's chief criticisms of his society: and it applies to ours today. His attitude to history in general was itself ahead of his time and would find favour with many now. For while he carefully researched dates, battles and treaties for *The Dynasts*, he was careful in that and in all his war poems to unveil a quite different order of "facts": the deeper human level where the war was felt by ordinary people – an aspect of history too often ignored in the telling.

This sensitivity to individual men and women, and to the constant necessary adjustment and revision of human experience, is shown in another area of social discussion today: the distortions caused by assuming the male to be the norm, and the female a deviation from, or appendage to, that norm. For his time, Hardy was commendably aware of women's largely powerless and marginalised condition – "the woman always pays". His markings show that, reading Comte's *General View of Positivism* in 1865, Hardy paid particular attention to the chapter on "The Influence of Positivism on Women".[23] Rather unusually, his version of history explicitly included the experience of the common woman, and he was sometimes more aware of limiting language than many today: "'man's inhumanity to man' – to woman". He even recognised that "God", or the Causer, creator of "male and female... in his own image", was too much beyond human understanding to be limited by gender definitions. Picking up (perhaps unknowingly) the forgotten thinking of some early religious writers and the medieval mystic Julian of Norwich, he too understood that the "Spinner of the Years" was likely to be of both feminine and masculine character:

> Such I ask you, Sir or Madam,
> (I know no more than Adam,
> Even vaguely, what your sex is, –
> Though feminine I had thought you
> Till seers as "Sire" besought you; –
> [*A Philosophical Fantasy*]

In this he was closer to theology current fifty years later than to that of his own time – and not in this alone. In a note of February 1898 Hardy postulates the idea of "a limited God of goodness":

> One not Omnipotent, but hampered: striving for our good, but unable to achieve it except occasionally.[24]

While the Christian doctrine of man and woman's free will implies a specific self-limitation by God, Hardy went further, both in this note and in, for example, his conversations with William Archer, about "a consciousness infinitely far off, at the other end of the chain of phenomena, always striving to express itself, and always baffled and blundering..."[25] Christian theology later in this century has more of an understanding of "the divine self-limitation in creation" (in the words of Leonard

Hodgson, lecturing at Oxford in mid-century). It has moved towards a Christian interpretation of post-quantum science and the balance of chance and necessity in the universe, which seems to suggest an infinitely more subtle evolutionary process than either Darwin or earlier Christian thought, based on an uncritical reading of Genesis, could have entertained. Hardy was probing in this direction, and would probably have welcomed such a theology.[26]

Perhaps at this point we should recapitulate. Hardy in his life and art reflected and spanned many of the divisions between classes and sexes, between traditions oral and written, urban and rural; between the exclusive claims of reason and a more integrated view of human beings and the nature of reality; between different kinds of "facts", "truth", and "values", and their writing of history; between mass unthinking certainties and thoughtful agnosticism. Every one of these gaps still yawns in the consciousness of Western/ Northern society towards the close of this century; and Hardy's re-assessments of his time's received opinions are still valuable for ours. As we have already seen, in many areas he seems strikingly modern.

"Being modern" had a glamour for him until he was an old man. He valued "modern thinking minds" and the "modern type", the "countenance of the future", which he embodied in Clym Yeobright.[27] For Hardy the modern face was one which showed the contemporary disillusionment with life. In his view of the absurdity of the human condition (including the absurdity of war)[28] he foreshadowed in many ways the philosophy of the Absurd, whose widest acceptance came in the mid-twentieth century. He would, for instance, have had much in common with Albert Camus: Camus' personal dilemmas between a deprived background and the social advancement brought by education and literary success, and between French and Algerian culture; Camus' recognition of the complexity of the world; his paramount concern for artistic truth; his assertion, through his Sisyphus,[29] that a dignified acceptance of the absurd laws of existence, a sense of the joy merely of being alive, a continued hope even without reason, were the best defiance – all these have a parallel in Hardy's attitudes.

He was, after all, writing most of his poetry during the time when the first shoots of what is called "modernism" were appearing above the ground. (Modernism, which loosely describes the international tendencies which began to be seen at the end of the nineteenth century, is a comprehensive term which covers many smaller "movements", from Symbolism, Impressionism, and Post-Impressionism to Dada and Surrealism. It has been well discussed elsewhere.[30] Here I use it in a more general, less technical sense, to suggest more simply the "modern", prevailing, climate in art today which is inevitably affected by the passage of all these movements.) In Graham Dunstan Martin's characterisation of it, Hardy is reflected in every phrase:

> In fact modernism has at any rate a recognizable frame of mind, asserting the importance of the individual, the uncertainty of truth, the difficulty of expression, the variousness and ambiguity of the world. Moreover this frame of mind is, as we have seen, in harmony with the modern scientist's picture of things.[31]

In varying degrees, we have met it in Hardy's poetry all along the way. Yet if poets like Ezra Pound, Yeats, and T.S. Eliot are taken as the chief exponents of different kinds of Modernism, it is also clear that another tradition in English poetry has continued quite independently, from the earliest days of English lyric verse: and in this tradition Hardy belongs. Unlike the highly symbolist, often obscure and fragmented poetry of Eliot which looks to, and quotes from, the whole breadth of European culture, this other tradition is particularly English, descriptive rather than symbolic, vernacular and rural rather than cosmopolitan or addressed to the intelligentsia, and regular in its form. Because its origins were in an ordered, rural, pre-Industrial Revolution society, it was concerned primarily with the relationship between men and women and their natural environment, with their personal experience of reality. This included the reality of the imagination and feelings, which are inexplicable, and of the metaphysical perceptions making us question the beyond, which are unanswerable. In this tradition can be seen Wordsworth, Coleridge, Keats, Crabbe, Clare, and others. From Hardy's time poets like Edward Thomas, the early D.H. Lawrence, Walter de la Mare, and Graves lead on in varying ways to later poets in something of the same tradition. Auden, for example, wrote in the dry, ironical, self-depreciatory, vernacular way which contemporary culture now expected and wanted: but in this Hardy was his precursor, as in Auden's latent idealism and quiet lyricism, his interest in verse technique, the primacy he gave to love and a sense of moral responsibility, and the Englishness of his landscapes.

In the next generation, the poets of the so-called "Movement" (published in Robert Conquest's 1956 *New Lines*) continued to trace the line from Hardy in their ironic understatement, their careful language, their search for complete honesty of feeling. This in some poets sprang partly from a fear of excessive emotion, a low-key desire to avoid the highbrow or the pompous, high idealism and an inflated claim for poetry. Hardy was not afraid of emotion – indeed, it was one of these poets, Philip Larkin, who said: "Hardy taught me to feel". Nor was he afraid of idealism, for a passionate ideal of human life and love burns through his poetry, and an unshakeable conviction of the enduring and immeasurable value of art. Hardy in fact seems to answer the need expressed by one modern critic in these terms:

> What poetry needs . . . is a new seriousness. I would define this seriousness simply as the poet's ability and willingness to face the full range of his experience with his full intelligence; not to take the easy exits of either the conventional response or choking incoherence.[32]

We know, at this end of our journey, that Hardy faced "the full range of his experience with his full intelligence"; that he faced it again and again, revising his understanding, and even following it down the dark tunnel of war to find the violence at the heart of human nature. We have seen his honesty and discipline, which refused to be side-tracked by technical cleverness or by a retreat into incoherence or lost innocence. We've seen how, starting from some slight incident or some deep experience, he brought his whole personality – passion and compassion, moral and every other kind of sensitivity, stoicism, humour, ironic detachment, love of beauty, and a long life's wisdom – to his own distillation of understanding. In that distillation – in "touch[ing] our hearts by showing his own"[33] – his own emotion becomes the universal, the essentially human in which we all share. In an age when they are widely negated, he affirms the importance of the individual and the costly values of human personality. Seeing the breakdown in the practice of the original ideals of Christendom, which we continue to watch in the disintegration of what has been experienced as European civilisation, Hardy can still find no other blueprint for living than the principle of loving-kindness, and the truth that has made him free. His poetry nourishes us.

Notes

1   James Reeves, *Understanding Poetry,* (London 1965), ch 18.

2   *Life* 180, 204. Like Matthew Arnold, E.M. Forster and others, Hardy only gives "two cheers for democracy", often fearing that what Plato called "the madness of the multitude" (copied by Hardy in his *Lit. Notes*, entry 1322) might lead to "the utter ruin of art and literature" (*Life*, 236 – the context is significant.) See Lennart Björk's interesting essay "Hardy's Reading", 114ff, in *A Writer and His Background, op cit.*

3   Paulin, *Thomas Hardy: The Poetry of Perception* (introduction to new paperback edition, London 1986)

4   *A Laodicean* turns on the then newly-invented telegraph: many poems are about the railway, which only reached Dorchester in 1847.

5   See for example John Polkinghorne, *One World* and *Science and Creation* (London 1986 and 1988)

6   Lesslie Newbigin, *Foolishness to the Greeks,* 31 (London 1986)

7   Ibid

8   Ibid 35, 36

9   *Life*, 148. The rest of the passage is rather inconclusive, concentrating on the idea that humanity should never have been created with emotions "in a world of defect". His extended grappling with the philosophical problems of the universe, humanity, and evil comes later, particularly in *The Dynasts.*

10   Comte, *Social Dynamics,* copied by Hardy, *Lit. Notes*, entries 666, 750.

11   Eg see the *Apology to Late Lyrics and Earlier*

12   Wm Archer, *Real Conversations*, 47

13   *Life*, 368, 406

14   See *On the Belgian Expatriation, Often When Warring, In Time of Wars and Tumults, To the Moon, "And There Was a Great Calm"*, etc. Dennis Taylor's chapter on "Hardy's Apocalypse" discusses this further.

15   *Life*, 285, 450

16   Hardy's speech in response to the award of the Royal Society of Literature's Gold Medal, as reported by *The Times*, 4 June 1912, *Orel*, 146–7

17   Arnold, *The Study of Poetry*, Essays in Criticism, 2nd Series.

18   See Björk, "Hardy's Reading," op cit, 120

19   Hardy's letter of 23 May 1906 to J.McT.E. McTaggart, philosopher.

20   G.D.Martin, *op cit*, 3

21   Wm Archer, *Real Conversations*, 32

22   See for example *The Woodlanders*, ch XVI, and *Jude the Obscure*, ch II

23   *Millgate*, 91, 588.

24   *Life*, 297. In his *Literary Notebooks* (vol II, entry 2359) Hardy had summarised his own conclusion: "The line of least resistance, then, as it seems to me, both in theology and in philosophy, is to accept, along with the superhuman consciousness, the notion that it is not all-embracing, the notion, in other words, that there is a God, but that he is quite finite either in power, or in knowledge, or in both at once."

25   Wm Archer, *Real Conversations*, 45–6

26   See Polkinghorne, *op cit, passim,* and Hans Küng, *Does God Exist?* (English translation, London 1980), pp 642–9

27   *Life*, 415; *The Return of the Native*, Bk III, ch 1

28   *Life*, 315, and many poems, some already instanced.

29   Camus, *Le Mythe de Sisyphe* (1942)

30   In eg Spender, *The Struggle of the Modern*; F. Kermode,

"Modernism", in *Modern Essays;* Bradbury and McFarlane (eds), *Modernism: 1890–1930*

31   G.D. Martin, *op cit,* 289; see also pp 278–9, 281.

32   Larkin, radio conversation edited for *The Listener,* 25 July 1968, also quoted *Casebook* 189–91; A Alvarez, *The New Poetry,* 28 (introductory essay to an anthology of that name, London, revd. 1966, reproduced by permission of Penguin Books Ltd.)

33   *Life,* 128: a quotation copied by Hardy from Leslie Stephen, which began: "The ultimate aim of the poet should be to touch our hearts by showing his own . . ."

INDEX

'Curtains Now Are Drawn, The', 81–2

'Darkling Thrush, The', 186; 'Daughter Returns, A', 265; 'Dawn After the Dance, The', 269; 'Dead Man Walking, The', 49; 'Dead Quire, The', 279; 'Death-Day Recalled, A', 140; 'Difference, The', 262; 'Division, The', 280; 'Domicilium', 20, 285–6; 'Doom and She', 160n32, 193–4; 'Dream Follower, The', 252; 'Dream is – Which?, The', 45, 63n11; 'Dream or No, A', 135–6, 140; 'Dream Question, A', 192–3; 'Drinking Song,' 191; 'Drummer Hodge', 21–2, 55, 182, 287; 'Duettist to her Pianoforte, A', 73–4; 'During Wind and Rain', 130, 169, 173–8, 288; 'Embarcation', 41; 'End of the Episode, The', 231–2, 277; 'Exeunt Omnes', (They all Leave'), 249; 'Experience, An', 270n26

'Face at the Casement, The', 87n5, 224; 'Figure in the Scene, The', 160n27, 168; 'First Sight of Her and After, 258–9, 270n22; 'Five Students, The', 169–70; 'Flirt's Tragedy, The', 287; 'Former Beauties', 65–6, 274; 'Four in the Morning', 283–4; 'Fragment' 47, 63–n13; 'Friends Beyond', 43, 55; 'For Life I Had Never Cared Greatly', 26, 37n10

'Garden Seat, The', 64n25; 'Genoa and the Mediterranean', 210–12; 'Geographical Knowledge', 20; 'God's Funeral', 215n3; 'Going, The', 114–5, 117, 123, 129, 132, 138, 142; 'Going of the Battery, The', 287; 'Great Things', 9–10, 269; 'Had You Wept', 250; 'Hap', 42, 63n7, 194–6, 273, 279; 'Harbour Bridge, The', 246, 269n3; 'Haunter, The', 58, 127–8, 132, 142, 287;

'Haunting Fingers', 64n25; 'Head above the Fog, The', 64n25; 'He Fears His Good Fortune', 224; 'He Never Expected Much', 225; 'He Prefers Her Earthly', 7, 15n4, 240; 'He Resolves to Say No More', 52, 242–3; 'Her Death and After' 264; 'Her Immortality', 87n3, 96; 'Her Initials', 228, 253, 266; 'His Immortality', 87n3; 'His Visitor', 132–3; 'Honeymoon Time at an Inn', 16, 109, 159n5, 260–1; 'House of Silence, The', 84–5, 255; 'How She Went to Ireland', 282–3; 'Hurried Meeting, A', 270n26

'I Found Her Out There', 122–3, 136; 'I Look Into My Glass', 1–3, 5, 7, 41, 48–9, 52, 182, 276, 287; 'I Looked Back', 262; 'I Looked Up From My Writing', 259; 'I Travel as a Phantom Now', 157, 161n44; 'Impercipient, The', 187–9, 267; 'In a Eweleaze near Weatherbury', 42, 63n8, 251, 270n9; 'In a Former Resort After Many Years', 177; 'In a Museum', 40; 'In a Waiting-Room', 16; 'In a Wood', 226–7; 'In Front of the Landscape', 176–7, 229, 289–291; 'In Her Precincts', 254; 'In Tenebris I', 49, 56, 223, 227, 253, 279; 'In Tenebris II', 7, 219, 227, 253; 'In Tenebris III', 269; 'In Sherborne Abbey', 261, 270n24; 'In the Cemetery', 60–1; 'In the Mind's Eye', 78, 88n13; 'In the Moonlight', 261, 270n24; 'In the Nuptial Chamber', 74–5, 202; 'In the Old Theatre, Fiesole', 33, 37n13, 251; 'In the Small Hours', 71–2; 'In the Vaulted Way', 250; 'In Time of "The Breaking of Nations"', 163–9; 'Inquiry, The', 30–1, 41, 182, 288; 'It Never Looks Like Summer Now', 168

'Jingle on the Times, A', 197; 'Joys of Memory', 72–3, 276;

A', 37n12; 'Seven Times, The', 265; 'Shadow on the Stone, The', 83, 111, 302; 'She Opened the Door', 253; 'She Revisits Alone the Church of Her Marriage', 267; 'She, to Him I', 63n7; 'She, to Him III', 87n1; 'Shelley's Skylark', 197-8, 210, 293; 'Shiver, The', 4-5, 252; 'Shut Out That Moon', 73, 268-9, 272; 'Sick Battle-God, The', 209, 288; 'Sign-Seeker, A', 55; 'Silences', 17, 68, 287; 'Singer Asleep, A', 25, 287; 'Sleep-Worker, The', 160n32; 'Snow in the Suburbs', 10-11, 211-2, 214, 274; 'Something Tapped', 64n26; 'Song to an Old Burden', 35-6, 287; 'Sound of Her, The', 134; 'Spell of the Rose, The', 153-4, 156; 'Spellbound Palace, A', 199-200, 214, 278; 'Strange House, The', 263; 'Sunshade, The', 28, 53, 256; 'Surview', 241-2

'Telegram, The', 258-9, 263-4, 270n22; 'Ten Years Since', 161n42, 265-6; 'Tess's Lament', 66-7, 69, 70, 182, 287; 'Thoughts of Phena', 85-6, 252, 274; 'To a Lady', 221; 'To a Well-Named Dwelling', 16-17; 'To an Unborn Pauper's Child', 183-5; 'To Carry Clavel', 277, 297n9; 'To My Father's Violin', 203-4, 274; 'To Louisa in the Lane', 86; 'To Sincerity', 219-20, 288; 'To-be-Forgotten, The', 87n3; 'Trampwoman's Tragedy, The', 71, 262; 'Transformations', 64n27; 'Tree and the Lady, The', 258-9; 'Two Rosalinds, The', 252; 'Two Serenades', 251, 270n9; 'Two-Years' Idyll, A', 106-7;

'Under High-Stoy Hill', 287; 'Under the Waterfall', 75-7, 105, 256, 288; 'Unrealized', 283; 'Upbraiding, An', 262

'Vatican, The: Sala delle Muse',

198; 'Voice, The', 58, 129-30, 132, 274; 'Voice of the Thorn, The', 88n7; 'Voice of Things, The', 267; 'Voices from Things Growing in a Churchyard', 22

'Walk, The', 119; 'War-Wife of Catknoll, The', 215n5; 'Wasted Illness, A', 270n26; 'Welcome Home', 265; 'Wet Night, A', 288; 'Wessex Heights', 56-7, 73, 227, 259; 'When I Set Out for Lyonnesse', 105; 'Where the Picnic Was', 155-8, 265, 276; 'Where Three Roads Joined', 259, 270n22; 'Where They Lived', 258; 'Whitewashed Wall, The', 11, 53, 231, 280; 'Why Did I Sketch?' 168; 'Wife Waits, A', 274 'Wind Blew Words, The', 304; 'Wind's Prophecy, The', 171-3, 179n12, 250, 255, 287; 'Winsome Woman, A', 251, 270n10; 'Without Ceremony', 124-5, 138; 'Woman Driving, A', 113, 159n13, 240

'Year's Awakening, The', 238-9; 'Yell'ham-Wood's Story', 192; 'Young Man's Exhortation, A', 228; 'Your Last Drive', 117-9, 177

STORIES *Life's Little Ironies:* 'Fiddler of the Reels, The', 74; *Wessex Tales:* 'Distracted Preacher, The', 205

Hardy and the Cell of Time, (Ingham), 48, 49
Hardy's Magian Retrospect, (Jacobus) 51, 64n17, 216n14
Hardy's Virgilian Purples, (Davie) 113, 143
Hebrew, 188, 216n8
Helen of Troy, 39, 111
Héloise, Abbess, 39
Henniker, Mrs. Florence, 88n15, 113, 159n15, 227
Herbert, George, 246
Hodgson, (Canon) Leonard, 306
Holder, Revd, Caddell, 103, 105-6

26

106
262
26
278 —